Degrees of Inequality

D1484282

Degrees of Inequality

*Culture, Class, and Gender
in American Higher Education*

Ann L. Mullen

The Johns Hopkins University Press
Baltimore

© 2010 The Johns Hopkins University Press
All rights reserved. Published 2010
Printed in the United States of America

Johns Hopkins Paperback edition, 2012
9 8 7 6 5 4 3 2 1

The Johns Hopkins University Press
2715 North Charles Street
Baltimore, Maryland 21218-4363
www.press.jhu.edu

*The Library of Congress has catalogued the hardcover edition of this book
as follows:*

Mullen, Ann L.
Degrees of inequality : culture, class, and gender in American higher
education / Ann L. Mullen.
        p.   cm.
    Includes bibliographical references and index.
    ISBN-13: 978-0-8018-9770-2 (hardcover : alk. paper)
    ISBN-10: 0-8018-9770-X (alk. paper)
      1. Education, Higher—Social aspects—United States.
2. Education—Economic aspects—United States. 3. College students—
Social networks—United States. 4. Educational equalization—Cross-
cultural studies. 5. Income distribution—Cross-cultural studies.
I. Title.
    LC67.62.M58 2010
      306.43'2—dc22   2010013271

A catalog record for this book is available from the British Library.

ISBN-13: 978-1-4214-0574-2
ISBN-10: 1-4214-0574-1

*Special discounts are available for bulk purchases of this book. For
more information, please contact Special Sales at 410-516-6936 or
specialsales@press.jhu.edu.*

The Johns Hopkins University Press uses environmentally friendly
book materials, including recycled text paper that is composed of at
least 30 percent post-consumer waste, whenever possible.

For my mother and my father

Contents

Acknowledgments

I did not realize it at the time, but this book has its roots in a chance conversation that took place in a small French restaurant in Truckee, California. I was working there as a lunch waitress the summer before my senior year at the University of California, Berkeley. One day my manager asked me what I was majoring in. When I told him I was a humanities major, he replied, "Oh, a cocktail conversation major." I spent much of the summer pondering this comment, wondering just what he meant, whether he actually imagined I might be studying something only for the purpose of making witty banter at parties or whether his comment was simply meant to dismiss the value of studying humanities because it wasn't useful in any applied kind of way. Little did I know that years later I would spend a great deal of time investigating just why liberal arts fields hold so little appeal for those who prize more practical pursuits.

The research and writing of this book span several years and four cities. Its completion owes much to those who have supported the project as well as those who have sustained me through the course of it. In the former category, I would first like to thank the National Academy of Education and the National Academy of Education/Spencer Postdoctoral Fellowship Program. The yearlong teaching release as well as the retreats held with the other fellows and National Academy of Education members were invaluable. The project was also supported by a Connaught Start-Up Award granted by the University of Toronto. I also thank the research assistants who helped with coding and much more: Jayne Baker, Ellie Hobuti, Rebecca (Sophie) Statzel, and Wendy Pereira. I thank David Denino at Southern Connecticut State University for facilitating the project and especially for providing space for conducting the interviews. I thank Linn Clark and Jane Cavolina for editorial assistance. At the Johns Hopkins University Press, I thank Ashleigh McKown. Kathleen Capels is a superb copyeditor, and this book benefited greatly from her attentions. I also thank Taylor & Francis for granting me permission to reprint portions of chapter 4, which appeared in an earlier version in 2009 as Ann L. Mullen, "Elite Destinations:

Pathways to Attending an Ivy League University," in the *British Journal of Sociology of Education* 30(1):15–27. Most important, I would like to thank all of the students who took time out from their busy schedules to be interviewed. Whether or not they agree with my interpretation of their words, I hope they will be able to discern the care I took with them.

I also owe many thanks to my mentors who provided encouragement and advice in the early stages of this project: Paul DiMaggio, Kai Erikson, Josh Gamson, and Jerry Jacobs. Paul DiMaggio deserves an extra note of thanks for seeing this project through from start to finish. He was not only indispensable in advising me on designing and starting the research but also tremendously helpful throughout the data analysis and writing stages.

The manuscript greatly benefited from the knowledgeable and insightful comments I received from a number of people who read portions of the manuscript at various stages or discussed the work with me. They are Monica Boyd, Steven Brint, Cynthia Cranford, Scott Davies, Kevin Dougherty, Neil Fiore, Kim Goyette, Eric Grodsky, Joe Hermanowicz, David Karen, Anna Korteweg, Kenneth Larson, Kathy Liddle, Sam Lucas, Julian Tanner, Scott Thomas, and Joseph Soares. I have tried though not always succeeded in doing justice to all of their helpful suggestions; of course, any errors or omissions are my own. I would also like to thank the members of the University of Toronto Department of Sociology Gender Group for reading and discussing an early draft of one of the chapters. In addition, I give a special thanks to Bonnie Erickson and Jane Gaskell for their mentorship and guidance.

Writing can be quite demanding, and a project of this scope requires declining many more enticing ways of spending time. I am grateful to my good-natured and generous friends who alternately provided encouragement and exhortation or cheer and diversion, as needed. First and foremost, I thank Anne Gebelein for her steadfast friendship, for accompanying me on each step of this journey, and for standing by with wise counsel and cake through many difficult moments. I thank Beth Lawrence for taking me on opportune garden tours, Deirdre Flynn for the many delicious dinners with her family, and Karl Kannstadter for saving the day. I also thank Frank Bakutis, the Barrios Eleuterio family, Gustavo Dias Bonfim, Kathie Carlson, Chris Chapman, Chris Cherniak, Gillian Corzine, Pat Cross, Iverson Griffin, Stephanie Hartwell, Paula Knepper, Minelle Mahtani, Kirk Peterkin, and Laurie Savastano.

I would also like to thank Maninho Costa and the members of the Batucada Carioca, a samba percussion group I joined during the last months of writing this book. Samba provided the perfect counterbalance to the solitary task of writing, and learning to play intricate samba rhythms at breakneck speed actually made writing seem easy by comparison.

Finally, I especially thank my family for their love and support and their patience with the countless conversations about the content of this book and the process of writing it.

Degrees of Inequality

Introduction

Every September, somewhere around 1300 young men and women from all across the country arrive in New Haven, Connecticut, to begin their college education at Yale University. They are the children of some of the wealthiest and most powerful families in the United States. Most of them cannot remember a time when going to college was not part of their future. Many of them attended exclusive college preparatory schools, such as Exeter, Andover, and Dalton. They come to study archaeology, political science, literature, chemistry, and history; to play tennis and row; to sing in Yale's renowned a cappella groups; to volunteer in soup kitchens; and to be involved with a host of student organizations. Most of them plan on entering graduate or professional programs after college. They aspire to be doctors, lawyers, writers, filmmakers, poets, and professors. They consider holding public office in the future. The men intend to make enough money to live in upscale neighborhoods, to send their children to private schools, and to take their families on ski vacations. The women plan to follow their intellectual passions into gratifying and meaningful careers. For most of them, those dreams will become reality when they graduate after four years with a degree that will be taken as proof not only of their intelligence, but of their intrinsic worthiness.

Just two miles away, at Southern Connecticut State University, a similar-sized class of first-year students begins their university education. Most of these students grew up in Connecticut. Their parents are shopkeepers, secretaries, teachers, and construction workers. About half of these students will be the first in their families to graduate from college. They come to college because they do not want to work in factories; because they want better jobs than their parents have; because they want to become social workers, teachers, and computer programmers. They choose Southern because it is relatively inexpensive, is convenient, and offers programs in the career fields of their choice. Most will live with their parents and commute to cut down on expenses. Rather than singing and rowing, these students will spend their time outside of the classroom working twenty to thirty hours a week to help pay for their education. College will be less about intellectual exploration and finding oneself and more about doing the work to pass courses and accumulate enough credits to graduate. In exchange, at the end of four years they will receive a credential entitling them, they hope, to a good, stable, white-collar job.

The contrast between the geographical proximity of the two universities and the disparity of the students and their experiences captures the central paradox of the higher educational system in the United States today. At the same time that more young adults than ever before enter higher education, the college experience has become more disparate, ranging from living in plush campus dormitories and studying the liberal arts at prestigious universities to commuting from home to the local college to earn a preprofessional degree. While access to college has become more egalitarian, *where* a student attends college and *what* she or he studies have become increasingly tied to social background and gender. Given the myriad routes through the stratified higher educational system, how do students make sense of and understand their own journeys? How do they make the decision to go to college in the first place? How do they choose where to apply and attend? How do they sift through course catalogs in order to select a major? What, ultimately, does their university education mean to them?

This book answers these questions by taking a close look at the educational experiences of college students at two universities: fifty men and women studying at Yale and fifty men and women earning degrees at Southern, a moderately selective, public comprehensive college. It reveals how college destinations, choices, and experiences are linked to social background and gender. It also explores the ways in which students make sense of their own place in the complex hierarchy of higher education by drawing on competing narratives about the purpose and value of education. These meanings range from the liberal arts ideal of producing an educated person to the vocational model of training an individual for a specific occupation. This introductory chapter situates my study by providing a brief history of the expansion of higher education, reviewing the relationship between social background and college access, and exploring the philosophical ideals about the purpose of education.

The Expansion of Higher Education

The second half of the twentieth century witnessed a remarkably successful campaign to increase the accessibility of higher education in the United States, premised on the value of offering young adults an equal opportunity for success on the basis of hard work and merit. Heavy federal, state, and private investments produced spectacular growth in the higher educational system. Between 1950 and 2000 the number of postsecondary institutions more than doubled, rising from 1851 to 4084. The fastest rate of expansion occurred in publicly funded institutions, with a new commitment to infrastructure matched by a number of financial aid initiatives. Generous federal student aid packages were provided, including the G.I. Bill for war veterans and a host of grant and loan programs. Public and private postsecondary institutions also rapidly stepped up their financial aid offerings during these years.

[handwritten margin note: increased college enrollment and financial aid from 1950–2000.]

As a result of both the growth in the number of institutions and improved financial aid, postsecondary enrollments rose dramatically. The number of students increased more than sixfold between 1950 and 2000, from 2.3 million to 15.3 million (Snyder, Tan, and Hoffman 2006). This expansion was largely independent of the overall population growth: in 1950, one out of seven eighteen- to twenty-four-year-olds was enrolled in a college or university; by 2000, this had risen to one out of three (Snyder 1993). For over a decade now, upward of 60 percent of all high school graduates enroll in a postsecondary institution within a year of graduation and 75 percent enroll within two years (Snyder, Tan, and Hoffman 2006).

The expansion of the postsecondary educational system promised to fulfill a central tenet of the American ideology of equal opportunity: achievement is not predicated on the luck of being born into a wealthy family; rather anyone can get ahead through hard work and persistence. Education has been widely perceived as one of the best means to make this dream possible. In the 1880s, Horace Mann, a congressman and well-known proponent of mandatory public education, called education, beyond any other human device, "the great equalizer of the conditions of men—the balance-wheel of the social machinery." The tremendous investment in higher education in the United States in the last half of the twentieth century embodies the most recent incarnation of this conviction. Making a college education widely accessible would ensure that neither social origin nor race nor gender would prevent a person from attaining success in life.

Has the promise of the expansion of higher education been fulfilled? By some measures, amply so. The burgeoning of the postsecondary system is an oft-told tale of triumph, claimed as evidence of a strong public commitment to equality of opportunity. A system that was once reserved primarily for white, middle- and upper-class males is now more accessible than ever before to women and to racial and ethnic minorities. Women made up only 32 percent of postsecondary enrollments in 1950, but 57 percent in 2008. In 1967 only 13 percent of black eighteen- to twenty-four-year-olds enrolled in college, compared with 32 percent in 2008; and in 1972, 13 percent of Hispanic eighteen- to twenty-four-year-olds enrolled, compared with 26 percent in 2008. Going to college has evolved from a rare privilege typically accorded only to the children (especially the white male children) of the middle and upper classes to a common part of the life course for a large segment of the U.S. population.

The simple version related here, however, masks a more complex reality, and these encouraging indicators belie other, less hopeful, dimensions of access. The rapid expansion of the U.S. postsecondary educational system has been accompanied by an increase in the hierarchical differentiation of institutions. Compared with the much flatter higher educational systems of Canada and most of Europe, that in the United States is distinctive for its steep prestige hierarchy (Davies and Hammack 2005). The U.S. system takes the form of a pyramid: at the top are a small number of highly selective colleges and universities, and at the bottom cluster a large number of institutions with either minimal or open admissions standards. The Ivy League reigns at the pinnacle of the pyramid, comprising eight private universities located in the northeastern part of the country: Brown, Columbia, Cornell,* Dartmouth, Harvard, Princeton, the University of Pennsylvania, and Yale. They are among the oldest universities in the country: Harvard was established in 1636, Cornell in 1865, and the other six in the 1700s. They are phenomenally richly resourced, hold outstanding academic reputations, admit students on an extremely selective basis, charge

* Cornell is a hybrid institution, part private and part public, with ten colleges, four of which receive state funding (Ehrenberg 2002).

famously expensive tuitions, and count among their alumni many of the most wealthy and powerful individuals in the country.

Lower in the hierarchy come other private universities; the elite, four-year liberal arts colleges; flagship public universities, such as the University of Wisconsin–Madison; and then the less regarded state and private institutions. At the bottom are a large number of two-year, or community, colleges, most with open-door acceptance policies, admitting anyone with a high school degree. For students and their parents who are not sure how to select an institution, *U.S. News & World Report* and a plethora of college guidebooks and Web sites publish annual rankings of colleges and universities. The rankings reflect different measures, but generally attempt to take into account institutions' quality and reputation.

Student competition for entry into the most prestigious institutions has increased, as mounting evidence indicates that the rewards gained from a college degree have become increasingly dependent on the name of the institution appearing on the diploma. Matriculants in more selective institutions enjoy many advantages. Compared with their peers at less selective institutions, they are more likely to graduate, earn higher salaries, enter more prestigious occupations, and move on to high-status positions, such as top corporate management; to pursue graduate education and do so in highly selective programs; and to experience higher levels of life satisfaction (Bowen and Bok 1998; Brewer and Ehrenberg 1996; Carnevale and Rose 2004; Kingston and Lewis 1990; Mullen, Goyette, and Soares 2003; Smart 1986, 1988). In addition, graduates of the Ivy League—especially Harvard, Yale, and Princeton (HYP)—have long been overrepresented in the American elite (Karabel 2005). Indeed, in forty-nine of the 110 years between 1900 and 2010, the president of the United States has been a graduate of HYP.

Returning to the question of access, because of the hierarchical nature of the U.S. higher educational system and the disparities in the rewards that it offers, it is no longer enough to simply look at who goes to college and who does not. To fully evaluate the promise expressed by the expansion of postsecondary education, one needs to examine the opportunities students of different backgrounds have to attend the various institutions within that system. In other words, we need to look not just at *who* goes to college, but at who goes *where* to college.

Social Background and College Access

A look at the composition of the student bodies at elite institutions shows that they are heavily skewed toward the upper classes. In the year 2000, students from families in the bottom 50 percent of the income distribution made up just 10 percent of new undergraduate students at Princeton and 12 percent at Harvard. Data on family incomes are not available for Yale students, but a similar distribution seems likely because, in that same year, only 8 percent of Yale freshmen came from families where neither parent attended college (Karabel 2005). These patterns extend to top-tier public institutions as well. At the University of Michigan in 2005, there were more students from families with annual incomes over $200,000 than there were from families with incomes of less than the national median of about $53,000 (D. Brooks 2005). Comparing the socioeconomic status (SES) of entering students across college tiers similarly reveals the strong connection between social origins and college destinations. Colleges and universities can be assigned to four tiers, based on their entering students' high school grade point averages, class rankings, and university entrance exam scores. Tier one institutions include the top 146 colleges, where entering students generally hold a high school grade point average of B or above and score 1240 or above (out of a total of 1600) on the SAT I: Reasoning Test (Carnevale and Rose 2004). Fourth-tier institutions are much less competitive and typically accept more than 85 percent of all applicants.

Table I.1 shows that three out of four students at tier one institutions come from families in the top quarter of the SES scale (74%), while less than 10 percent come from families in the bottom half and just 3 percent come from families in the lowest quartile. The proportions from each SES quartile follow a standard progression across institutional tier levels: as institutions become less competitive, the proportion of lower-SES students increases while the proportion of upper-SES students decreases. At fourth-tier institutions, the proportion of students from each SES quartile becomes roughly balanced.

Further, trends suggest that students from wealthy families have increased their proportional representation at highly selective institutions. A study of twenty-eight colleges and universities with academically selective admissions policies (including four of the eight Ivy League institutions) reveals that students from families in the top income quartile grew from 39 percent to 50 percent of the student body between 1976 and 1995 (see table I.2). The proportion of students from families in the bottom income quartile did not increase at all during this time, but held steady at about 10 percent (Bowen, Kurzweil, and Tobin 2005). Even net of high school academic achievement, students from more highly educated families are four times more likely to enroll in elite institutions than their peers from less educated families, a ratio which has been

Table I.1   Socioeconomic status of entering classes by institutional tiers
(in percentages)

SES quartiles	Tier one	Tier two	Tier three	Tier four
Top	74	46	35	35
Upper middle	17	29	36	28
Lower middle	6	18	19	21
Bottom	3	7	10	16
Total	100	100	100	100

Source: Based on Carnevale and Rose 2004, p. 106, table 3.1.

growing since the 1970s (Roksa et al. 2007). A study by Astin and Oseguera (2004) confirms these trends. Students from wealthy and highly educated families increased their representation at highly selective institutions from 1971 to 2000, displacing those from middle-income families. The authors conclude that "American higher education . . . is more socioeconomically stratified today than at any time during the past three decades" (p. 338).

Similarly, between the years 1980 and 1992, the relative effects of family background (especially father's education and parental income) on the selectivity of the institutions attended by their children approximately doubled (Karen 2002). Further, while women and African-Americans increased their representation at elite institutions between 1966 and 1986, working-class youth did not make the same inroads. Indeed, students from families with low levels of education appear to have become more heavily concentrated in the lowest tier of institutions during these years (Karen 1991).

If the students at elite institutions come primarily from the upper reaches of the social structure, they also come predominantly from white and Asian-American families. African-American and Hispanic students make up just 6 percent and 7 percent, respectively, of the student bodies at Harvard and Yale, but they each represent about 12 percent of the general population (Harvard University 2007; Yale University 2007c). However, these racial disparities can be largely attributed to differences in social background and its relation to academic achievement. Variation in social background accounts for almost all of the inequality in college entry among minority and white high school graduates (Bowen, Kurzweil, and Tobin 2005; Gamoran 2001), and, once controlling for high school academic achievement, black students are no less likely than whites to enter elite colleges (Roksa et al. 2007). Women are also underrepresented among elite or top-tier institutions (Davies and Guppy 1997; Jacobs 1999), though the gender gap is modest compared with that of race and class.

Table I.2   Distribution of enrolled students at academically selective colleges and
universities, by 1989 national income quartiles (in percentages)

Cohort	Bottom quartile	Second quartile	Third quartile	Top quartile
1976	10	26	25	39
1989	9	23	23	46
1995	11	22	17	50

Source: Bowen, Kurzweil, and Tobin 2005, p. 291. Rows may not sum to 100 due to rounding.

Where do students from low-SES families attend college? They cluster at
the bottom of the educational hierarchy, particularly in two-year institutions.
The sector that most benefited from the expansion of the higher education
system during the last half of the twentieth century was the two-year college.
While only 12 percent of postsecondary students attended two-year institutions
in 1956, by 2000 this percentage had more than tripled, to 39 percent (Snyder
and Hoffman 2002). Some of these institutions offer certificates in applied fields
of study, such as hairdressing. Others ostensibly prepare their students to move
on to four-year institutions. In actuality, transfer rates are low, causing some
to call two-year institutions dumping grounds for poor students. Of the high
school graduates in 1992 who entered a two-year institution with the intention
of transferring to a four-year college, only 27 percent had earned a bachelor's
degree by 2000 (Hoachlander, Sikora, and Horn 2003).

Table I.3 shows how social background influences whether a student begins
at a four-year or a two-year institution. Of those students who continued their
education after high school, almost half of the low-income students enrolled in a
public two-year institution, compared with 41 percent of middle-income students
and only 18 percent of high-income students. A similar relationship is found for
their parents' educational level. Fifty-six percent of the students whose parents
had a high school degree or less entered a public two-year institution, compared
with just 23 percent of the students who had at least one parent with a college
degree. Similarly, the higher one's family income and the better educated one's
parents, the more likely one is to enroll in a four-year institution. Over 80 percent
of high-income students began their college careers at a four-year institution.

Overall, these findings underscore the degree to which college destinations
are tied to social background. If one could map the hierarchy of colleges and
universities in the United States and superimpose upon it a map of the class and
race structure, one would find a disconcertingly neat, though not perfect, fit.

Table I.3 1994 postsecondary enrollment by family background characteristics for 1992 high school graduates (in percentages)

	Public two-year or other less-than-four-year institution	Any four-year institution
Family income		
Low (less than $25,000)	48.8	51.2
Middle ($25,000–$74,999)	40.5	59.5
High ($75,000 or above)	17.7	82.2
Parents' highest level of education		
High school graduate or less	56.1	43.7
Some college	45.1	54.9
College graduate	22.8	77.2

Source: Adapted from Berkner and Chavez 1997, p. 7, table 2. Percentages may not sum to 100 due to rounding.

The institutions at the top of the hierarchy graduate children of privilege, by both race and class, while the ones at the bottom educate those less fortunate, disproportionately students of color and of less advantaged social origin. Social background has become less important for predicting college attendance, but more important for the type of college or university one attends.

A second axis of stratification cuts through fields of study. While women now earn a slightly higher share of bachelor's degrees than men, the fields in which men and women earn their degrees vary tremendously. In 2005, for example, women earned 79 percent of the degrees in education, 78 percent in psychology, and 87 percent in the nursing and health professions, but only 32 percent in economics, 30 percent in philosophy, and 20 percent in engineering (Snyder 2007). Segregation indicators, such as the index of dissimilarity, demonstrate that about a third of all college students (either male or female) would have to change majors in order for men and women to be evenly distributed across fields (England and Li 2006; Jacobs 1995). In addition, a twenty-year trend toward the narrowing of the gender gap ground to a halt in the mid–1980s (Jacobs 1995; Turner and Bowen 1999) and has held remarkably steady since then (England and Li 2006). Indeed, if it were not for the growth of business, the trend toward gender integration would have actually reversed between 1985 and 1990, with fields of study becoming more segregated than they were previously (Jacobs 1995). This gender segregation of major fields of study has been found to be directly linked *both* to the occupational segregation of men and women and to gender disparities in earnings (Bradley 2000; C. Brown and Corcoran 1997; Snyder and Hoffman 2002). Traditionally female majors lead to traditionally female jobs, and these jobs tend to pay much less than traditionally male jobs. Those with bachelor's degrees in education, for example, earn only about 60 percent as much as those with degrees in engineering. The gender segregation of fields of study cuts across social background: men and women of privileged social origins are as likely to choose different fields as are first-generation students (Goyette and Mullen 2006).* As institutions of higher education have become stratified by class, fields within these institutions remain strikingly stratified by gender.

Between these two axes of stratification lies the great paradox of the U.S. higher educational system at the beginning of the twenty-first century. A social institution regarded as critical for ensuring equal opportunity is marked by powerful patterns of inequality that both reflect and perpetuate social stratification. While a higher proportion of high school graduates than ever before now pursue bachelor's degrees, whether a student goes to college, where a student attends, and what she or he studies depends heavily on gender and social background. Moreover, the general expansion of higher education has done little to change long-standing patterns of educational stratification (Roksa et al. 2007; Shavit and Blossfeld 1993). Thus, while education has become the best means of getting ahead, the low levels of equality in educational opportunity serve to limit mobility for those who are least advantaged (Beller and Hout 2006; Hout 1988). Further, while the educational attainment of women now equals that of men, the kinds of work women do still remain largely different from the kinds of work men do, and the gender gap in earnings has only moderately improved over the past several decades (Padavic and Reskin 2002).

Similar to diagramming complex traffic patterns, sociologists document these educational trends with data collected from colleges and universities, along with national survey data. However, while these bird's-eye views tell us much about what kinds of students attend which kinds of institutions, they reveal little of the lived experiences of the students themselves. If the stratification of higher education is in part a result of unequal life chances, it is also the result of a multitude of individual choices. Each of the more than ten million students currently enrolled in a four-year institution made a decision to go to college and selected where to go. Each of the roughly one-and-a-half million students earning bachelor's degrees this year selected a field of study. For all of them, these were meaningful choices. How is it that an educational system can accom-

---

* The term "first-generation student" refers to an individual who will be the first in his or her family to graduate from college. One or both of that student's parents may have attended college, but neither would have graduated with a four-year degree.

modate so much inequality, encompass such disparate experiences, and yet still be meaningful? One of the central questions guiding this book concerns how students make sense of their own place in the hierarchy of higher education, and how they think through and make decisions at each crossroads.

Educational Narratives

Higher education has evolved around two quite different sets of cultural understandings about the purpose and value of education. The source for these competing narratives can be traced to dual philosophical perspectives concerning the ideal of a college education, as reflected in the content of college curricula, which range along a spectrum from applied studies to liberal arts offerings. Applied or preprofessional fields include business, nursing, education, computer programming, social work, and engineering. The intent of preprofessional education lies in equipping students with knowledge and a set of skills that can be readily transferred into a particular occupation. A degree in one of these areas is valued primarily for its usefulness in the marketplace. In contrast, the classic liberal arts curriculum (as articulated in the nineteenth century) consisted of Latin, Greek, philosophy, history, and math; it now typically includes the arts and humanities, the social sciences, math, and the natural and physical sciences. Traditionally, a liberal arts education was designed to equip elite students with the qualities needed to govern political institutions or to serve as a preprofessional education for careers in law, medicine, the clergy, or higher education (Brint 1998; Kerr 1991; Levine 1986; Soares 1999).

The intent of a liberal arts education reaches far beyond the practical goals of vocational training; it emphasizes breadth of knowledge over narrow specialization and advocates learning for its own sake, rather than for utilitarian ends. Instead of preparing a student for a particular niche in the labor market, a liberal arts education concerns itself with the intellectual and moral development of the individual. By providing a well-rounded education comprised of studying society's major achievements in art, literature, and science, coupled with a specialization in one of these areas, a student gains a well-developed intellect, strong verbal and written communication skills, and a refined moral vision. The study of the liberal arts is considered important both for developing mental qualities, such as reason and judgment, and for strengthening a student's character and sense of public obligation. The result of the successful completion of a liberal arts course of study is a person well prepared for responsible participation and leadership in society (Katchadourian and Boli 1985). While a preprofessional education produces a pretrained, labor-market-ready employee, a liberal arts education ostensibly produces an educated person.

Fierce debates over the content of the college curriculum mark the history of U.S. higher education. The result of the clashes between liberal arts advocates and those promoting preprofessional training is a U.S. higher educational system that currently favors preprofessional training but runs the gamut from one approach to the other. At one end are colleges and universities offering primarily liberal arts fields. In the large middle ground are institutions offering a mix of both liberal arts and preprofessional fields, often requiring some liberal arts courses for all students. At the other end are colleges and universities mainly training students in preprofessional fields. This spectrum closely aligns with institutional rankings: the most prestigious universities grant primarily liberal arts degrees; the least prestigious offer mostly occupationally oriented degrees (Brint et al. 2005). Given the correspondence of the class structure to the institutional hierarchy, children from high-SES families are more likely to study the liberal arts and sciences, while less privileged students will disproportionately enter applied fields.

These two broad meanings of higher education influence every aspect of the educational experience, from the perceived purpose of education, to the type of knowledge most valued, to the roles of the student and the professor. As students make their way through the higher educational hierarchy, they weave stories about their own trajectories around these competing narratives. One of the aims of this book is to uncover the ways in which the material resources, academic training, and social backgrounds of students work together to form dispositions to draw on different conceptions of education.

The Study

Though students at Southern Connecticut State University and Yale University will spend four years studying within two miles of each other, their experiences will be worlds apart. In addition, when they graduate, their trajectories will angle toward very different destinations. Yale graduates can expect to either enter top graduate and professional programs or sign on to fast-tracked and high-paying jobs, their futures stretching before them without limit. Southern graduates will enter steady, white-collar jobs with incomes around the national mean; some will go on for master's degrees and a few will enter doctoral programs; and most will fulfill the dream of owning their own home. The men from both institutions will get higher-paying and more prestigious jobs than their female counterparts.

Why do lower-class youth end up at less prestigious colleges and universities, compared with their more socially privileged counterparts, and why do they set out on applied tracks that will lead them only as far as a solid, white-collar job? Why do women from all classes consistently choose those fields with the lowest labor market payoffs? This book draws on in-depth interviews with a diverse group of students to investigate these persistent patterns. In analyzing the students' personal and academic histories, it shows how a combination of family influences, superior secondary schools, and the economic resources of privileged students results in a powerful bundling of advantages, launching these youngsters into the most elite colleges and onto the pathway of success. For those less fortunate in their family circumstances, graduation from inadequately equipped and uninspiring high schools, coupled with a limited knowledge of the college admissions process and sharp financial constraints, makes mass public education their most likely track. Once at college, the academic experiences of these two groups of students strikingly diverge. While most of the privileged students adopt a liberal arts approach to their education, reinforcing their sense of intellectual merit and entitlement, their less fortunate peers take a vocational approach, resulting in a more limited set of future occupational choices. By taking a close look at the competing narratives these students use to make sense of their college education, and uncovering the incorporation of these narratives into the institutions themselves, my research illuminates the important role of cultural understandings in supporting and justifying educational inequalities. Ultimately, this book aims to help uncover the ways in which higher education ends up perpetuating the very patterns of social stratification that it was designed to ameliorate.

My work is informed by a body of critical educational theory, originating with the French sociologist Pierre Bourdieu. Bourdieu's work illustrates how the French educational system manages to help reproduce class relations, all the while maintaining a guise of meritocracy. Privileged families stay ahead by passing on educational credentials to their children; their ability to do so is facilitated by a symbolic system that inevitably runs in their favor. The language, knowledge, and cultural styles of the upper classes arbitrarily become more highly valued and can thus be used as a form of capital. Children with these resources succeed in school and are perceived as being more intelligent because of the ways in which schools legitimize these resources (Bourdieu and Passeron 1977). Bourdieu's early work on this topic set off a torrent of research and debate. One contested issue centers on the extent to which students are regarded as passive dupes of a deterministic system or as autonomous individuals with the capacity to resist (Gaskell 1992; MacLeod 1987; Willis 1977). My book pays close attention to the real structural constraints facing students, as well as to the ways in which students actively maneuver around those constraints. Like Giroux (1983), I see the importance in "understand[ing] more thoroughly the complex ways in which people mediate and respond to the interface between their own lived experiences and structures of domination and constraint" (p. 108). To that end, the intention of this book is to look carefully at the ways in which its actors understand and negotiate their situations. Each student's location—at Yale or at Southern—represents, to some extent, the culmination of eighteen years of relative privilege or disadvantage. Yet while these students' chances can be predicted in part by their social origins, they are also the product of their own choices. Regardless of how and why a student arrives at a particular location, the choices he or she makes will be meaningful, based on a set of understandings about education and opportunity.

Yale and Southern were chosen because, as comparison points, they underscore the inequalities present in American higher education. While elite universities form only a tiny part of the U.S. higher educational system, enrolling just a fraction of all students, they exemplify important aspects of the educational landscape. They are the sites where we see the densest concentration of social privilege. Understanding the workings of education in this arena means that we gain a better understanding of the whole. It is also no coincidence that elite universities uphold the purest version of a liberal arts education. Exploring the liberal arts vision from the perspective of its entanglement with privilege tells us much about how power is conveyed and transmitted through education. Southern falls much closer to the norm in higher education, both in terms of its student body and in its institutionalized educational philosophy. The majority of U.S. university students more closely resemble those at Southern than those at Yale.

The data for this book come from one hundred in-depth, semistructured interviews with random samples of fifty junior- and senior-year men and women from Yale and fifty junior- and senior-year men and women from Southern (see the note on methodology for details of the research design). Although there is some variation in social background within each institution, the students attending Yale come predominantly from highly privileged backgrounds, while half of the students at Southern come from families where neither parent completed a college degree. Along with collecting information on their parents' education, occupation, and family earnings, the interviews included a comprehensive history of each student's schooling. Questions were asked about where the students went to high school and their academic and extracurricular experiences during high school. The interviews then explored their decisions to go to college and their choices of where to apply. Further questions covered the students' academic and extracurricular activities during college. A particular focus of the interviews concerned the choice of a major. The students were asked to tell the whole story of how they had come to select their college major, including the fields they had originally considered and later rejected; the range of factors linked to their final choice of a major; their current views on their decision; and what they most liked and disliked about their field. The interviews concluded with questions about the kinds of jobs the students hoped to find, how much money they imagined they would earn, and their plans, if any, to continue their education beyond a bachelor's degree.

Organization of This Book

Chapter 1 introduces the reader to the two institutions in the study, Yale University and Southern Connecticut State University, and provides brief histories of them. From there, we take a closer look at their respective student populations. Chapter 2 elaborates on the theoretical framework guiding this study and then compares the high school experiences of the Yale and Southern students in my sample. To situate the students' early educational trajectories, the chapter also explores the connections between social background, investments in schooling, and academic achievement, as well as the complex relationships between families and schools that contribute to these connections. Chapters 3 and 4 take up the question of how the students ended up at Yale and Southern: chapter 3 looks at the students' decisions to attend college in the first place, and chapter 4 compares how the students decided where to apply. Chapters 5 and 6 turn to what the students actually did in college: chapter 5 considers differences in how the students spent their college years, and chapter 6 examines both how the students chose their fields of study and how they viewed the knowledge they gained during college. The concluding chapter summarizes the findings from this research, discusses its policy implications, and suggests how it advances our understanding of stratification and higher education.

CHAPTER ONE

Yale and Southern

In the several months I spent traveling the short distance back and forth between Yale and Southern to conduct the interviews for this book, I was struck by the near-complete isolation of each university from the other. Very few members of the academic community at Yale even knew that Southern existed. On meeting a student from Yale for the first time, I would explain a little about my project and would inevitably be asked "Southern? Where is that?" Most had never heard of it or of any of the other seven colleges and universities in the immediate vicinity of New Haven. The obliviousness of the Yale community to its nearest academic neighbor turned almost comical when the Women's Studies Program at Southern held a conference on global justice featuring a keynote speech by Nobel Prize winner Rigoberta Menchu Tum. Yale learned of this event only a few days before it occurred and, surprised that such an eminent speaker was visiting Southern and not Yale, immediately tried to incorporate part of the event at Yale. Unfortunately for them, Menchu's schedule had already been filled and they were left only with the option of attending the talk at Southern. Faculty and administrators alike, however, had never visited Southern and, although it was just two miles away, did not know where it was located or how to get there. Southern finally had to fax them a map.

In some ways, Yale was just as distant for those at Southern. The Southern students had heard of Yale, but few had ever visited the university or knew anyone who had attended it. Moreover, the short geographic distance was over-shadowed by a significant social distance. While the students held Yale in high esteem, they also largely viewed it as a place for rich, snobby kids. These views were not unfounded, as can be seen in the account of what happened when a Southern student visited Yale's art gallery.

> This actually happened to me. I went to the [Yale University] art gallery, and they thought I was from Yale at first, and then when I told them that I wasn't from Yale, they completely just changed their attitude towards me. They didn't want to like talk or anything . . . so it was just really . . . annoying.*

Yale's relationship with the New Haven community has not been smooth, and locals resent Yalies' sense of entitlement and lack of awareness of the city they live in. Although written two decades before my own research began, one observer's description incisively captures the ongoing set of tensions still experienced on a daily basis as townspeople drive home after work through the city streets that cross the Yale campus.

> The Yalies always seemed quietly ruthless and unself-consciously confident in their khaki slacks, blue oxford-cloth shirts, sleeves rolled twice, ties flapping in the breeze, running off to classes or dinner, crossing Elm Street, not bothering about traffic, oblivious. The townspeople resented this terribly . . . driving home in cars that are falling apart but not yet paid for, the last straw for these working-class people is for some smart-ass-rich Yalie to cross in front of a car in defiance of traffic rules, courtesy, or decent responsibility. It is too much. These privileged creatures seemed to make the whole world stop for them, wait for them, fear them. (Glennon 1978, pp. 30–31)

The divide between the two institutions was also apparent in the rooms where I conducted the interviews. When I met students at Yale, I had to wait on the sidewalk outside the college until a student with a scan card unlocked the heavy

---

* The quoted material presented in this book comes from the verbatim transcriptions of the taped interviews, although I have removed false starts and extraneous utterances. I use ellipses to indicate where I have omitted a segment of the interview or where a student has paused. In some cases, I have changed identifying details to protect confidentiality. My interview questions appear in italics.

wrought-iron gate for me.* The interviews were held either in the common room—a spacious room with dark, oak-paneled walls, lead-paned windows, and thick oriental rugs, where we sat in plush, red leather armchairs—or in one of the simpler basement rooms, with plain white walls fitted with blackboards, dark-carpeted floors, and solid oak tables and chairs. At Southern, we usually met in a small administrative room in a large, boxy, cinder block building where we sat together on beige plastic chairs.

The interviews themselves also differed. The Yale students tended to have the composure, confidence, and verbal fluency that come with privilege; they were comfortable and articulate speaking about themselves and expected their views and opinions to be worth listening to. Bourdieu and Passeron (1977) depict this as "the ease that is called 'natural' [which] affirms the well-mastered mastery of language in the casualness of the delivery, the evenness of the tone, and the stylistic under-statement" (p. 119). Tobias Wolff's (2003) novel about upper-class boys at an elite private boarding school also keenly portrays the manner of these students.

> Class was a fact. Not just the clothes a boy wore, but how he wore them. How he spent his summers. The sports he knew how to play. His way of turning cold at the mention of money, or at the spectacle of ambition too nakedly revealed. You felt it as a depth of ease in certain boys, their innate, affable assurance that they would not have to struggle for a place in the world, that it had already been reserved for them. (pp. 15–16)

The interviews with the Southern students inevitably seemed stiffer, at times awkward, and were shorter, on average, than those with the Yale students. The Southern students were generally more tentative and sometimes clearly uncomfortable with the experience of being interviewed, anxious about getting it right. They were more likely to follow up their responses by checking to make sure that they had adequately answered the question. Part of the difference also related to the interview questions themselves. For the Yale students, steeped in a culture that extols the importance of learning and knowledge, the interview questions connected easily to much of what they had thus far spent their lives pursuing. Also, because most of them were academic superstars, the questions provided them with an opportunity to convey their already positive sense of themselves as

---

* Modeling itself on Oxford and Cambridge, Yale assigns every undergraduate student to one of twelve residential colleges. Each college surrounds a gated courtyard and provides a community where students live, eat, and engage in academic and extracurricular activities.

students. The Southern students seemed to have spent less time reflecting on the course of their own education, and the questions sometimes seemed to require more mental review before they could be answered. Also, some of the questions asked about their favorite courses and what kinds of students they were in high school, but many of the Southern students had not particularly enjoyed high school and could not remember a single course that stood out positively. Likewise, many students reported "skating through" or "just doing enough to get by." While they did not seem particularly bashful about sharing these observations, I wondered to what extent being asked was uncomfortable for them.

These observations of the physical assets of the two campuses, the kinds of awareness each does or does not hold of the other, and the dynamics of the interviews begin to create a picture of some of the ways these institutions can be distinguished from each other. The remainder of this chapter fills out this picture by reviewing the histories of the two universities and comparing their student bodies. A central difference between Yale and Southern, besides the variation in their current constituencies, can be found in the way the two institutions go about the business of educating young adults, as reflected in their curricula. The Carnegie Foundation for the Advancement of Teaching, in its 1977 commentary on the missions of college curricula, emphasized that "the curriculum is the major statement any institution of higher education makes about itself, about what it can contribute to the intellectual development of students, about what it thinks is important in its teaching service to society" (quoted in Southern Connecticut State University 1983, p. 21). Yale embraces the notion and practice of a liberal arts education, while Southern crafts an uneasy balance between the liberal arts ideal and a vocational model of education.

Southern Connecticut State University

Southern Connecticut State University began in 1893 as the New Haven State Normal School, a two-year teachers college. In 1937 it became a four-year college and began granting bachelor's degrees; ten years later it began offering a master of science degree. In 1959 the college again expanded and began offering liberal arts programs leading to bachelor's degrees in the arts and sciences; it was also renamed Southern Connecticut State College. Finally, in 1983, the college became part of the Connecticut State University system and was rechristened Southern Connecticut State University. Today about 12,000 students attend Southern; about half of those are full-time undergraduates, while the remainder are part-time and graduate students. The current full-time tuition is $7,578 per year for students who live in-state and $17,270 for students from out of state. Room and board costs another $9,469.

Unlike Yale, Southern offers degrees in several preprofessional fields. The university comprises five schools, four of which (the schools of business, education, health and human services, and communication information and library sciences) offer degrees in applied fields. The remaining school, arts and sciences, awards degrees in a wide range of liberal arts fields. However, while students may obtain degrees in preprofessional fields, the curriculum at Southern also adheres to the liberal arts philosophy. Students are required to take about a third of their courses in the humanities, the social sciences, the natural sciences, math, and foreign languages, along with a few courses in communications, physical education, and health, selecting from a range of courses within these categories to fulfill those requirements. This All-University Curriculum has been in place since 1970, when the university adopted a liberalization of its existing curriculum, reducing the number of courses required for graduation and replacing nearly all specific course requirements with area requirements (Southern Connecticut State University 1983).

In several university documents, the justification for the All-University requirements rests squarely on liberal arts notions. The requirements were meant to provide students with a solid grounding in the liberal arts and to serve as a foundation for their degree programs. A 1983 document detailing a then-current review of the curriculum invoked the ideal of training students to be lifelong learners and declared that "the traditional tenets of a liberal education have been successful in producing adaptable, educated citizens" (Southern Connecticut State University 1983, p. 22). A 1996 Strategic Plan contains a long list of general education objectives (Southern Connecticut State University 2002, p. 32), including the following items:

- impart useful knowledge, skills, and understandings to students to develop the ability and desire to continue reading, pondering, and acting upon issues of professional and societal concern;
- impart useful knowledge, skills, and understandings to students to develop a sense of the interconnectedness of ideas and knowledge, such that living as liberally education [*sic*] human beings is possible; and
- influence students to develop a willingness for intellectual exploration and the risk this involves.

While the administrators and faculty at Southern seemingly advocate the notion of a liberal arts education, these documents also suggest a mismatch between their views and those of the students. The 1983 review states that

> the liberal arts portion of the student's education may ultimately prove to be the most important and valuable part of the curriculum. One of the primary tasks of concerned faculty is to convince students of these conclusions so that they view these requirements in proper perspective and give them the attention and study they deserve. (Southern Connecticut State University 1983, p. 22)

In 2002, the General Education Subcommittee at Southern wrote that "students fail to see a purpose to liberal education and so lack interest in their general education classes" (Southern Connecticut State University 2002, p. 2). The report goes on to outline the results of a survey of alumni five years after graduation that revealed students' discontent with the general education program. Alumni made comments such as "Eliminate the university requirements. Let us focus on our intended major" and "[Requirements] limit the amount of time that students can put into classes that will affect their career goals" (p. 8). Their report also cites the difficulties of maintaining a liberal arts education with a "diverse student body," as opposed to the homogeneous student bodies found at small liberal arts colleges (p. 14).

The disjuncture between the stated liberal arts goals of the university and the more career-oriented motivations of its students comes across in the online descriptions of fields of study. Even for students majoring in liberal arts, the university emphasizes the marketable characteristics of these fields. Under their description of the fine arts, for example, the following advice is offered:

> An artist might paint or sculpt, design a magazine or a Web site, teach a child. A musician might perform or compose, manage or promote concerts, repair instruments. A theatre person might star on Broadway, paint sets, sew costumes, launch a community theatre, or write reviews. All of them are doing what they love. All of them are making art possible.
>
> The fine arts graduate might do all of this and much more. (Southern Connecticut State University 2009b)

Prospective humanities students are advised that they will "develop . . . the ability to reason and communicate with strength and subtlety, in one or more languages." The fields are then closely linked to more practical applications: "Many professions welcome people trained in the humanities—journalism, business, education, and law are but a few" (Southern Connecticut State University 2009c).

Yale University

Yale University was founded in 1701, with the idea of maintaining the tradition of European liberal education in the New World. It is about the same size as Southern, currently enrolling just over 11,000 students, about half undergraduate and half graduate and professional students. The university is extraordinarily wealthy and boasts an endowment of over $15 billion, about two thousand times greater than Southern's $8 million endowment. Full-time tuition for one year runs at $36,500, nearly five times more than Southern's in-state tuition, plus another $11,000 for room and board. Yale does, however, offer "needs-blind" admissions and guarantees that any admitted student will receive sufficient financial aid to cover the cost of attending Yale.

Unlike Southern, Yale has emphasized the centrality of liberal arts learning from its inception. Founded as an institution " 'wherein Youth may be instructed in the Arts and Sciences [and] through the blessing of the Almighty God may be fitted for Publick employment both in Church and Civil State' " (all quotations from Yale University 2005a, a self-study report), the liberal arts doctrine has been perennially reaffirmed. The Yale Report of 1828, for example, declared that "the two great points to be gained in intellectual culture are the discipline and the furniture of the mind: expanding its powers, and storing it with knowledge." Noah Porter, president of Yale from 1871–86, stated that "higher education should aim at intellectual culture and training rather than at the acquisition of knowledge, and it should respect remote rather than immediate results." In the 1950s, A. Whitney Griswold, Yale's president at the time, reinforced this theme.

> The purpose of the liberal arts is not to teach businessmen business, or grammarians grammar, or college students Greek and Latin . . . It is to awaken and develop the intellectual and spiritual powers in the individual before he enters upon his chosen career, so that he may bring to that career the greatest possible assets of intelligence, resourcefulness, judgment and character.

The self-study report portrays Yale's mission and purpose as twofold. The first emphasizes liberal arts instruction in order to "develop the freedom to think critically and independently, to cultivate one's mind to its fullest potential."

The second and related objective is an "emphasis on instruction in the liberal arts for service to the larger society." Here, the report goes on to discuss the development of the "whole person," by training "active and energetic citizens," and character formation, defined as the "development of a quality of mind and spirit that transcend [*sic*] the acquisition or creation of knowledge per se." A person thus educated should be better prepared to serve the larger society. Likewise, the report's current mission statement for Yale College (the undergraduate program) begins with this exalted declaration:

> The mission of Yale College is to seek exceptionally promising students of all backgrounds from across the nation and around the world and to educate them, through mental discipline and social experience, to develop their intellectual, moral, civic, and creative capacities to the fullest. The aim of this education is the cultivation of citizens with a rich awareness of our human heritage to lead and serve in every sphere of human activity.

Underscoring this point, the Yale course catalog, published every year, begins by reminding students that

> Yale College offers a liberal arts education, one that aims to train a broadly based, highly disciplined intellect without specifying in advance how that intellect will be used . . . The college does not primarily train students in the particulars of a given career . . . Instead, its main goal is to instill in students the development of skills that they can bring to bear in whatever work they eventually choose. (Yale University 2005b)

Throughout its three-hundred-year history, Yale has consistently positioned itself as a liberal arts institution, in both its mission statements and its undergraduate curriculum. While Southern also draws on liberal arts notions of what it means to educate students and seeks to provide all students with a well-rounded, general academic curriculum, the major difference between the two lies in Southern's extensive applied-program offerings. At the undergraduate level, Yale offers a single applied field, engineering, while Southern has a broad range of preprofessional fields, in combination with a balanced series of general education requirements.

The differences in the curricula between Yale and Southern reflect a national pattern whereby the most prestigious institutions offer the highest proportion of degrees in liberal arts fields, while the least prestigious offer predominantly applied fields (Brint et al. 2005). Indeed, the lowest-status postsecondary institutions, two-year colleges, almost exclusively provide degrees in vocational fields. The liberal arts convey status through an association with a higher level of intelligence (Lewis 1993; Rose 2008; Sanderson 1993). As Rose (2008) explains, "the academic course of study, not the vocational . . . has been identified as the place where intelligence is manifest . . . a language of abstraction, smarts, and big ideas surrounds the academic course of study, which is symbolically, structurally, and often geographically on the other side of the campus from the domain of the manual, the concrete, the practical, the gritty" (p. 635).

Despite its association with status, a liberal arts education has not been fully embraced by much of the American student population. Only about 40 percent of all undergraduate students major in the liberal arts, down from around 55 percent in the mid-1960s (Brint et al. 2005). This may be in part related to changes in educational values. Trend data from an annual survey of freshman students at U.S. colleges and universities show notable shifts in students' values between 1966 and 1996. During this period, the value given by freshmen to "developing a meaningful philosophy of life" and "being very well-off financially" essentially reversed. In the late 1960s, more than 80 percent of entering freshmen ranked developing a meaningful philosophy of life as an "essential" or "very important" goal, while only 45 percent of freshmen saw being very well-off financially as an important or essential life goal. The pattern had reversed by the late 1980s and has since held constant, with nearly 75 percent of all students endorsing the importance of being very well off financially and only 42 percent valuing the development of a meaningful philosophy of life (Astin 1998). Further, most students (79%) remain unclear about the goals of a liberal arts education and also believe that a liberal arts degree will not help in getting a job because of the perception that it does not provide marketable career skills (Pascarella et al. 2005). Many report that developing career skills remains the most important aspect of higher education.

While most students now pursuing higher education major in applied fields in order to prepare for a specific career, there are exceptions. Students from higher-SES families, as well as students in more prestigious institutions, independent of their SES, are more likely to select a liberal arts field of study (Goyette and Mullen 2006). This raises questions about why these students continue to study the liberal arts, when most students have turned toward preprofessional training, and about the possible influence of their institutions. One of the topics this book takes up in later chapters is the degree of correspondence between the educational missions of Yale and Southern and the ambitions and motivations of their students. For now, this chapter looks at the kinds of students who attend these two institutions.

The Students at Yale and Southern

As expected, Yale students by and large come from exceptionally privileged social origins. More than half of the students in my sample reported annual family incomes in excess of $135,000, placing them in the top 15 percent of the income scale (see table 1.1). Almost 80 percent of the Yale students had parents with a bachelor's degree or more, and a little over two-thirds had parents with some form of graduate education. Almost half of them listed their parents' occupations as doctor, lawyer, scientist, or professor. In comparison, just 10 percent of the Southern students reported family incomes of $135,000 or higher, and only a little over a fifth of them came from families where at least one parent has a graduate degree. Conversely, more than half of the Southern students would be the first in their families to graduate from college, compared with 21 percent of the Yale students. There are also large gaps in the prior levels of academic achievement for the two groups of students. The average combined SAT score of all Yale students was 1490 (out of a total of 1600), compared with 935 for all Southern students. In terms of retention, 96 percent of all Yale students will graduate within six years, compared with just a third of all Southern students (Connecticut Department of Higher Education 2007). At both Southern and Yale, about 70 percent of the students are white. Women comprise 60 percent of the student body at Southern, but only 47 percent at Yale. Finally, at Yale, over 90 percent of the students come from out of state; at Southern, over 90 percent are in-state.

In comparison with the Yale students in my study, the Southern students came from families with considerably less education and much lower incomes. However, there were also important distinctions within each group. At Southern, the most significant division was the line between those students who were first-generation college students and those who were not. The occupations of the parents of the first-generation students clustered mainly in the manual labor and service fields. Their fathers were factory workers, firemen, and truck drivers, while their mothers were secretaries, teacher's aides, and day-care providers. In contrast, the fathers of the non-first-generation students tended to be businessmen or salesmen, while their mothers were teachers, nurses, and accountants. Only one of the first-generation students at Southern reported a family income

Table 1.1   Students' family and academic backgrounds, by number of students and percentages (in parentheses)

	Southern	Yale
Parents' highest level of education		
Less than a college degree	26 (52)	10 (21)
College degree	13 (26)	5 (11)
Graduate degree	11 (22)	32 (68)
Annual family income*		
Less than $54,000	11 (22)	6 (15)
$54,000–$134,999	33 (67)	13 (33)
$135,000 or above	5 (10)	21 (53)
Average SAT score (out of a total of 1600)†	935	1490

Note: N = 100; 3 missing cases for parents' education, 11 missing cases for family income.

*In the United States as a whole, 39 percent of the families had household incomes under $54,000, 46 percent had incomes between $54,000 and $134,999, and 15 percent had incomes of $135,000 and above (U.S. Census Bureau 2000). Dollar amounts are given in 2008 dollars.

†Figures represent the average score of all entering students in the fall of 2006 (National Center for Education Statistics).

in the top category, compared with four of the non-first-generation students. The distinction between first-generation students and their peers with higher levels of family education related to many facets of the students' educational experiences.

In my Yale sample, about a quarter of the students reported an uncommon set of educational and family circumstances. Almost all of these students listed family incomes in excess of $135,000 and came from families where both parents had professional or advanced degrees. Their parents', especially their fathers', occupations were in the top professional ranks: doctors, lawyers, bankers, professors, and executives. These privileged families had also invested heavily in their children's education, long before beginning to pay Yale's tuition, as almost all of the students in this group attended private, nonparochial high schools. A second group of students, about half of the Yalies in the sample, came from solid middle- and upper-middle-class professional families. About half of this group attended private and the other half public high schools. Finally, twelve of the students (eight women and four men) came from families in which neither parent completed college. Their parents held clerical and blue-collar jobs, such as receptionist, custodian, machinist, and electrician. Their family incomes were much lower than those of the other Yale students; only one of them listed a family income in the top income bracket. The majority of these students attended public or Catholic high schools; only two attended private schools. They were the most diverse group of students at Yale: of the twelve, three were white, two Asian, three black, and four Hispanic. Three of the students were first-generation immigrants (all three had attended at least high school in the United States, a requirement for selection into the sample).

Seven students in the Yale sample (all male) mentioned having been recruited through athletics to come to Yale (though it was not clear whether they had been given admissions preference or whether they had been merely sought out and encouraged to apply because of their athletic abilities). Of the seven, three were first-generation college students. Two came from middle-class families and two came from the lower middle class. One of the seven was African-American and the other six were white. Because the place of athletes at institutions of higher education generally, and in the Ivy League in particular, has received a great deal of scholarly and popular attention in the past several years (Bowen and Levin 2003; Shulman and Bowen 2001; Wolfe 2004), this group deserves further discussion.

Student-Athletes at Yale

While athletics have long been regarded as an important part of campus life and as an enriching experience for the athletes themselves, in recent years concern has grown about the widening divide between intercollegiate athletics and the academic mission. Critics have questioned the prominent place reserved for athletics at top colleges, voicing worries over its threat to educational values (Bowen and Levin 2003; Shulman and Bowen 2001; Wolfe 2004). The issue has come to the forefront for two central reasons: first, the recruitment of athletes, and second, their academic performance once in college.

Ivy League universities, by their own choice, do not offer athletic scholarships. However, they do actively recruit potential student-athletes. In the recruitment process, college athletics coaches at these institutions review the athletic records of promising high school athletes and initiate contact with those who best fit their current needs. Then, having identified the students they like who appear to have the necessary academic qualifications, the coaches compile a list of these names and submit the preferred list directly to the admissions office (Bowen and Levin 2003; Shulman and Bowen 2001; Stevens 2007). These students then receive a hefty admissions advantage. In 1999, both male and female athletes at Ivy League universities were found to have an over 50 percent better chance of being admitted than other students, controlling for differences in SAT scores (Bowen and Levin 2003). In one selective university (again controlling for SAT scores), athletes had a 48 percent better chance of being admitted than the average student, while legacy students had a 25 percent admissions advantage and minority students had only an 18 percent admissions advantage (Shulman and Bowen 2001). Thus the advantage provided to athletes is about twice as much as that provided to legacy or minority students. Shulman and Bowen also find that the admissions advantage given to athletes has increased dramatically since 1976. By 1995, recruited athletes made up 16 percent of the entering male cohort and 11 percent of the female cohort at Ivy League universities, and in some sports (such as the high-profile sports of football, basketball, and men's ice hockey), 82 percent of the male athletes participating in them were recruited (Bowen and Levin 2003).

Concerns over the recruitment process have been fueled by the academic performance of student-athletes. Both male and female recruited athletes earn significantly lower grade point averages (GPAs) than other students (Bowen and Levin 2003), and their academic underperformance cannot be explained by race, socioeconomic status, field of study, or even SAT scores (Shulman and Bowen 2001). The effect is stronger for male athletes and for athletes in high-profile sports. Indeed, 81 percent of high-profile male athletes rank in the bottom third of their class (Bowen and Levin 2003). Further, tendencies toward academic underperformance have become more pronounced over time (Shulman and Bowen 2001).

Student-athletes also differ in other notable ways from their peers. Politically, male athletes are less likely to be liberals or on the far left. They are also more concerned with money; athletes are more likely than their peers to rank being very well off financially as a very important or essential goal. This finding cannot be explained by social background but holds even when controlling for the educational attainment of their fathers (Shulman and Bowen 2001). Perhaps because of the greater importance they attribute to financial success, athletes are more likely to be interested in pursuing business careers. They, and particularly male athletes, also differ from other students in their choices of fields of study. Athletes at Ivy League universities tend to concentrate in the social sciences and in business, rather than in the humanities, science, or engineering. Fifty-six percent of high-profile male athletes recruited in the 1995 entering cohort of students at Ivy League universities selected social science or business majors, compared with only 34 percent of their peers (Bowen and Levin 2003). Finally, student-athletes tend to build friendships and room with other athletes, creating consternation that athletes have become a segregated group on campus (Shulman and Bowen 2001). Taken together, these findings suggest the possibility of an athletic culture on college campuses, where athletes share similar values, concentrate in the same majors, and socialize and room together. Concerns have grown that this athletic culture may be at odds with the academic culture; the athletes themselves may be ill served by not taking full advantage of academic opportunities, and academic standards may be lowered to support athletes.

The significant reported differences between student-athletes and their peers at elite institutions make it important to explore this potential source of variation within my sample of Yale students. As we will see in later chapters, the student-athletes I interviewed for this study stand out from their peers in a number of ways. (At Southern, there were too few student-athletes in my sample to discern any meaningful differences from the other students.)

•   •   •

This chapter brings the distance between these two New Haven universities into view. One institution evolved around the purpose of training leaders; one began with the mission of training teachers. One maintains a liberal arts curriculum; one blends an applied focus with general education requirements. One educates primarily children of wealth and privilege; one serves youth from much further down the SES scale. These differences exemplify the inequalities characteristic of the higher educational system in the United States, a system in which the richest and most prestigious universities enroll children from the richest and most prestigious families.

They also underscore the relationship between privilege and curriculum. The historic purpose of the liberal arts curriculum was to educate young men to be civil and religious leaders (Pascarella et al. 2005). This position rests on a long history that differentiates between education for the ruling classes and education for the masses (Lewis 1993; Sanderson 1993), between liberal arts and vocational education, between people who work with their minds and people who work with their hands, or, more recently, between knowledge workers and skill workers. Yale and the other Ivy League institutions have fulfilled the liberal arts ideal, producing more leaders in the nineteenth century than all other colleges combined and continuing to lead all others through the first half of the twentieth century (Geiger 2008). Historically, however, the leadership-training component of the liberal arts ideal entirely excluded women and minorities. For almost all of its more than 300-year history, the leaders produced by Yale were white Protestant men. None of the Ivies began matriculating women until the late 1960s, and there were very few racial or ethnic minority students until around the same time. When Yale did begin to admit women, instead of lowering the number of men admitted, it simply expanded the size of new entering classes in order to keep its avowed commitment to producing 1,000 male leaders every year (*Time* 1972).

Yale continues to link the notion of a liberal arts education to leadership training, taking as its mission preparing students to "lead and serve in every sphere of human activity" (Yale University 2005a). While Yale produces leaders, Southern produces labor power, stating as a primary objective meeting the "workforce needs of the state's economy" (Connecticut Department of Higher Education 2009, p. 3). The figurative distance I observed between the two institutions undoubtedly persists in the social distance between the graduates of these institutions. More likely than not, many of the owners and managers of the organizations in which the Southern students I interviewed will find jobs, and the political leaders they will vote for, will be graduates from Yale and other Ivy League institutions.

How is it that students are sorted into these institutions? How is it that Yale easily fills its entering class every year with the most academically talented *and* the most socially advantaged youth? The next three chapters take as their task disentangling the complex forces behind the "seamless web of circumstance" that accounts for how social privilege so often translates into academic privilege (Central Advisory Council for Education 1967, pp. 50).

CHAPTER TWO

The High School Years

By the time students hit high school, they are well along the educational trajectories that will take them to their final destinations. Some will graduate from high school and enroll in a top university or other four-year institution, while others will enter community colleges. Still others will end their education with high school, and some may not even finish high school. These trajectories can be linked to profound class-based differences in levels of academic achievement, motivation, educational expectations, and even a sense of what it means to be a student. Because the patterns already established in high school hold such importance for students' postsecondary educational futures, this chapter takes a close look at the descriptions the students in my study gave of their high school experiences. Before turning to the stories of the students, however, it is important to explore the connections between social background and academic outcomes, and the complicated relationships between families and schools that contribute to them.

Studies consistently document wide discrepancies in academic achievement by social background. High school seniors from high-SES families are three to four times more likely to demonstrate advanced proficiency in reading, science, and math than their peers from low-SES families. On the other end of the scale, nearly a third of low-SES students score at the below-basic level in science proficiency, and almost half score at the lowest level of math proficiency, compared with much smaller fractions of students from medium- and high-SES families (Green et al. 1995). In terms of course selection, although the formal tracking system where students were separated into groups for all academic subjects was largely dismantled by the mid-1970s, most schools continue to offer different series of courses, ranging from advanced and college preparatory to general, vocational and technical (Lucas 1999). These streams of study vary by subject and, unlike the previous, more rigid tracking system, students may enroll in different subjects at different levels (for example, taking college-preparatory English classes but general-level math courses). Students may also move between tracks from year to year, moving up into more advanced levels or down to the general levels. Social background corresponds closely to high school course enrollment. For example, half of the 2003–04 high school graduates in the highest SES quartile had taken Advanced Placement (AP) or International Baccalaureate courses, compared with only 16 percent of the students in the lowest SES quartile (Planty, Bozick, and Ingels 2006). Similarly, students in the top SES quartile were more than three times as likely as the others to concentrate their studies in academic courses (42% versus 13%, respectively) and much less likely than the others to concentrate in vocational areas (8% versus 21%). Statistics about high school programs and academic achievement actually understate the real disparities by SES, because low-SES students, and in particular those with a low level of academic achievement, are more likely to drop out of high school and are therefore not included in such studies.

Nearly all students highly value education; independent of SES, around 90 percent of high school seniors rate getting a good education as "very important." However, while students converge in the value they place on education, and most students plan to continue their education in some form after high school, postsecondary expectations differ. Low-SES students are much more likely to set their sights on two-year degrees, while high-SES students are more apt to plan on a four-year degree followed by a graduate program; just over half (53%) of high-SES students indicated plans to go to graduate school, compared with only 31 percent and 22 percent of medium- and low-SES students, respectively. Conversely, 27 percent of low-SES students planned to attain only a two-year degree, compared with only 7 percent of high-SES students (Ingels, Planty and Bozick 2005).

Going hand in hand with these patterns, for several decades scholars have documented variations in students' commitment or opposition to the official ideology of schools. Students who identify strongly with their school and fully participate in it tend to come from relatively privileged backgrounds, while students who are disengaged or even alienated are more likely to come from low-SES families. In his classic work on the British educational system, Bernstein (1975) identified five ordered categories of what he termed "pupil role involvements": commitment, detachment, deferment, estrangement, and alienation. Students' positioning within these categories depends on the extent to which they accept their school's values and processes, which in turn depends on their family's alignment with the school's values. While there are certainly exceptions, children from middle-class families are more likely to be committed to the school's values, while alienated students, who stand in opposition to such values, more typically come from working-class families. Willis (1977), in his well-known study of working-class boys at a British school, found that some boys developed a counterculture perspective that opposed the values and norms embraced by the school. Because of their cognizance of the low probability of their eventual entry into the white-collar world, they regarded academic work as having little value and thus, instead of investing in school, preferred to amuse themselves by "having a laff." Ironically, their opposition to the achievement ideology ensured their confinement to working-class jobs. In a study of American high schools, Eckert (1989) uncovered similar dynamics. She identified two primary groups of students: "jocks," who were college-bound, middle-class students who participated in sports and other school activities; and "burnouts," who were disaffected working-class students who maintained an adversarial relationship with the school.

What accounts for these firmly entrenched, class-based patterns of achievement, educational expectations, and student identity? Why are children from privileged families far more likely to do better in school, take more academic courses, and plan to attend a four-year college before going on to graduate school? Sociologists who have investigated the links between social background and academic achievement have identified three sets of resources that families utilize to contribute to their children's academic success: economic, social, and cultural. In addition, it is important to examine the relationships between families and schools that further support these class-based dynamics, such as the way that middle-class norms and values become inculcated in schools.

Family Resources: Economic, Social, and Cultural

A family's economic resources affect the quality of the schools their children attend. Wealthier families will be able to pay for private schools or afford housing in the middle-class neighborhoods that have better public schools (the effects of the schools themselves are discussed later). Devine (2004) shows how families from higher social strata intentionally settle in neighborhoods with better public schools; the affluent physicians she interviewed in her study explicitly stated that their choice of residence was influenced first and foremost by the local school system. Realtors use the quality of local public schools as a selling point, and some families move from one neighborhood to another for the sole purpose of enrolling their children in the best schools. Wealthy parents also have the means to pay for out-of-school activities that facilitate academic achievement, such as summer camps and dance, music, and art lessons (Lareau 2003). They keep more books and magazines in their homes, can afford to purchase computers for their children, and have homes large enough to include a quiet study area, all of which can improve grades (Roscigno and Ainsworth-Darnell 1999). In cases where their children encounter difficulties in school, wealthier families may hire private tutors to provide extra assistance for their children (Lareau 1987). While all families may wish to help their children academically, families with economic resources that they can mobilize may do so more effectively.

Families may also draw on social resources to support their children's educational success (Bourdieu 1986; Coleman 1988; Zhou 1997). Middle-class families benefit from having a wider and more diverse social network of friends, colleagues, neighbors, and relatives. During dinner parties and office water-cooler conversations they can exchange valuable information about the neighborhoods with the best schools, the best teachers within those schools, or tips for successful applications to private schools (Devine 2004). Knowledge shared in this way is easier to gather and less time-consuming than other methods of research, and families tend to trust the information because it comes from people they know. Families also benefit from the social pressure for academic success conveyed through the academic ethos of their friends. In this way, social networks serve as more than just channels of information; they may also influence both educational expectations and choices.

Finally, a family's cultural resources contribute toward academic success. The French sociologist Pierre Bourdieu (1984) attributed academic achievement largely to the type and quantity of cultural capital passed down to children by their families, as opposed to being the result of innate intelligence. Cultural capital includes a wide array of linguistic competencies, general cultural awareness, preferences, and information about the schooling system. Although Bourdieu's theory, and its applicability to North America, still receive extensive debate (Kingston 2001; Lareau and Weininger 2003; Swartz 1997), research supports the premise that cultural capital affects academic success. For example, knowledge about or participation in highbrow cultural forms or activities positively predicts students' grades in school (Aschaffenburg and Maas 1997; DiMaggio 1982). Class-based differences in language patterns also contribute to gaps in educational achievement. Bernstein (1975), for example, shows how the speech patterns of working-class families rest on the assumption of collectively shared meanings and thus utilize restricted codes that contain implicit subject and object references. A working-class child might say, for example, "They're playing football and he kicks it and it goes through there and it breaks the window," assuming her listeners have knowledge of the implicit references. In contrast, middle-class families, because their communication is less tied to local relationships, employ more explicit, or elaborated, speech codes. A middle-class child would more likely say, "Three boys are playing football and one boy kicks the ball and it goes through the window and the ball breaks the window." These differences in speech patterns become problematic for working-class children, because the linguistic norms of educational institutions correspond to the elaborated codes of the middle class, leaving working-class children at a considerable disadvantage. Similarly, Heath (1983) conducted an ethnographic study of black and white working-class communities in the Carolinas and identified differences in language patterns that affect success in school. The white families in her study more actively taught their children from a young age to engage in conversation and encouraged them to label and name objects and to respond to direct informational questions. In contrast, the black families tended to engage their children as conversational partners less frequently and were more likely to ask questions that required answers in the form of analogies, rather than specific bits of factual information. Consequently, the black working-class children in Heath's study received less socialization in the language patterns used in schools, resulting in lower academic achievement.

An important theoretical component of all of these studies is what Bourdieu and Passeron (1977) refer to as the "cultural arbitrary." According to these authors, the cultural standards of dominant groups establish the cultural standards employed in schools. However, the cultural standards of any group are fundamentally arbitrary and do not reflect intrinsically higher forms of knowledge or values. If this is so, then schools could just as easily value the ability to communicate through analogy rather than through factual information, value restricted codes rather than elaborated ones, or value knowledge of lowbrow rather than highbrow cultural forms. Therefore, one major way that the dominant groups in society maintain their position is by successfully establishing cultural standards in schools that correspond to their own arbitrary standards, ensuring a built-in level of advantage for their children. Not only do these children already have higher levels of the kinds of cultural and linguistic capital that are legitimated and rewarded in schools, but teachers also perceive these children as having more innate intelligence and ability than children without these kinds of cultural resources.

Culture can also work as a resource in the way that it influences decision making and behavior. Bourdieu (1984) defines the concept of habitus as a set of dispositions that structure perceptions, practices, and lines of action. One of the most significant ways in which this occurs is through expectations. Habitus expresses itself in "a practical anticipation of objective limits acquired by experience of objective limits, a sense of 'one's place' which leads one to exclude oneself from the goods, persons, places and so forth from which one is excluded" (p. 471). In other words, the evaluation of objective chances influences the choices that appear unthinkable, possible, or probable, shaping the aspirations and expectations that guide decision making and action.

Lareau's (2003) study of class-based philosophies and practices of childrearing illustrates how parents transmit different habitus and cultural capital to their children. According to Lareau, middle-class families tend to adopt the ideal of *cultivating* the talents of their children, while working-class families follow a process of allowing the *natural growth* of their children. Everyday parenting routines differ according to these logics, with middle-class families spending more time talking directly to their children and soliciting their views and opinions. In the process, these children obtain greater verbal facility and larger vocabularies. Middle-class parents also teach their children to interact in more confident ways with authority figures, such as shaking hands with adults and looking them in the eye. While both types of childrearing offer different kinds of advantages and disadvantages, the practices of middle-class families are accorded more social value by institutions such as schools. Thus the cultural practices associated with concerted cultivation provide benefits to children that other cultural practices do not. Among other aspects, middle-class children develop and value an individualized sense of self and a strong sense of entitlement.

Another way that families contribute to the development of their children's habitus is through the educational expectations they hold for them. Families vary in how much education they expect their children to receive. Over 80 percent of the families where the annual income is more than $75,000 or where at least one parent has a bachelor's degree expect their children to obtain a bachelor's degree. Conversely, in families where the annual income is $25,000 or less or where parents have only a high school degree, less than 50 percent expect their children to earn a bachelor's degree (Lippman et al. 2008). Parents pass on these expectations to their children, influencing how likely the children are to envision the possibility of going to college (Looker and Pineo 1983). When a child is raised in a family where both parents attended college, as well as most of their parents' friends and relatives, going to college may be regarded as an almost inevitable part of growing up.

The Effects of Schools

Differences in schooling also play a role in contributing to uneven educational achievement. As noted above, wealthy parents are more likely to send their children to private schools or live in neighborhoods with high-quality public schools. One of the most important reasons why students do better in these schools is the social composition of the student body. All students do better when they attend a middle-class school, regardless of family background (for a review, see Kahlenberg 2001). This finding was first established in a major national study commissioned by the U.S. Congress, *Equality of Educational Opportunity*, also referred to as the Coleman Report (Coleman et al. 1966). Coleman (1967) observed that children from a given family background achieve at different levels when attending schools of different social compositions and concluded that "the educational resources provided by a child's fellow students are more important for his achievement than are the resources provided by the school board" (p. 21). Furthermore, "the social composition of the student body is more highly related to achievement, independent of the student's own social background, than is any school factor" (Coleman et al. 1966, cited in Kahlenberg 2001, p. 26). Coleman's conclusion that the resources provided by the social composition of schools are more important for student performance than other kinds of school resources (such as teacher salaries and expenditures per student) has since been confirmed by hundreds of other studies (summarized in Gamoran and Long 2006; Hanushek 1997, 1998).

Why does the social composition of the student body make such a big difference? One reason is that high-SES students have more ambitious educational expectations and a greater motivation to do well academically, which help raise the expectations and motivation of all students. In short, motivated students with high expectations are a good influence on other students. From the opposite perspective, if a student attends a school where many students drop out, that option may come to be regarded as a more viable possibility than if he or she attends a school with a very low dropout rate (Coleman et al. 1966). Second, students from high-SES families tend to be higher achievers and help their peers by sharing knowledge and language facility, such as vocabulary.

While differences in teacher salaries, teacher-to-student ratios, and expenditures per student show weak or inconsistent effects on academic success (Hanushek 1997), some characteristics of schools do make a difference. Just as parents' and peers' expectations play a role in shaping a student's own expectations, so, too, do the expectations of teachers. Teachers' expectations have a direct bearing on students' achievement levels (Dougherty 1996), and the higher the overall social class of the student body, the greater the expectations that teachers hold for students (Kahlenberg 2001). In addition, teachers have higher expectations for students on academic tracks, even controlling for initial differences in academic aptitude. This has been identified as one reason why students placed in these tracks perform better than students on lower tracks (Dougherty 1996).

Remarkably, academic aptitude does not explain the majority of track placements, while social class plays a significant role. Students in academic tracks take more math and science courses, study more complex material, and cover more material overall. Not surprisingly, Dougherty found that students in the top, or academic, tracks then score higher on tests than their counterparts in vocational or lower-ability tracks, even after controlling for the students' backgrounds, initial academic aptitudes, and educational expectations. Academic standards, rigor, and teaching styles also differ by school. Again, schools with a higher-SES student body tend to provide more challenging curricula, as well as to place more emphasis on open-ended discussions and independent thinking and less on rote learning and memorization (Gamoran 1987; Kahlenberg 2001). For all of these reasons, private schools and schools in wealthier neighborhoods produce higher-performing students.

In the end, children of privilege do better academically because of a multitude of advantages arising from their families and schools. The performance gap between rich and poor students is small in kindergarten, but the accumulation of advantages over time manifests itself in wide gaps in academic achievement by the end of high school. A close look at the high school educational experiences of Southern and Yale students explores some of the ways these differences contribute toward setting students on diverging educational trajectories.

The High School Years of Yale and Southern Students

The accounts the Yale and the Southern students gave of their high school years bore little resemblance to each other. For the most part, the Yale students were highly motivated academic standouts who also participated in a full complement of extracurricular activities. A standard description of high school for a Yale student went like this:

> I got one B in all of high school. I was student body president, varsity athlete in three different sports, sang in choir, did German club, went to Germany. I mean, people at Yale do, like, everything in high school. That's one of the reasons why they come here.

Maintaining high grade point averages while staying involved with sports and other activities meant packed schedules and a lot of hard work. With the exceptions of some of the student-athletes, who I will turn to later in this chapter, and a few Yale students who mentioned breezing through high school, most Yalies recounted the tremendous effort and dedication they put into their studies and school activities.

> I worked really hard, I killed myself. I worked harder than I work here.

> You were in classes from 9 a.m. to 3:30 and then, I mean, this is what I did, and then I'd play on a sports team every season, 'til like 5:30, and then rehearsals for a play or a musical 'til like 8:30, you know, or working on the school paper. Just that you did a million things, and you know, like student government, just doing all these extracurricular activities, in addition to having classes all day with no break.

> I was extremely diligent . . . I worked, well, as much as you can say 24/7, I worked constantly . . . I was a very hard worker.

> I worked very hard. I took like a whole bunch of courses. Like there was one year that I took six courses and most of the other years I took five when all you really had to take was four. And, I don't know, I just, I always did all my homework.

At Southern, only about a quarter of the students shared similar experiences, taking honors courses, earning mostly As, and involving themselves in several extracurricular activities. Instead, the majority of the Southern students described a vastly different kind of high school experience, characterized by doing the bare minimum, or just enough to get by. When asked what kinds of students they were in high school, typical replies went like this:

> Cs, straight Cs, just did enough.

> I didn't try, just kind of skated through. I didn't really do much.

> I just slid by, I did what I had to do to get by. I didn't put much effort into it.

> Average. I didn't really do all my work all that great, I just did what I had to to get by, so I got my basic Bs.

> I was an average student. You know, I didn't care that much at that time, about school and stuff.

For some Southern students, the main objective was simply passing their courses.

> I would just do things just to pass, wouldn't put any extra effort really to, you know, to ace, or you know, I did what I thought was necessary to pass the course.

> I guess I was a good student. I did probably the bare minimum to get by, but, I mean, I passed so that was good.

Although there were exceptions in both groups, most of the Yale students matched Bernstein's ideal of the committed student, while the Southern students, for the most part, did not "apply themselves," as they often put it. The roots of this divergence in motivation and involvement often could be seen in the educational expectations held by the students and their families. While their families may have been similar in valuing education, the families differed in the degree to which they emphasized this value and expected their children to be good students, and the students differed in how much their own identities became tied to a sense of *being* a good student. The college expectations of the students also varied, ranging from uncertainty about going to college at all to the certainty of attending an Ivy League university. Each of these elements worked to create motivation or indifference. Yet if the source of commitment to schooling came first from expectations passed down from their families, the students' high schools then played an important role in either further activating, or, as was often the case with the Southern students, diminishing motivation. The initial differences in educational expectations between the Yale and the Southern students became magnified through the students' experiences with their high schools.

Yale Students: Being a Good Student and Getting into a Good School

Compared with the Southern students, the Yale students more frequently remarked about the educational expectations their families held for them. Several comments revealed the families' emphasis on getting a good education and being a good student; they also highlighted the influence of these factors on the students' academic performances.

> I'd say I was a typical student, but all through my life my parents always stressed education, that's just the way they are. They're really big on education, so that's like, I've always done well in school.

> It's always been, academics have been the most important thing in my family.

> Parents definitely played a role in [motivating me] . . . My father saw it this way, that if I worked as hard as I could, then I would do as well as I possibly could . . . that's what made me work really hard, so, it was definitely, though, parents were driving that.

While the formation of high educational expectations first developed largely within their families, early experiences of academic success contributed to the students' internalization of these expectations, leading them to develop identities around doing well in school or being a good student. Expectations of success were such a core part of this identity that their continued success became a natural extension of their early school achievements.

> I think that, my parents have a very, they have a strong work ethic, and they've always thought of me as a good student and I know that. I guess it sort of started in elementary school even.

> I was a very dedicated student, very focused . . . I'd just sort of done well, like prior to that, so when I got to [high] school, I just sort of continued I guess.

In addition to expressing high expectations for their children's academic performances, some families also provided hands-on assistance with schoolwork, similar to the families in Lareau's study (2003). This combination helps ensure early success, which then sets students on a trajectory of superior educational achievement. One student reflected on how his mother's help, along with her desire to see him do well, contributed both to his success in school and, more importantly, to developing the habit of doing well.

> *What was motivating you in school?*
>
> I guess my parents through grade school. My mom always helped me with my work and that kind of thing. She kind of wanted me to do well, so I'd gotten used to that and then I just wanted to continue. I was just used to it, out of habit, I guess.

For other students, internalized expectations accompanied perceptions of a continuing external pressure to succeed.

> I think from grammar school I had always been at the top of my class, and so it was expected, that was another motivating factor, it was expected for me to, you know, not only do the work but be at the top, and so it's like, you know, I can't, it would disappoint me and it would also disappoint the rest of the, you know, the world, it seemed, so I had to.

These remarks show how, in addition to internalized expectations stemming from having always been at the top, this student felt the pressure of external expectations so strongly that she feared disappointing "the world" if she were not to meet those expectations. Her use of this term suggested the extent to which she lived in an environment where everyone held high expectations for her, including her immediate and extended family, friends, and teachers. Such external and internal pressure to succeed, combined with early successes, may be one way that small class differences in achievement early on become magnified over time.

In cases where they went to schools employing tracking, the students who were placed in top-track courses in their early years of schooling became accustomed to this position and then "just kind of" followed this pattern through high school.

> I was, you know, very motivated and diligent with my work.
>
> *What was driving you, what was behind that?*

I don't know. I guess, from the time when I was really . . . I guess when tracking started in third and fourth grade, that was when they started dividing us up into, you know, the different levels of the math groups, and the different English groups. And I guess I was just always used to being in the top group and doing well in that group and it just kind of became a pattern that I followed through high school.

This student became used to being in the top academic groups, and that position became part of how she identified herself as a student. This example shows how being placed in a top track early on can work in a student's favor; beyond the academic benefits, there is a motivational benefit in creating the desire to maintain that top position. It also helps establish the pattern of doing well in school, which then becomes a habit, something a student simply becomes used to. Similarly, though not related to tracking, other students spoke of doing well even in courses they did not find particularly interesting, because it was the thing to do.

School has always come pretty easily for me. And so most of it was what I was interested in, but also I wasn't particularly interested in bio[logy] but I still did well in it, just because that was the thing to do I guess.

And then, the classes that I didn't like, I guess it was sort of reinforcing, though, just the prophecy that I was doing well in my other classes, why should I shank and just totally flake on this one even though I don't really like it that much?

Going hand-in-hand with considering oneself a good student, most of the Yalies actually enjoyed high school, recalling with enthusiasm favorite courses and moments of intellectual excitement. Coming to actually *like* school, rather than experiencing it as onerous, may be one of the greatest accomplishments of class privilege.

I loved [my courses]. I had a great time while I was there. I never felt like the work was a burden or that I didn't enjoy the academics.

I guess it was like, intellectually, it was really exciting . . . It was in high school that I was really exposed to like Western civilization, intensively. And I just remember being so excited by like American history and like Modern European history and literature and I really liked math, too . . . It was a lot of work, and I worked pretty hard, but it was also really interesting to me.

I guess, well, as far as like my academic interests, I had, my senior year, a biological anthropology class and I loved the subject.

I enjoyed most of the classes I was taking. My high school allowed you to really select what you wanted to take so I took a lot of things that I didn't have an opportunity to take when I was in grade school, so, really fun stuff, and the AP classes I took were really like exciting.

I thought all of the concepts fascinating. I always wanted to push into new territory and just explore new mathematical concepts.

Internalizing the high educational expectations from one's family, doing well in school, and enjoying school would have probably been enough to ensure a strong level of commitment to academic achievement. Yet most of the Yale students had one more potent incentive for academic success: they wanted to go to top colleges, and to do so, they had to meet highly competitive admissions requirements. At Yale, an average of 20,000 applicants each year vie for about 2000 incoming spots. Those who are accepted hold outstanding academic records, with average SAT scores in the top 1 percent of all SAT test takers. Academic achievement alone is not enough; admissions committees at highly selective institutions also expect "athletic ability, demonstrated artistic accomplishment, and formally recognized philanthropic service" (Stevens 2007, p. 15). The Yale students did not pursue extracurricular activities solely for enjoyment, but as part of a conscious strategy of building a strong résumé for college admissions. As one student explained about his involvement in student government, "It was good for my résumé. I'm not gonna lie."

Many of the Yale students I interviewed were aiming for an Ivy League or other top college from the time they were small children, and almost all of them, with the exception of some of the student-athletes and first-generation students, had settled on that goal by the time they started high school. Tastes for top colleges often come from families, communicated early on to children by pointing them toward elite colleges and universities (Devine 2004; Stevens 2007). Most of the Yale students spent their high school years with their eyes on the final prize, acceptance at the college of their choice, and in some cases the goal of college acceptance became their primary motivation.

What kind of student were you?

I guess I was pretty good.

What motivated you?

At that point . . . it was probably just getting into college. I really wasn't, I don't think, that motivated by the work itself, usually.

In the end, the Yale students did well in school because of the confluence of several factors. For each student, some fortuitous combination of their families' expectations, their own expectations, a growing sense of self tied to being a good student, and their need to do well in order to get into a good college came together to produce a commitment to academic excellence. In addition, most of them truly enjoyed their schooling. The first account below points to the powerful pull of an identity built around academic success coupled with the goal of getting into a good college and a genuine enjoyment of academics. By the time this student transferred to a new school in ninth grade, his way of proving himself came through demonstrating his academic prowess to his peers and teachers.

I was sort of looking towards college, and I knew that if I worked hard and I did well, I would get into a good college, but like, I wouldn't say that was my primary motivation. I guess, like, I wanted to prove to myself and others that I could do well and that was important to me, because I was new in ninth grade, and like I felt like I had to sort of establish my identity in like this new community, especially because a lot of the people had been going to school together for a long time. Yeah, I guess that's it. And on top of that I found . . . a lot of those reasons might have been reasons why I started working hard but I couldn't have sustained it if I hadn't enjoyed the material.

The following commentaries illustrate different ways in which various sources of motivation can come together. All three of these students talked about their desire to get into a good college in conjunction with family expectations, valuing a good education, or enjoying academics.

I've always been a pretty serious student. Like I said, my parents both stressed it a lot, being a good student, getting a good education, and I always knew it was a good thing to do, just to get into a good school.

My parents definitely always pushed me to do well academically. I think part of it is definitely that I had to get good grades for my parents, they'll be disappointed. Probably a big motivating factor. Also, wanting to get into Stanford [his first choice institution]. And wanting to do something with my life, too.

I was a good student, I guess, that's how I ended up here. Yeah, I mean, I did my work.

What was behind it, what was motivating you?

I guess that I think probably part of it was 'cause you knew college applications would come up eventually, but . . . Yeah, I remember liking the work and the reading and liking doing well, too, you know.

Southern Students: Having Fun and Getting By

Like the Yale students, a few of the Southern students also attributed their high school academic success in part to the influence of their families.

I was a good student. I finished high school with about a 3.8 [GPA].

What was motivating you?

I was expected to do this. As I said, my parents never really pushed me, they just sort of taught me to do that sort of thing.

I did very well. I was an honor student all through school.

What was motivating you?

I guess I knew I had a natural ability and so I needed to work to that. My parents also had high expectations for me, you know, but mostly it was myself.

By and large, though, the Southern students rarely mentioned their families when discussing high school or, when they did, they were as likely to note the absence of any real encouragement or support as they were to remember a positive influence. One student, when describing what kind of a student he had been, connected his disinterest in schooling to his family and commented on the advantages for other students of having an involved family.

Average, I didn't, average. I didn't really try in high school. Actually, I probably didn't even open a book. I was just more social. I didn't take it seriously, maybe 'cause my family didn't, like the people that were like valedictorians and all that stuff and athletes, they had people to, it was like handed down to them, that's how they were.

What do you mean, handed down to them?

Like people's parents, they encourage them to get into sports and to study, to do, you know, for college.

Likewise, a student from an immigrant family associated her own average school performance with her family situation, specifically, the lack of help she received because her mother worked nights.

> I was average. It's hard for someone who's from an immigrant home, because I knew that all the other kids, "Oh, my parents help me," or "If I need extra help, my parents will help me." I didn't have anybody else, I was all by myself. And my mom worked nights, so I had to come home and I had to help around the house . . . I was all on my own.

In regards to student identity, while a small proportion of the high-achieving students also came to identify themselves as good students, the majority related an emphasis on the social aspects of schooling over the academic. Many explained that seeing friends and having fun took precedence over academics, similar to the students in Willis's (1977) study, just trying to "have a laff."

> [High school] was just like a hang out, actually, that's all I remember. Just go there to see friends, that's what it was to me.

> I didn't do anything much [in high school] . . . I don't know, I'd just go just to hang out with my friends there.

> It was a ball. It was a ball for me, you know. I didn't take school too seriously, I just showed up . . . I had lots of friends, played baseball, it was fun.

> I had a lot of fun. I really didn't do too much work and my study skills were pretty weak, and I'm paying for that now, but I just went to parties every weekend. I remember the parties more than the school itself.

> I just wasn't really into school. I mean I did well, but like a C average. I was just an average student. I got like a 79 for my average grade. I mean, I would not do my homework and stuff like that . . . I was more focused on having fun.

In some cases, particularly for the men, their athletic involvement had been far more important than academics. Though not having much to say about their teachers, they spoke highly of coaches who shaped their characters and taught them real-life lessons.

He [the wrestling coach] instilled in us a lot of discipline, and taught us just how to be motivated, you know, and that you always got to work with what you have, 'cause not everybody has all the resources, so whatever you have, work with it, because most of the time, somebody else is worse off than you anyway . . . If there's anything I dedicated myself to in high school, it was wrestling. And I respected him a lot, I looked up to him . . . And he looked out for us, not just on the wrestling mat, but also academically. You know, there was that factor where, "If your grades aren't right, you're not wrestling."

Are there any teachers from high school that stand out in your mind?

No, but my coach was very, he molded me . . . He taught you a lot about life. He would incorporate things you did on the field to life . . . It wasn't so much about winning all the time, just learning to do things the right way.

While most of the students actually enjoyed school, even if primarily for social reasons, there were also a sizable group of Southern students who made it clear that they did not like school, or were not "into" school, at least in terms of education.

I went to a small Catholic high school in Waterbury.

What was that like?

In high school, it was fun, I guess. I didn't really care about, as far as education-wise, I didn't care.

I wonder why?

I don't know.

It wasn't of interest to you?

No, I didn't like school.

What did you like about high school?

I don't really know. I don't know what was good about it. It wasn't a bad experience, I guess, so that's why it was a good experience. Like if something really bad happened . . .

What was your favorite part about high school?

Senior year when we got to leave halfway through the day. They let us out early . . . The last two periods were optional and you could just go home.

To tell you the truth, honestly, I don't like school, period. I never have, ever since I was a little kid. I don't like it now. It's a big chore to me. I'd much rather work and learn like on the job. I'm a very hands-on person so I like a lot of lab work stuff, that kind of thing. I don't do too well, unless it's very interesting, I don't do too well sitting and listening, but I mean, you got to do it.

As with the Yale students, the academic motivation of the Southern students derived in part from their college goals. Those students who had always planned on going to college tended to be more committed to their schooling. Even so, while some students had initially aspired to more prestigious institutions than Southern, none had seriously entertained the idea of applying to a top college. At the time of this study, Southern accepted nearly 75 percent of all freshman applicants (Southern Connecticut State University 2009a). On average, successful applicants had SAT scores of just under the national average, and they ranked just over the fiftieth percentile in their high school classes gradewise. Connecticut community colleges offer an open-door policy, admitting anyone with a high school degree or an equivalency diploma and not requiring SAT scores. Given these more lenient requirements, the Southern students lacked the sharp incentive of most of the Yale students to push themselves in high school. Rather, the students directed the level of their efforts toward the type of college they wanted to attend. As one student explained, he planned to go to college, but he never aimed for the Ivy League and was satisfied with his modest SAT score.

I wasn't gunning for an Ivy League education. I was just, like, "Just get me into college," and when I took my SATs I got a 970, eligible for college athletics, so that works, you know.

Another student, who had decided in junior high to go to college in order to get into the corporate world, described himself as a C student in high school, explaining that he just wanted to pass his courses. I asked about the apparent contradiction between his college plans and his high school performance.

Well, what they drummed into my head was that there's a college out there for everybody, so no matter what grades you get, you can get into a college.

Other students had not initially anticipated going to college at all. Their motivation increased only after they made the decision to go to college. Students who had described themselves as "sliding by" reported an improvement in their marks and more extracurricular involvement once they decided to go to college.

And when it came time, like when you go to your college fairs when you're in high school, you start talking about college, and now college has kind of dawned on you, and you're like, "Well, maybe I should, you know, not slack so much," trying, you know, "I want to get into school."

At first, I wasn't all that great, you know. I really didn't care about how I did, you know, I just was going to school. I didn't feel that I needed to do too good, I don't know, you know. That's when I didn't know what I was gonna do . . . After that, when I finally decided that college was gonna have to be in my future, that's when I started doing better. I started improving my grades. I remember . . . I even joined the math club.

In some cases, the students brought up their marks so that they could enter a four-year rather than a two-year college.

High school was pretty much . . . my first two years I just looked at it as, "Get me through, get me out of here." I barely passed my sophomore year, I just didn't care about it at all . . . not 'til my senior year. My senior year I made honor roll on all four semesters.

What made the turnaround?

I guess just the realization that I really needed to get my act together and now was the time, 'cause if I didn't, I wouldn't get into any colleges I really wanted to get into or go to a two-year community school first, that kind of thing.

As these examples attest, college goals help define performance in high school. Students who barely passed their first years of high school can turn into honor roll students once they make the decision to go to a four-year college. Ironically, we often think about it the other way around, that how well a student does in high school determines whether he or she will go to college, placing the emphasis on merit. In fact, expectations drive achievement for these students. When students do not imagine ever going to college, then doing just enough to pass high school is a reasonable plan. If and when they decide that college is in their future, then their efforts rise to meet that goal. At that point, the degree of effort will be geared toward the admissions requirements of the types of institutions they hope to attend.

Overall, these accounts of the Yale and the Southern students' high school years expose the significant class advantage of family educational expectations passed down to children. The expectations communicated by parents, and their assistance with school work, contributed to the Yale students doing well in school and internalizing their families' educational expectations, which in turn increased their likelihood of building identities around being good students, learning to enjoy academics and making a habit out of success. Once harnessed to the goal of gaining admission to a top college, it is little wonder that the Yale students excelled in high school. Likewise, without these factors, school became more about having fun and seeing friends for the Southern students; there was less motivation to do well because one's identity did not hinge on being a good student. Even if one intended to go to college, in the absence of Ivy League aspirations, getting into a local four-year college could be handily accomplished with average grades and test scores and little extracurricular involvement.

The Influence of the Schools: Activating or Diminishing Motivation

While differences in commitment to schooling and academic achievement have their roots in the family, the kinds of high schools attended by the Southern and the Yale students deepened these disparities. The academic standards and expectations conveyed by schools work either toward enhancing students' academic commitment or reducing their investment in school work. For most of the Yale students, motivation levels stemming from their family background became even more highly activated by their high school environments. Unfortunately for most of the Southern students, aspects of their schooling often served to dampen their motivation. Thus, besides passing down educational expectations, the most powerful contribution families make to their children's academic success comes in the type of high school education they secure for their children.

Nationwide, the vast majority of students (91%) attend public high schools, 7 percent attend private religious schools, and only 2 percent attend private secular schools (Broughman and Pugh 2004; Snyder and Hoffman 2002). The figures for Southern are roughly congruent with the national averages, with 84 percent of the students attending public schools and 16 percent attending private religious schools. In contrast, an exceptionally high proportion of Yale students attend private high schools; in my sample, 47 percent of the students attended private secular schools, 10 percent private religious schools, and the remaining 43 percent public schools (these percentages are comparable with those for the entire Yale student body). These figures testify to the expansive resources of the Yale students' families: the cultural capital and social networks necessary for understanding the importance of private high schools; knowing how to find them and how to get their children into them; and the finances to pay for them. The average tuition for day students at independent private schools is now $35,000 per year; for independent private boarding schools, this price soars to $41,000 (National Association of Independent Schools 2010). Not only did such a high proportion of the Yale students attend private schools, but many of them attended the best private schools in the country, as the students did not hesitate to tell me: "It was a boarding school, in Exeter, in New Hampshire. And its reputation is, I guess, the best in the nation."

Whether public or private, the key difference between the schools attended by most of the Yale students and those attended by most of the Southern students lay in the proportion of the student body going on to four-year colleges. Most of the Yale students went to high schools where nearly everyone graduated and went directly to college. The Yale students repeatedly noted their high schools' emphasis on preparing students for college and on sending students to top colleges.

> And even the high school I went to, it was one of the best in California. It was top fifteen, and, you know, a little private school where they put a lot of emphasis on people going to college, like just about every senior class, 100 percent matriculate in college.

> It was an all-boys Catholic school. Like they say that they're trying to condition you to go to, well, pretty much everyone from that high school went to, like really, one of the top colleges I guess. They really do try to prepare you for college.

> In the New York Metropolitan area, it was the top-of-the-totem-pole school, and so it would draw people from Manhattan, Westchester, and New Jersey, like people would commute for up to like an hour and a half to get there and it was really the joint where any sort of professional parents, like you got all these investment banking/lawyer/doctor parents all over that area and all of them, who went to Harvard and Yale and wherever, and they're all just trying to get their kids into whatever high school they can. And it was pretty much the one at the top, just because it had the best numbers.

This last quote provides a lively illustration of the dynamics at work in these schools. This student pointed to the professional backgrounds of the parents and their own elite university degrees. He also noted the energy these parents put into getting their children into school and then driving them there every day, sometimes commuting for three hours a day in an effort to ensure that their children got the best education available. His last comment, about the school having the "best numbers," refers to the school's track record of sending graduates on to top colleges and universities, statistics on which the reputation of these schools rests. As he pointed out, his school was considered the top school because of its numbers.

In cases where the Yalies' families did not send their children to private schools, many lived in affluent neighborhoods with high-quality public schools where most students were college bound. Public school students often described their schools in similar ways.

> Public, about 1200, pretty affluent area, suburb of New York City. As I said, essentially all college bound.

> Public high school, 1600 students. I lived on the North Shore of Chicago, the north side of Lake Michigan. Affluent background. I think 98 percent or something like that go on to four-year colleges.

> I went to Stuyvesant High School [public magnet school] . . . It's a fairly competitive high school. We had to take an exam to get in, and that's the sort of place where people are just expected to go to college.

The characteristics these students chose to include in their descriptions show how the students themselves regarded the salient features of their schools as the social background of the student body and the proportion going on to college.

Like the families in Devine's study (2004), some of the Yale students' families purposely moved to a neighborhood with a highly ranked public school. One student described her own mother making this choice and drew a connection between the rank of the school and the social background of the families in the neighborhood.

> I went to a public suburban high school in Wisconsin. It was in a fairly wealthy area. It was upper middle class, you know, a lot of doctors and lawyers . . . My mom moved into the suburb so that I could go to the school system. It was very highly ranked.

Whether moving to neighborhoods with better schools or paying to send their children to private schools, these parents sent a strong message to their children about the importance of their education. Moreover, by choosing schools geared explicitly toward college preparation, the parents ensured that the educational expectations established in the home were bolstered by their children's schools. In this way, the parents indirectly conveyed their own expectations. For instance, the following student noted how even though his parents never verbally expressed an expectation that he go to college, he assumed that was the case because of the norms of his high school. Not only were almost all of the students going on to college, but, in his reference to people not going to technical schools, he also indicated that the students were, for the most part, going to four-year colleges.

> Actually, when I think about it, my parents never, when I was in high school, mentioned that they expected me to come to college, although I sort of assumed that's the way it was, primarily because the high school I went to was a prep school and pretty much everyone in the graduating class was going to college in some form and there weren't too many people that went on to technical schools or to different types of things or to work right out of high school, so really I think it was just a result of my high school education more than anything else.

Where parents did push, the schools added reinforcement to expectations coming from home.

> *What was motivating you in high school?*
>
> Getting into college, definitely. My whole high school had that mentality. As well as my parents pushing me on that regard, too.

In contrast to the Yale students, the Southern students tended to report much lower college-going rates in their high schools, with many of the students either going into the workforce or the military after high school. For those students who did continue their education, many entered two-year instead of four-year colleges.

> The kids I hung around, it was only maybe a little more than half went to college, whereas about half went straight into the workforce or the army.

Academic Standards, Curricular Offerings, and School Activities

Schools geared towards preparing all students for college hold strict academic standards and require students to follow a rigorous academic curriculum. The primary benefit of high academic standards is preparing students for college admissions tests and college-level work. However, an important secondary benefit is that these high standards mean students do not need to rely solely on their own internal motivation to succeed. Most private schools and public schools in affluent neighborhoods have only one track, the college-preparatory, or college-prep, track, leaving students without the option of choosing an easier curriculum. Regardless of the students' interest or desire in taking advanced math or science, for example, they will be compelled to take the school's required courses in these areas. The Yale students often described the rigor of their schools and related "having to take" or even being "forced to take" advanced courses.

It was very, very focused on academics and really intense courses.

It seems as if there's pretty much a set curriculum that most prep schools follow where throughout high school they encourage students to, a lot of times more than just encourage, but force students to take, you know, courses in all different fields, math, science, English, history, and a foreign language. In general, that was pretty much what my high school curriculum was. And, English was a lot of reading, books, a lot of the books that I'm sure everyone reads in high school: *Catcher in the Rye*, and the *Great Gatsby*, and a little bit of Shakespeare. So, I'd say it was just more-or-less standard New England prep school education.

The high school is pretty strict academically. I had to take a lot of science courses, at advanced levels, so it was a lot of work.

In contrast, while about a fourth of the Southern students reported taking honors and AP courses during high school, the majority of them described much lower academic standards and much less challenging courses.

I thought the teachers dumbed down the classes, which really, really annoyed me, so I ended up doing a lot of independent study stuff, too.

It was easy, I mean, I thought high school was easy. You could study for a test in the morning and have it in the afternoon and get a good grade. That's why I think my study habits are totally messed up right now.

Me, personally, I found [honors track] high school really easy, that's why I had such a hard time when I went to college, because I never really had to study in high school, and I didn't really find much of a challenge kind of thing, and when I got to college, I had a hard time my first year.

I mean, I knew that I could do better I think than that. I wasn't being really challenged. That was it, pretty much.

To be sure, the Southern students' expectations for doing well were generally lower than those of the Yale students, and for some, their intention was merely passing. Nevertheless, to be able to get a "good grade," however defined, on a test for which one studied only a few hours beforehand suggests that these schools did indeed require less work. Several of the Southern students also mentioned working harder in more demanding courses, suggesting both their capability to do this kind of work and how a school's standards influence student behavior.

> There was like maybe . . . two classes, three that I took in high school that actually, that I worked hard, that I could say, "Hey, I worked." Chemistry, physics, and geometry.
>
> *Why did you work hard in those?*
>
> They were tough classes, you know, they posed challenges for me, so I was like, "Hey, I want to take 'em on," so I did and I took 'em, you know, and I did well.

Beyond the differences in standards, the Yale students mentioned a much wider range of course offerings to choose from, such as Chinese, theatre, the history of art, and religion in history. In contrast, the course selection for some of the Southern students was much slimmer. One Southern student described how she lost her motivation in her senior year because there were no courses she was interested in taking.

> I wasn't really into doing good. I did at first but then I didn't want to . . . I lost my motivation, I guess.
>
> *Why do you think that was?*
>
> I don't know, 'cause my classes during senior year, they weren't involved, they weren't interesting, there was nothing. It was just literature, like reading and reading, and there was nothing really that I wanted to take. It was just math and reading and that's about it.

Finally, schools differed in the extent of extracurricular activities available to students and in the encouragement they received to pursue those activities. The Yale students noted a wide range of extracurricular activities and, in some cases, exceptional facilities open to students. They also recounted receiving guidance from teachers and counselors, not just on which classes to take, but also about the extracurricular activities that would improve their college applications.

> I did a lot of astronomy there, which was really good because it was a really hands-on class. We had really good astronomical facilities, and so I spent a lot of time

taking pictures and stuff. I spent most of my, I mean, my last two years there I'd say I spent like about half my nights just up there taking pictures.

I was involved in everything that you can think of, like every club, and, like, I ran track and cross country and I also did, I was president of this club, FOCUS, and it was Forum on Cultures and Urban Societies, and we worked with elementary schools kids . . . and I also did Model UN.

They [high school teachers] not only taught but they really guided you in telling you what tests to take, and take this class next year, and you should really think about doing volunteer work, because, you know, it looks good for your college application.

While some of the Southern students did participate in extracurricular activities, many others described a dearth of opportunities.

It was mostly cheerleaders. It's a really football-oriented high school, so there wasn't . . . it was just football, football, football, so you didn't have many choices to do something else. I ran cross country and there wasn't a lot of money for [it]. We had outfits from like the '70s 'cause all their money went to football.

I don't think they had enough extracurricular activities. It was basically you go to school for English, math, reading, the basic subjects. There wasn't like extracurricular, like extra programs or whatever.

Thus the structural features of college-prep high schools, in terms of the ethos of preparing everyone for college, requiring a rigorous curriculum, and offering a broad range of extracurricular activities, facilitated their students' academic achievement and school involvement. The students themselves sometimes commented on the difference in standards, particularly between private and public schools. One Yale student, for example, had attended public school through tenth grade and then transferred into a private school. She described the difference in the amount of work required at the two schools and how her own efforts changed in response to her schools. Without having gone to a private high school, she doubted that she would have been prepared enough to attend Yale.

I was having a lot of fun in [public] high school through tenth grade and had sort of stopped doing work, in a way, and it had no real effect on my grades. And my sister went to a private school for four years, so I sort of had an indication that I wasn't working as much as I'd seen her work . . . I had a really hard time my first semester . . . in private school. And did miserably. And that was a wake-up call to myself. Other than that, I was a good student . . . I really think that academically, I would have been so much less prepared if I hadn't gone there, and maybe not prepared at all.

Other Yale students expressed regret at not having attended a private school, particularly after discovering how unprepared they were relative to private high school students.

The only thing that I didn't like [about high school] was sort of the lack of preparation for me for college. I was sort of at a disadvantage when I first got here. My math and science was [*sic*] . . . even though I took everything we had at our high school, it was still not on par with most other people, especially people from either large high schools or especially private schools, and . . . I sort of have this little regret that I didn't take the opportunity when I had it to go to a private school.

Teachers, Tracking, and Expectations

Besides the structural features of the study participants' schools, the teachers in the schools also influenced the students' motivation and achievement. The Yale students more commonly described having supportive relationships with teachers who held high expectations and who pushed them. While some of the Southern students' descriptions paralleled those of the Yalies, on the whole the Southern students encountered teachers who had lower expectations for them than they themselves had. Thus, in addition to the formal standards of a school, on a day-to-day level it is the teachers who communicate expectations to the students and enhance motivation.

During the interviews, I asked students whether any of their high school teachers stood out in their minds. Almost all of the Yale students answered this question with enthusiastic descriptions of two or three favorite teachers. These teachers were often portrayed as caring and supportive, not just academically, but socially and emotionally.

I really liked him because he was the kind of person who always, he cared about his students and he made sure he knew who they were and what they were all about, and . . . he actually, he tries really hard to help people out with like, you know, and he's somebody who really cares about the students and just about teaching and giving them an education.

I had a teacher for sophomore English . . . and she was just different because she was a friend, she was into not just your academic development but your personal and social and emotional development . . . I liked her a lot because she was very supportive.

Well, my high school was like, you know, the reason it's ranked so high is because teachers are very, you know, personal, like that's one reason why they're hired. It's not just, "I'm your teacher and I'm gonna teach you the material and that's it," but a lot of times the teachers are your friends, and they coach a lot of the sports there, too, so you really get to know them well, and they really encourage you, not just in the academics but whatever else you're doing. They truly try to get to know you.

In some cases, the kinds of bonds students developed with teachers prompted these students to work harder as they became invested in their teachers' opinions of them.

What was motivating you?

I think by junior, senior year it came down to a lot of, well . . . I mean, a lot of it was that you wanted to get into the school that you wanted to get into, that's important, but not so much. I mean, I think a lot of it, as I said, I got very emotionally wrapped up in my papers, especially, I mean, English was one of my best subjects and I worked so hard on that because my relationships with my English teachers were very important, and what they thought of me was tremendously important. And I think had I been in a big school, even if I had wanted to get into a certain college, I don't know that I would have worked as hard and as intently.

Besides caring and involved teachers, the Yale students often described teachers who took them seriously and both recognized and encouraged their intellectual potential. By showing interest in their work and seeing their promise, the teachers also expressed their own expectations for their students, helping to build their students' confidence.

I had a great English teacher, who encouraged me to write more and . . . she just took us very seriously as young adults but also as possible writers.

He [chemistry teacher] was really very into chemistry. He really respected us as students. He was like, "Well, we're doing microscale organic lab here, and this is a very difficult course and someday you're going to be publishing and this . . ." and just that he expected such high performance from us and that somehow we all managed to earn his respect after a while.

The classroom environment like every day was pretty much across the board really stimulating and I had teachers that I really respected and learned a lot from, and who were really interested in what I had to say, or what I was writing, or in helping improve my writing.

These examples show teachers who communicated the possibility of being writers and scientists to their students. By reflecting these options, the teachers conveyed their confidence in the students and helped the students begin to envision these kinds of high-level careers for themselves. In this way, the teachers' attitudes played a powerful role in the development of the students' aspirations and sense of confidence.

[My] history teacher . . . was this sort of incredible woman . . . she just was the most dynamic sort of intellectual force I ever had, sort of, in high school, in terms of just being that, like, pushing you to answer real questions and like really thinking . . . And I think what was really great about her is that I don't think I took myself academically very seriously, or intellectually very seriously, until I was in her classroom. And she was like "You can write," like "You are good," like "You will do something." And I've always been sort of interested in whatever I was learning about, but I think I never really took it seriously or with the kind of confidence that I did after I'd been in her classes for a couple years. And I think it made a huge difference.

The Yale students also frequently remarked about how their teachers had pushed them in high school.

My teachers were just outstanding. I mean, the way that they approached teaching was just very, at least as far as I could tell, innovative, in that they really got your attention and made you think a lot, and made you work extremely hard, and that was something that really just pushed me to a level where I was very competent in my English writing, and in fact it's come back to help me a lot here.

I had a teacher in math . . . He was really good. He was always very much pushing you to, like, use your mind, and expand it, and don't just settle, like, "Oh, I can't do it," you know, "Keep pushing," and he was, I think he was really, really good that way, very, knew how to push his students but also knew how to be, you know, supportive and help you if you were having problems . . . I had an English teacher . . . just [the] same thing, where he would just sort of go beyond the standard education . . . I think it's really easy to settle into "This is what's expected of me and this is what I'll put out," even as a teacher or a student, either one, and he sort of went beyond that. He would like try to go beyond the standard way you would teach an English class or whatever and try to do some challenging, different things, and also try to get us to do some things that were more challenging . . . expand your mind a little.

My AP history professor, he was a great guy, he was like a friend to me, basically, and he was the one who sort of kept boosting my ego and trying to push me harder and harder to get me to do more. He was, I think at least in part, one of the reasons why I wanted to continue my education at a high level.

Each of these excerpts speaks to how these teachers motivated their students to work harder. These teachers *made* their students work, getting them to do more and not settle for doing just enough for a good grade. Instead of working only to meet the typical standards, the students went beyond by raising their work level to their teachers' expectations.

The Southern students, too, had positive comments about their teachers. However, they tended to focus on how their teachers made courses fun or entertaining.

I had a biology teacher my senior year . . . he was great.
What was so great about him?
Oh, he was just . . . kind of like ridiculous. He would make jokes, like if you got a wrong answer, he's like, "What, what!" you know, and he wouldn't make you feel stupid but he would help you all the time and he was really funny, he was really nice, he was like a grandfather type, you know, he was really a great teacher.

Then there was a history teacher. I had him for history and technology, two different years, but he was really good. I really liked him. He like had a way of teaching history where it was almost like gossip, like just the way he went about it and stuff like that, it was just really fun.

Only rarely did the Southern students describe being pushed by their teachers, while many had the opposite experience. Indeed, it was more common for the Southern students to talk about the low expectations their teachers held for them.

I suppose the teaching, the teaching style, wasn't something I particularly enjoyed. I didn't feel that they, they ever, they didn't push you, they didn't, it was very dumbed down, I felt. And I'd go to some classes and I'd sit in the back and read a book of my own that I'd brought and not pay attention to what they were saying, because some of it was just, it was just very dumbed down. It didn't appeal to me very often.

I don't want to knock my old school, but, you know, I think I could have done, I would have done a lot better if they thought that I could do it.

Numerous Southern students gave examples of how their teachers' expectations varied according to track. Students not in academic tracks recounted much lower expectations from their teachers or just being allowed "to fall," as one student put it.

None of [my teachers] really pushed me in any way, they just kind of let you fall.
Did your school have tracks?
Yeah, I was in track two.

I didn't like the way it was run in the sense that if you were in Level I classes, then they just assumed you were going to college, and if you weren't, then they just assumed that you weren't, and it didn't seem like the effort was put . . . I was put in there [lower track] accidentally and then I got switched out, and it was a total different attitude that teachers had about you, it was really weird. If you were in Level I or honors classes, you were going to college, like the minute you walked in the door, that's what they did, and if you weren't, they were like, "Well, you might, but . . ." They didn't push you as hard and the classes weren't as hard, and it was really weird . . . It was just, overall, it wasn't a push, it wasn't like, you know, "Oh, all right, you did your homework, that was good," but it wasn't as hard, it wasn't like this big "All right, you have to push to try to go to college." 'Cause just 'cause you were in Level II didn't mean you weren't smart enough to make college, but it seemed like that was their attitude. You were probably going to work and you weren't going to college, so don't worry about it.

The perceptions of these Southern students were echoed by a Yale student who also attended a public school but was placed in the top track. She commented on the disadvantages for students in lower tracks, particularly for students without families pushing them academically.

I think something that I was always disappointed in was just the fact that I feel that [in my high school], people are put into categories, like the whole tracking system. I really don't like that. And then teacher expectations for their students are really low, and I think that it's like a self-fulfilling prophecy kind of, like if you tell somebody he's dumb, you know, he's not going to do well . . . And I really think that at [name of her school], there were a lot of teachers who just did not care and didn't really try to motivate the students, or even challenge them in any way. And, uh, if you don't get that at home, like I did, then, it's just like, why, you know, even continue?

Several of the Southern students also noted the difficulties they faced in trying to enter college-prep courses after having been assigned to courses in other tracks.

> My personal guidance counselor was garbage. He was just like, "Why don't you take this class?" I'm like, "'Cause that's not a college-prep class." "Well, I don't think you can," and I was like, "Well, if you don't feel that I can take this, I'll just have my father come in and you can talk to my father about what I can take." So, you know what I mean, like I said, not the school as a whole, but there was [*sic*] individuals in positions where you would assume they would have motivated a kid, you know, like I wanted to take the physics class, and he was like, "Well, you don't have to to graduate, why don't you just take something else?" I'm like, "That's what I want to take." "Well, are you sure, you think you can handle it?" "Yeah, I can handle it, that's why I'm taking it."

Like the Yale students, the Southern students adjusted the level of their effort in response to the expectations of their teachers, working harder for demanding courses and less for easier courses.

> The teachers that I had they didn't expect much, so I didn't give them a lot, but then when I got to my senior year, I was getting like As in the classes, 'cause the teachers wanted work.

> I remember my junior year I had this one teacher on the first day that said, "This is the level of class where you might, or you probably won't, go to college," so I didn't do anything for her. And I got a C+ in that English class, and then I went to Level I English class junior year and I was getting As. I don't think she meant to say that, but she did.

> Usually . . . the ones that demanded a lot more were the ones that I would get an A for.

Overall, the Yale and the Southern students related striking differences in their experiences with teachers. With few exceptions, the Yale students reported that they had teachers who supported them both as individuals and as students, who communicated high expectations, and who encouraged and pushed them to meet high standards. While a small minority of the Southern students also benefited from these kinds of teachers, most of them described how little their teachers expected from them, particularly for those students not taking courses in advanced tracks. While the two groups experienced very different kinds of teachers and teaching styles, they were similar in their sensitivity to their teachers' expectations. Both the Yale and the Southern students recounted how they geared their academic efforts to meet the expectations of their teachers.

Peers

The final advantage of attending a private school or a public school where the majority of students go on to college comes from the student body. Students' friends and classmates in high school play a significant role in shaping and reinforcing their own educational expectations. The students in the schools attended by most of the Yale students shared a common goal of getting into good colleges. This, in turn, fostered a level of competition among the students, as most of them were highly motivated and many sought to attain the status of a top student. Because of this, while these schools still had cliques and friendship groups, they did not seem to have the wide divisions among students described by authors such as Eckert (1989). Indeed, in terms of motivation, the Yale students described a nearly homogeneous student body.

> I went through a high school where people were completely obsessed about getting into college and there was, I'd say, there was a definite attitude that people were just fighting as hard as they could. Not fighting one another, but just sort of internally competitive as much as they could be in order to get into the best college they could.

> The students were really interesting. They were really intelligent students and really motivated students.

> Cutthroat. Very, very cutthroat. Because everybody else was also aiming to be a top student.

> I think we all tended to do well, because you had to take a, you had to apply to get in, and we were all motivated, but [some] people to lesser degrees than others, so I was one of the more, like, self-motivated ones.

By and large, the Southern students attended high schools with a more diverse student body, and many students attributed their own lack of motivation to their friendship groups.

[I was] a C student. I didn't, I just did the work to get by. I mean, the crowd I hung around with was like that, too. I mean, we played sports.

I don't know. And the thing is that it wasn't just me, all of us, we were on this like cloud, it was just like, you know, you got a test tomorrow, study the night before, you got a paper due for whatever, do it the night before.

I think I would have learned it if I did apply myself, but I was just with my friends, sitting in the back of the class, making noise.

Why were you not so motivated? Were you just not that interested?
At that point, I really didn't know what I was gonna do when I got out . . . and, well, I had a group of friends that didn't seem to care.
So it didn't seem worthwhile?
No, not at all.

These accounts highlight an additional challenge faced by some public school students, one from which private school students are largely immune. Students' motivation in part depends on their peer group, and in schools with a higher proportion of students not expecting to go to college, students were more likely to form friendships with classmates with low aspirations, consequently normalizing these kinds of aspirations. The influence of peers is underscored by the accounts of the Yale students who attended public schools with more diverse student bodies and had to contend with just these kinds of divisions. One Yale student described the divide between the "jocks" and the "nerds" at his public school and mentioned his concern that his academics would suffer as a result of seeking popularity with the non-academically oriented athlete group. In making the decision to switch into a private school, he also noted the benefits of attending a school where everyone had to play a sport *and* do well academically.

Well, I went to one high school for freshman year, to a public school . . . and it's a good public school . . . I think basically the reason I left was just because I had problems with my friends there, because I played sports and I was in, they divided the class into advanced, upper-standard, and standard, so I was in all advanced classes and I played sports and most of the other people in all advanced classes didn't play sports. So I had sort of two groups of friends, and you always had one group calling the other group sort of idiot jocks and the other group calling the other one a bunch of nerds. So I guess maybe my leaving was kind of a cop-out, but I really just didn't, it was just kind of stressful the whole time and I think if I'd stayed, I probably would have, in an attempt to be popular or something, done worse, maybe. Or at least not really put myself, exerted myself, as much as I should have. So when I left, I went to somewhere that kind of everyone was, I guess people were more similar because everyone, you had to play a sport and you had to do well.

Other students coped with these differences by choosing to affiliate themselves with only a small group of like-minded peers. Three of the Yale students, for example, had attended public schools where only about half or less of the students went on to college. Their response to this environment was to limit their friendship groups.

> It was kind of a strange environment, I guess. I was pretty much only friends with a certain group of people.

> I remember being on the track team, which was a lot of fun and took up a lot of my life. And I also just remember the last couple of years of AP classes, with sort of a minority of the population there, kind of already started closing me off from most of the people.

> I think in a way [I was] a bit of an exception, because a lot of students in my school do not go on to college. They get the forty-hour-a-week job, five days a week, get married. So many of my classmates are married already, have kids, and I, that's just never been my priority. I mean, I want that at some point in my life, but I wanted my education first, so I did everything I could to prepare myself to get into a school like Yale. And that pretty much set me apart. So I guess I remember being different.

Another public school student provided a vivid glimpse into the kinds of pressures she experienced from students with a lower set of academic goals than her own.

> [High school] was okay, like they had a really good advanced placement program so you could learn a lot academically, but it was sort of weird to want to come to a place like Yale, 'cause everyone just goes to University of Kansas or Kansas State

or community college. And people look at you kind of funny, like "Why don't you go out and party more and just go to the state school? It's easy to get into and it's still a good school."

Thus, beyond the structural differences in the high schools and the qualitative differences in the kinds of teachers they encountered, the Yale and the Southern students attended high schools with very different student bodies. By and large, the Yale students benefited from going to school with like-minded groups of students, intent on academic excellence and the pursuit of higher education, while the Southern students generally attended schools with a more mixed student body. The Yale students who did attend mixed schools coped by either limiting their friendship groups or, in some cases, transferring to private schools when they perceived that their academics might suffer. The Southern students, on the other hand, often explained their own lack of motivation in the context of their friendship groups. Being affiliated with friends with low educational expectations seemed to legitimize their own performance.

Overall, the students' descriptions of their high school experiences point to a set of educational benefits more commonly available to the Yale students than to the Southern students. However, it is important to emphasize that not every Yale student attended an elite private school, had uniformly encouraging teachers, and was surrounded by peers with high aspirations; likewise, not every Southern student recounted having teachers with low expectations or being relegated to nonacademic tracks. Indeed, it is worth repeating here that about a fifth of the Southern students were as academically engaged as their Yale peers and had mostly positive comments about their teachers and classmates. While this chapter intentionally focuses on the broad set of differences between the groups, there was also variation within each group. In particular, some, though certainly not all, of the student-athletes stood out among the Yale students, in that athletics clearly took first priority for them during high school, while academics ranked a distant second place. In comparison with most other Yale students, their studies were of relatively little interest to them. Rarely did they express enthusiasm about high school courses or teachers, and rarely did they mention involvement in extracurricular activities besides sports. Instead, these students described their demanding training schedules and talked of skating by or just doing enough in their classes.

> I guess I was the type of [high school] student where I honestly didn't do a lot of work. I basically did enough to get by . . . And I guess because I play hockey so

much, you know, I don't even know if it wasn't that I didn't have time, but I always made myself feel like, "I really don't have the time to do this, so I can just kind of like slide by." And I mean, luckily it was enough to get me by, but I never really enjoyed school. I mean, I don't enjoy school. I like being out and doing things, you know, practically, instead of like being in the classroom, reading books and stuff.

Certainly, at that time I wasn't going to school to learn. I was going to school to be with my friends, and because I'd rather be there than sitting at home. And I had to go there so I could play football. If I wasn't in class, I couldn't play football, and if I wasn't in class, I couldn't play lacrosse. But I had good teachers and it wasn't painful to sit through class for me.

I've always been a good student, but a lot of times I'd just kind of skate by and kind of get by however I could.

• • •

In illuminating the educational trajectories that carried one set of students to Southern and one to Yale, this chapter underscores the exceptional circumstances required to produce academic excellence. The four years both groups spent in high school bore little resemblance to one other. The Yale students benefited from just the kinds of family and schooling advantages identified with high academic achievement and predictably became top students. Their experiences highlight the role of expectations. Students do better in school when their families expect it, when their teachers expect it, when their friends expect it, and when they themselves come to expect it. We also saw how doing well in school connects with college-going aspirations. Students expecting to go to college also expect to do well in high school. This exemplifies the habitus of middle-class families where college going has become the norm, as Bourdieu and Passeron (1977) explain:

> Depending on whether access to higher education is collectively felt, even in a diffuse way, as an impossible, possible, probable, normal, or banal future, everything in the conduct of the families and the children (particularly their conduct and performance at school) will vary, because behaviour tends to be governed by what it is "reasonable" to expect. (p. 226)

The students' accounts of their high school years support Bourdieu's theory of expectations driving school behavior. However, expectations alone are not enough to account for behavior, and these findings point to a crucial yet undertheorized mechanism between expectations and behavior: motivation. Academic excellence requires not just high expectations, but the motivation to work hard. For example, many of the Yale students expected to go to a good college, yet their day-to-day motivation depended on the demands of their schools and teachers. A related principle is that while expectations are generally theorized as stable, motivation is far more fragile and malleable, varying from year to year and even from course to course for some students. Both groups of students attuned their performance in accordance with signals coming from their schools and teachers, working harder for those teachers who demanded it and easing up in other courses. Two Yale students spoke of working much harder after changing schools. Even though their college-going expectations remained constant, their degree of motivation rose and fell. However, within this pattern of variation, most of the Yale students attended high schools that supported their own expectations and generally activated their motivation to succeed. They had teachers who possessed high standards, valorized their efforts and accomplishments, and expressed confidence in their future endeavors. For many of the Southern students, the low expectations conveyed by their teachers served to diminish their motivation, often resulting in the students "giving them nothing."

Many of the Southern students aspired to attend college, yet they were not greatly concerned with their high school grades. Rosenbaum has identified this pattern as an inadvertently negative effect of "college-for-all" norms (Rosenbaum 1997, 2001). In an effort to promote college attendance among all youth, high school personnel may encourage college aspirations without stressing the academic preparation necessary to achieve these goals. Rosenbaum finds that many students now expect to enter college, yet do not see their performance in high school as being relevant and thus often exert little effort. College-for-all norms, though well intentioned, end up encouraging students to believe they can attend college, even with low grades.

Predictably, the two groups of students in my study varied in terms of their identification with schooling. While the Yale students largely aligned themselves with the goals of their schools, a large proportion of the Southern students remained disengaged, concluding that they did not like school or that it simply was not important to them. However, many earlier studies note how low-SES students' experiences with education lead them to have a deficient sense of themselves as students or to think that they are not capable of succeeding academically. This did not seem to be the case for the students in my study. Indeed, a number of the low-performing Southern students noted that they could have done better if they had only applied themselves.

I just did enough to get by, where I think if I really applied myself, I could have done better.

It was very easy, it really was. If I actually applied myself, I would have done a lot better, I imagine, but it was just easy just to get by, you know, get a C for sleeping, so, that was pretty much what I did.

Oh, I was a B student. Basically I slacked off and sometimes didn't do my homework when I should have or whatever . . . I know with most things I probably could have had As in all of 'em but I got Bs instead, because I chose not to do some homework.

I did what I had to to just get by. I really didn't put all that I have into classes.

While these students did not attribute their lack of success to a lack of ability, they did tend to assign the blame for their mediocre performance to their own lack of motivation, only occasionally pointing to a lack of encouragement from their teachers and families. In this way, these students left high school believing that their academic records reflected their personal qualities.

The Yale students, on the other hand, came away from their high school years perceiving not the favorable circumstances supporting their schooling thus far, but rather the link between their talents and educational accomplishments. Indeed, they had the external indicators to validate this belief in their own abilities: strong grade point averages, high SAT scores, a list of awards and honors, and acceptance into a top university. From this vantage point, they were unable to recognize how many cards were already stacked in their favor, helping to ensure their success. Instead, the Yale students left high school with a sense of their own deservedness.

From this complex set of dynamics, we see the emergence of different models of what being a student and what learning mean. For the Yale students, their sense of themselves became bound to their academic accomplishments. They built an identity around what kind of students they were and around their specific academic talents and interests. While most of the Yale students clearly worked hard during their high school years, their successes become an intrinsic part of themselves, establishing their identity as a "good student," meaning someone who is smart and capable. They found learning enjoyable. The Southern students were less likely to invest their high school learning with meaning and more likely to perceive it simply as "work." (Later chapters will explore how these early schooling identities map onto the liberal learning tradition at Yale and the vocational orientation of Southern.)

In light of these findings, it is also important to keep in mind that they are based on student populations at two universities and not on a sample of high school students. There are undoubtedly many students from public high schools in Connecticut who are more successful academically than the students presented on these pages and go on to top colleges. Indeed, my study had examples of students who came from humble social origins, attended public schools, and yet still ended up at Yale. Likewise, not all privileged children get ahead. As Devine (2004) points out, the reproduction of privilege is often a messy, uneven process, and even with an abundance of advantages, many high-SES students, for whatever reason, do not succeed academically. Caution must be taken to not view the accounts presented here as suggesting a deterministic relationship between social origins and academic success. Instead, these accounts help us understand the way that privilege facilitates, but does not ensure, academic success.

CHAPTER THREE

Deciding to Go to College

Going to college is firmly tied to social background. Children from affluent and educated families are now almost certain to graduate from high school and immediately enroll in a four-year college or university. For children whose parents did not attend college, only one out of four will enroll in a four-year institution (Berkner and Chavez 1997). Given how strongly social background influences the likelihood of attending college, how might students from different backgrounds vary in when and how they make the decision to go to college? Or in the kinds of reasoning that guide their choice? I expected that most students would offer a mix of practical and intellectual reasons, with the Yale students more likely to invoke liberal arts ideals of becoming an educated person and the Southern students relying more heavily on vocationalist narratives. Yet how strongly did the students draw on these ideals, how much did each weigh in their decisions, and how wide was the difference between the two groups of students?

The answers from both the Yale and the Southern students to the question of "Why did you decide to come to college?" came as a surprise. First, most of the Yale students had in fact never actually decided to go to college; it was simply the next step in their lives, one not requiring a rationale. The Southern students, on the other hand, had made a decision, one linked to the pragmatic goal of getting a good job. Rather than balancing intellectual and practical concerns, the Southern students set their sights almost exclusively on acquiring a credential that would launch them not just into specific careers, but out of the blue-collar working world and into the white-collar one. For a large segment of these students, college was about escaping from the limited job opportunities of their families and moving up into better and higher-paying jobs.

Finding out *why* some of the students decided to attend college and some never needed to make a decision became just as relevant as comparing differences in *how* the students made the decision. Exploring this latter distinction illuminated some important differences in the ways that the two groups of students thought about attending college. Because going to college was simply the next step for the Yale students, one deeply ingrained in their habitus, they were less prepared to offer a rationale for their choice. They had always presumed they would attend college. Nonetheless, their answers to the question of why they came to college revealed that the assumption did not rest directly on the extrinsic goal of getting a good job or preparing for a specific career; rather, college was simply what one did, suggesting a broader purpose framed around building a particular kind of self rather than preparing for a particular profession.

While this approach toward education was generally endorsed by their families and by their high schools, another significant factor shaping how the Yale students thought about their college education, and indeed an important difference between the Yale and the Southern students, was that the Yale students did not attach a goal of social mobility to their education. Rather than trying to climb out of one social stratum and into another, most of the Yale students simply sought to maintain their position within the class hierarchy. They hoped to live in the same kinds of neighborhoods they grew up in, and the future jobs they imagined for themselves were not so different from those held by their parents. The Southern students, on the other hand, were actively engaged in a quest to get ahead and firmly harnessed their college education toward that goal.

Asking how they had decided to come to college thus revealed two distinctive ways that the students' social backgrounds shaped their approaches to education. First, behind the Yalies' easy assumption of college as the next step could be seen the supporting role of a number of advantages in their lives. By and large, these students came from highly educated families and existed in social worlds that took a college education for granted. This fostered the expectation that they, too, would attend college. Because of their parents' solid economic positions, coupled with their knowledge of financial aid opportunities, most of these students never had to question whether there would be sufficient funds for them to attend college. That they would meet the academic requirements for college was also not an issue, guaranteed by their first-rate high school education. Second, most of these students were not compelled by the objective of improving their social-class position, because they were already stationed near the top of the social hierarchy. This freedom allowed them to approach their education from a broader perspective than their peers at Southern. These advantages highlighted the social distance between the two groups of students and demonstrated how one's ideals about education are shaped in part by one's position in the social-class structure.

Going to College: The Next Step

For most of the Yale students, the question of why they had decided to come to college was met with a pause and a quizzical look. One student was so baffled by the question she responded with: "Did I decide? Yeah, no, I guess I did. It was just kind of the next step from high school." Many of them asked whether I meant the decision to come to Yale or the decision to come to college in general. In fact, for most of them (forty out of fifty), the question did not make sense, because there was never a decision to be made. Going to college after high school was simply the next step, a deep-seated assumption held as far back as they could remember.

> Well, it wasn't even a question. I always knew I was going to go to college, like I never made a decision to do so.

> I guess I've always known. It was just like a given.

> Because it seemed like the next step. I thought it was fairly obvious that you go to high school, you go to college.

> As far back as I can remember it was just never a question.

> I never really assumed there was any other option.

> I never considered not, I guess. I just, it never crossed my mind to do anything else.

What explains their taken-for-granted assumption of college as the next step? As the students elaborated on the topic, the powerful role of their families emerged as one of the key factors. For most of these students, their parents and older siblings, if they had them, had graduated from college. Not only did this set an example, but it also contributed toward forming the natural assumption that the student would go, too.

> I'd say it was pretty much something that was so hammered into me from the very beginning, like as far back as I can remember, that it was just never a question. My parents both had education through grad. school, so it seemed to be pretty apparent that if I was going to be doing anything with my life, then I'd be headed in that direction.

> I'm lucky enough to have both parents, they both went to college, and it was just something I kind of assumed was going to happen just on [that] basis. My father has been to, he went to both Duke and University of North Carolina–Chapel Hill, Columbia, Albert Einstein, Harvard, and my mom went to a small college in Wisconsin, so it was kind of an inevitable thing in my mind.

These students, particularly those from the middle class and upward, did not describe their parents as pushing or even encouraging them to go to college; rather, the expectation had become ingrained.

> I think my parents wanted me to go to college probably as soon as I was born. So they sort of, you know, as parents can, sort of teach you that that's what you're going to do, and there's never any question in your mind that that's what you're going to do.

> My parents both went to college and they both expected it, and I did too.

> Both of my parents are doctors, so I have a very academically oriented family. So it was always just expected that I would go to college.

> Like everyone you know, your parents had gone to college, your brother and sister went to college. So it was not a question of "if college," but "which college."

The first-generation students at Yale, while just as likely to think of college as the next step, often recalled more active pressure from their parents.

> Only my father has been to college and he didn't finish, and both of them [parents] have always really stressed education with me and all of my siblings, so I knew that [ever] since I was a little girl, that I would go to college.

The influence of their families was bolstered by their broader social environment. Most of the Yale students attended high schools where nearly all of the students planned to attend college.

> I don't know of anybody in the years that I was in high school who didn't go to school or college.

> My high school, almost everybody went to college.

> I was at a boarding school and everyone went to college.

This helps explain why some of the students' parents did not need to explicitly convey their educational expectations to their children. The parents could convey these expectations indirectly by ensuring their child attended a school where almost everyone goes on to college.

Beyond the expectations of parents, peers, and schools, going to college has become so common for those from the middle class and above that it was simply considered the "logical progression of things." Two students described this broader influence.

> I've thought about how I didn't really decide to. For me, I kind of feel I was bereft of ever making that decision. It was, in the environment I grew up in, it wasn't even expected of you that you were going to go to college, it was just the logical progression of things . . . Being from a middle-class family in New York City, I think it's just one of the expectations that, you know, your parents have built in.

> Oh, wow, I never considered doing anything else. I mean, it's just like something expected of middle-class suburbanites, that they'll go to college.

When attending college is simply the taken-for-granted next step, it does not require much justification. Indeed, many of the students in my sample did not go beyond explaining that they had never imagined doing anything else. Nonetheless, some of the students did elaborate on their answers, adding that the love of learning, or the desire to become an educated person, motivated their decision.

> It seemed like the next step, and I love reading and learning, and it was something expected in my family, and, you know, it just made sense to me.

> Just because I expressed an interest in learning sort of throughout school. And I wanted to. I enjoyed studying, and it seemed only natural.

> I love learning, I love, well, books, reading, all that. I always liked school.

I liked education, and I liked learning new things, and there was never any question in my mind, in my parent's mind, in anybody's mind, that I was gonna go to college.

I guess I've always just enjoyed studying, so it was a place that I would get to go and study what I wanted to study . . . supposedly.

When I got out of high school, I guess I was kind of idealistic, and I felt like, I really believed in, like, pursuing knowledge. I was a very hard worker and I thought when I came here I would scale the heights of knowledge and I would like learn all these fun and exciting things.

Some of the Yale students, twenty out of the fifty, also attached a practical explanation related to future employment opportunities. These explanations were often linked to the ideal of professional jobs, such as doctors and lawyers, rather than to the semiprofessional or general white-collar occupations envisioned by the Southern students.

Well, since I was young, I've been in a society where people are always either doctors, lawyers, something that's very professional, you know. They always wear suits and stuff to work, so naturally I've grown up, you know, wanting to be either a doctor or lawyer or business person, 'cause that's how it's been in my family.

Higher education, the importance of getting a job later on in life, the quality of the job that I can get, is probably dependent on what type of an education you can get, so putting those factors together. I also figured, four more years of education, why not? Before you have to enter the real world.

Well, I figured whatever I wanted to do in life involved going to college and getting a degree, and it was the prerequisite for whatever career choice I would choose. I didn't know what I wanted to be yet when I went to college, like doctor, lawyer, whatever, you know, but it was definitely something that required a degree.

I guess, also, it's the typical, to get to maybe where I wanted to be, you need to go to college, so . . . Maybe the things that I wanted to do, later in life, everybody always says, "You have to go to college, you have to have the college degree if you want to get this type of job, or if you want to end up here" or whatever.

Finally, some of the Yale student-athletes chose to go to college for an entirely different set of reasons. For these students, their primary aim was to pursue sports on a professional level, and going to college could be an important part of that progression.

I play ice hockey, which, if you play hockey, and you live in the United States, like the big thing to do, like the highest step for the most part, besides playing professional, is playing college, so that actually had a big part, because when I was younger, I was more into hockey than I was into school so that was kind of a major push for that.

While some student-athletes came to Yale as a strategic career step, on the whole Yale students go to college because a sufficient number of influences make it part of the natural course of life. Not all students have every advantage, but each has some lucky combination of educated parents, family economic resources, inculcated expectations or active encouragement, college-prep schooling, and like-minded peers. For those fortunate enough to enjoy all of these advantages, college going indeed becomes almost inevitable.

It was kind of an easy decision [to go to college], because it was everything that, everything I'd always done kind of led up to going to college. I went to a good private school for grade school, and then I went to boarding school in New England, and I think 99 percent of my class went to college, and the other 1 percent, the two people took like the year off and are in college now, basically. It's, I don't know, it's something that, both my parents were heavily schooled, and it's something that I'd always seen older people, like older friends, people that I'd looked up to when I was a little kid, doing. And everybody had such a great experience and, mostly socially, everybody loved it so much. And academically, I'd always kind of taken the hard route and wanted to keep doing that and see what I could do. And I guess also it's the typical, to get to maybe where I wanted to be, you need to go to college.

For most of the Yale students, education was not tightly linked to preparing for a specific career (though it certainly would increase their employability). Instead, education was about preparing to be a certain kind of person. When the students said that "it was just the next step," they meant going to college was just what one does. The kind of person they were becoming was the kind of person who attended college.

Going to College: Getting a Job

The question about how they made the decision to go to college held much more relevance for the Southern students. For almost all of these students (forty-five out of fifty), there actually had been a decision made at some point, usually during the later years of high school. For the Southern students, college was not the taken-for-granted next step; it was a conscious decision made by weighing the alternatives of not going to college. In fact, many of these students had not particularly enjoyed high school and had decided that schooling was not for them. Yet in evaluating the employment options available to them with only a high school degree, these students decided that the credential and the skills they would receive with a college education, and the path toward the future that these would ensure, made college their most reasonable option. Unlike the Yale students, for most of the Southern students going to college did not represent a path toward assuming one's identity so much as an escape from one's destiny.

A large proportion of the Southern students neither had college-educated parents nor graduated from high schools where most students planned to attend college. Thus, unlike the Yale students, these students did not grow up in an environment that conveyed the expectation of going to college. For the Southern students, college was a practical decision. They chose college primarily for economic reasons, based around the goal of getting a good job. Indeed, almost all of these students (forty-five out of fifty) cited getting a better job as their key reason for coming to college:

> If you're gonna get a good job, you have to go to college.

> There's really not much you can do without higher education.

> You're not looked at without a college degree.

> A high school diploma can't really get you to where you want to go.

> Because most jobs out there now require a college education.

> The whole, hopefully getting a better job kind of thing, getting more money, hopefully.

Conversely, the Southern students were clear about the jobs that would be available to them *without* a college degree. The jobs they were seeking to avoid were low-level service, blue-collar, or factory jobs, the occupations held by many of their parents.

> Because I didn't want to earn, you know, $4.50 an hour or whatever, flipping burgers, and college is where that all starts.

> 'Cause I didn't want to do blue-collar work.

Well, I know that when I leave here I'll be able to get a better job. I won't have to go work in a factory like my parents did.

It's better than working construction.

Some of the students had already come face to face with the limited job options open to them with just a high school degree and, on that basis, made the decision to go to college.

After high school, I took two years off, and I worked full time in a very low-paying job, and I decided I had to get myself back to school.

The following student had tried college and hated it. However, she also hated the job she got after leaving college, and eventually decided that to get a job she liked, she would have to go back to get her degree. It is interesting that her main complaint about her first college experience was in not knowing what she wanted to do, underscoring the extent to which college holds little meaning in and of itself unless linked to a particular career objective.

My first two years out of high school, I went to Central [Central Connecticut State University], and then I took a couple years off.

Why did you stop after two years?

I hated it. I didn't want to be there. I didn't know what I wanted to do, and I thought it was a waste of time to be there if I didn't know why I was there.

Why did you decide to come back?

Because I hated the job that I had had over the past couple years, and I knew that if I wanted to do something that I liked, I would have to go to school.

Some of the Southern students, about 20 percent, came to college because of specific occupational goals. All of these students planned to be teachers.

Well, I thought I wanted to be a teacher when I graduated from high school.

Well, I knew that I wanted to be a teacher, and I knew that that would be the only way I could do it.

Finally, a handful of students, all male, had also considered the possibility of the military and then chosen college.

I suppose it was either that or the military, so, I wasn't about to go join in the military, so I figured I'd go to college.

I was like, it's either that [college] or go into the military. My mom really did not want me to go into the military.

The decisions of the Southern students also bore the marks of family influence. Whereas the parents of most of the Yale students seemingly conveyed the expectation of college without ever issuing a directive, the Southern students were more likely to report neither expectation nor encouragement, but pressure. For nearly a third of these students, the decision to attend college was the result of explicit parental pressure, if not coercion.

I was told to, by my dad. I had no choice. It was either that or go to work.

Well, my parents encouraged me a lot to go to college. They wanted me to go to college or either work at Burger King. So I said, "Well, you know, college is a better choice for me then."

Well, my parents made me. They just said that I had to go to college.

Well, my parents basically said I would have to either pay rent or move out if I didn't go to school.

I think I was forced. I know that's awful to say, but out of high school I was forced, kind of. My parents expected me to go right to college.

A few students noted the encouragement they had received from high school teachers to apply for college. This encouragement seemed especially important for those students with concerns about their ability to do college-level academic work. In some cases, having their confidence bolstered by high school teachers proved pivotal in their decision to apply to college.

Like I said, that one teacher that told me, she was like, "You have a lot of potential." I never liked her but it always stayed in my mind. She was telling me, "You have what it takes to go to college, and then some."

That must have meant a lot to you.

Yeah, that meant a lot to me, 'cause I was a freshman in high school, and I didn't know any better, you know what I mean? You think about college, but you don't really think about it, you know. So she said that and that was cool . . . when somebody outside of the family, somebody that's really a stranger to you is like, "Hey, you're intelligent, you've got potential." Oh, wow, this person that I don't even know, that I don't even like, is telling me that I can be somebody. That means something.

Without a history of college going in their families or attendance at a college-prep high school, a teacher's positive assessment of their intelligence and capability of handling college work could be vital.

While the better part of their focus was on the prize of getting a good job after graduation, the Southern students also occasionally touched on the status associated with earning a university degree. The notion of raising one's status was bound together with their descriptions of "furthering" or "bettering," terms that came up at Southern but not at Yale. The terms were applied in two ways. First, some students used them in relation to their education, as in: "Well, I wanted to further my education and get a good job after college." These students simply meant increasing their education. However, some students used these terms in a way that related the furthering not simply to their educational credentials, but to themselves.

> Well, our society nowadays is structured. You're not looked at without a college degree, so . . . that's first and foremost, whether you did well in college or no. Employers look at whether you have the bachelor's degree, and then obviously the education factor, you know. I wanted to further myself.

This student used the term to suggest that not only would he get a better job with a college degree, but beyond that, more broadly, his own value would increase by adding in the "education factor." Independently of the job benefits, he would have improved himself in a significant way by becoming an educated person.

Some of the more lengthy responses from students about why they decided to go to college revealed this secondary aim of getting an education. The following student saw both her brother and sister drop out of high school. She envisioned college as providing not just a way out of the kind of work her father and aunt did, but also opening up bigger doors for her, allowing her to grow and get more out of life.

> There's three of us, and so we basically grew up with my father, and he tried to provide the best he could for us, but my brother chose to hang around and drop out of high school, and my sister the same thing, and with me, I didn't, yeah, I had my friends, I did my partying and everything, but I didn't want to drop out of school. I was like, "You know, if I drop out, what next?" you know, and it was funny 'cause I didn't want to end up in a factory, 'cause I had an aunt and she used to work at a factory, and I used to say, "No, that's not the job for me, you know, I don't want

to struggle." And I see how hard it is for my father, just getting up every day and having to work outside in the cold, doing, you know, hard work, hard labor, and not getting any respect, not, not moving, and I want so much out of life. I want, there's so much out there, just that we close ourselves to, we get stuck in our little, and I don't want that, I want more, I want to grow.

Another student drew similar comparisons. He made a distinction between working with his hands versus his head. College was portrayed as the means, the most practical way, of making that switch in his life, but it also represented a way of bettering himself, because he would be paid for the value of his intelligence.

> I think I came, chose to go to college, same reason everybody did, to improve their way of living, way of life. I come from a just, a blue-collar, you know, lower-class family, where they just worked their whole lives with their hands, and they've always motivated me to go to school, to higher learning, to better myself, 'cause that would be the most practical way of doing it. So that would have to be the number one reason, for me to better myself . . . They felt that, you know, "Why are you going to work in a factory, why are you going to work fifty, sixty hours a week, you know, and wear yourself out? You're a bright kid, go to school, study, you know, and use your brain. And get paid for the value of your intelligence." So that's always been the emphasis for my family.

• • •

Statistics show that the likelihood of attending a four-year college largely depends on social background. What they do not show is that the decision-making process also differs. For the students at Yale, college was never really a decision, but simply the expected next step after high school, an expectation made natural by the combined and often indirect influences of their families, friends, and schools. Perhaps because it was simply part of a natural progression that did not require much thought, the Yale students did not give much justification for their decision. When they did, most explained that they liked learning and that it was something at which they excelled. Less than half also added a practical justification, linked to their future careers. Going to college had simply become a taken-for-granted part of their life course. Most of the Southern students, on the other hand, did not take college for granted and instead chose a college education in order to secure better job opportunities and avoid the fate of their parents. Rather than attending out of a love of learning, they often went in spite of an aversion to schooling. Privilege, then, influences both whether one goes to college and whether it is a nondecision or a strategic choice.

CHAPTER FOUR

Choosing Colleges

Whether going to college is a nondecision or a strategic decision, students must choose which college to attend. The college application process is often portrayed as a grand competition, with students fighting for entrance into the most prestigious colleges. Indeed, for many students, the final and most important project of their high school years *is* getting into college, and these students mount an intensive campaign to select and then apply to appropriate institutions. This undertaking involves carefully researching the characteristics of various colleges, visiting several different campuses, calculating the chances of admission at each, and then making a final strategic selection. However, contrary to the image of students competitively vying for spots at the best institutions, in reality approximately 74 percent of all undergraduates attend their first-choice college, and 20 percent their second-choice one (Astin, Green, and Korn 1987; Sax et al. 1996), with only 6 percent of students facing the disappointment of not being able to attend their first- or second-choice institution. These statistics indicate that nearly all students select institutions willing to admit them and, thus, that students' aspirations largely correspond to the college opportunities available to them.

This general trend varies in the case of applications to elite colleges and universities. Even when they are equally talented academically, low-SES students are considerably less likely to apply to elite institutions than are their more privileged peers. A study of the application behavior of students scoring 1300 or above on the combined SATs (placing them in approximately the top 10% of all test takers) found a direct connection between income and the likelihood of applying to a group of thirty-one highly selective institutions, including all of the Ivy League universities (McPherson and Schapiro 1991). Of those with annual family incomes of $90,000 and above, a full 85 percent applied, compared with only 50 percent of those students with family incomes of less than $20,000. Likewise, only one-third of all high-testing, low-income students applied to a group of forty selective colleges, compared with over half of high-testing, high-income students (Spies1973). Further, after controlling for SAT scores, low-income students are as likely as high-income students to be admitted to highly selective institutions and are slightly *more* likely to accept the offer and enroll (Bowen, Kurzweil, and Tobin 2005). Thus one reason for the underrepresentation of low-SES students at elite institutions is that they are much less likely to apply. Moreover, while these studies emphasize the underapplication behavior of low-SES students, they also point to the overapplication behavior of high-SES students.

Bourdieu's (1984) concept of habitus suggests that these class differences in educational choice may be partly explained in terms of the perception of one's chances for success.

> Objective limits become a sense of limits, a practical anticipation of objective limits acquired by experience of objective limits, a "sense of one's place" which leads one to exclude oneself from the goods, persons, places, and so forth from which one is excluded. (p. 471)

Bourdieu further clarifies the idea of a sense of limits by explaining that the process of self-exclusion may occur through a perception that "that's not for the likes of us" and a consequent adjustment of expectations to chances. Because habitus varies with class status, due to differences in objective chances, it helps explain class-based educational self-selection. Bourdieu argues that working-class youth may resign themselves to lower levels of educational attainment because of their knowledge of their limited opportunities for success, whereas the higher probabilities of success for upper-class children result in higher educational expectations. An important point is that students' low educational aspirations are conceived of as the product, not the cause, of their low likelihood of success (DiMaggio 1979).

Several researchers have located habitus as an important site of educational decision making. Reay, David, and Ball (2005) find evidence of habitus in the "absence of decisions" or the "decision to go to university [as] a non-decision" (p. 33) for many middle-class young people, in contrast to the very deliberate decision making of many working-class youth. Even the choice of an institution for privileged students is one that is "ingrained, tacit, taken for granted" (p. 33). Likewise, McDonough (1997) introduces the concept of "entitlement" as one aspect of habitus: privileged students believe they are entitled to the best kind of education they can secure, while less privileged students feel worthy of either local options or community colleges. Entitlement for privileged students is seen at work in their easy assumptions (rather than calculated choices) of attending one of the more selective private colleges.

While a "sense of one's place" may guide the kinds of college options students consider reasonable for themselves, studies on educational decision making highlight how families, schools, friendships, and costs also influence students' choices. Privileged families hold more knowledge of the college application process, and in particular for the elite sector of education, an important type of cultural capital (Lamont and Lareau 1988; McDonough 1997). McDonough (1997) shows this form of cultural capital at work, with the high-SES families in her study demonstrating more perspicacity concerning the admissions process and the means to increase their children's likelihood of acceptance through such tactics as employing private college-admissions counselors and SAT tutors. Students from high-SES families are also more strategic in how they approach the college choice process and apply to more institutions (Hurtado et al. 1997). Perhaps for these reasons, parental cultural capital has been found to be an important predictor of attendance at an elite versus a non-elite college, even after controlling for academic ability (Kaufman and Gabler 2004). Families with less higher educational experience not only lack knowledge of college application procedures, but may also express ambivalence about their children attending college or about them leaving home for colleges in other cities (Lubrano 2004).

In his study of the admissions process at a liberal arts college, Stevens (2007) makes the point that in general, only the relatively wealthy can afford the infrastructure that produces the kinds of accomplishments in children required for admission to an elite college. Because of their awareness of the elite-college admissions process, "privileged parents do everything in their power to make their children into ideal applicants" (p. 15). We have already seen how higher-SES families are more likely to invest in private schooling or move to neighborhoods with better public schools (Devine 2004). Stevens (2007) outlines several other ways in which affluent parents dedicate themselves to nurturing their children's athletic and academic talent, through travel, field trips, books, and youth sports programs. He argues that affluent families "fashion an entire way of life organized around the 'production of measurable virtue' in children" (p. 15).

Some privileged families may also foster a tradition of sending their children to the same elite institutions that they themselves attended (and sometimes even their parents or grandparents before them). Institutions acknowledge this process by giving preferences in admissions to "legacy" students, a policy designed in part to enhance the likelihood of ongoing monetary gifts to the university (Karabel 2005; Soares 2007). Thus, in the case of elite universities, we may find a different kind of family influence at work: that of parents conveying the expectation to their children that they will attend a parent's alma mater or inculcating this expectation by familiarizing their children with that institution through campus visits or alumni functions.

A second source of influence on students' choices comes from their high schools. McDonough (1997) and Reay, David, and Ball (2001, 2005) document differences in the college application support given to students by their schools. High schools attended by higher-SES students tend to provide more extensive guidance counseling and other forms of support through the college application process. High schools, either through school culture or institutional habitus (Power et al. 2003; Reay, David, and Ball 2005), may also convey particular views of higher educational opportunities to their students, which include norms regarding appropriate college destinations and "tastes" for specific institutions. These influences connect with family-based resources to situate the framework for the college choice process.

Besides these general effects from schools, there is also a strong link between elite high schools and elite universities, well documented in the United States and Britain. These schools not only provide their students with the rigorous academic training necessary to meet the admissions requirements at elite institutions, they also supply an important form of socialization that helps prepare their students to assume positions of power in society, beginning with their education at a top-tier university (Cookson and Persell 1985b). Graduates of private boarding schools attend colleges that are more selective, even after taking into account differences in their family backgrounds and SAT scores (Cookson

1981). In part this may be because many private schools have long-standing relationships with elite colleges, which increase their students' chances of admission (Cookson and Persell 1985; Karabel 2005; Power et al. 2003; Reay, David, and Ball 2001). Highly developed social networks between the schools' college advisors and the admissions officers from elite colleges smooth the process and allow for a subtle negotiation of admissions cases (Cookson and Persell 1985; Stevens 2007).

Friendships also influence the college selection process (R. Brooks 2003; McDonough 1997). Friends that come from the same social circle tend to hold similar aspirations and help reinforce each other's goals and plans. Friends can also be an important source of information on potential colleges and on the application process. In some cases, students whose parents lack knowledge about college options may rely on friends from a higher-SES group as a pivotal source of support and information (McDonough 1997).

Finally, the cost of college and the availability of financial aid also play a role in the decision-making process (Hossler and Gallagher 1987). The vast majority of students attending public and private four-year institutions now receive some form of financial aid. For example, in the 2003–04 academic year, 89 percent of students attending private, nonprofit, four-year institutions received financial aid in the form of grants and loans, at an average amount of $16,300 (Berkner and Wei 2006). However, many students make their comparisons on the full sticker price advertised by each institution (Avery and Kane 2004). Their likely misperceptions of the real cost of attending various institutions is not surprising, as a number of national surveys reveal that the general public holds distorted views of the costs of attending college (Grodsky and Jones 2006; Ikenberry and Hartle 1998). In addition, knowledge of tuition and fees varies dramatically by parents' education levels. One study shows that only 20 percent of parents with a high school degree had obtained information about the costs of tuition and fees, compared with 43 percent of parents with graduate degrees (Horn, Chen, and Chapman 2003). These latter parents were also three times as likely to have spoken with someone or read information about financial aid. In terms of how financial aid relates to choice, the availability of state merit-aid programs and federal tax-credit programs influence whether students attend two-year versus four-year institutions or choose colleges with greater resources and higher tuitions (Dynarski 2004; Long 2004). Likewise, with the exception of students from very affluent families, students make decisions based in part on the financial aid packages offered to them (Avery and Hoxby 2004).

All of these influences occur over time, often beginning in the early high school years. In their comprehensive model of college choice, Hossler and Gallagher (1987) identify three distinct phases in the process: predisposition, search, and choice. In each phase, students' social backgrounds, abilities, attitudes, aspirations, and activities interact to influence decision making. In the final phase, that of actually choosing institutions to which to apply, students evaluate the institutions they are considering and rank them according to their preferences. Factors such as cost and the availability of financial aid, location, size, academic programs, perceptions of quality, and the students' interactions with the college may influence the ranking process (Erdman 1983; Hossler and Gallagher 1987; Hossler, Schmit, and Vesper 1999).

A comparison of the selection processes of the Yale and the Southern students considers these various influences, clarifying how these students chose those institutions most likely to accept them and showing why high-SES students were more likely to apply to elite institutions. I start by exploring the pathways taken to Yale, looking at how the students described their choice to apply and comparing the accounts of students from different social backgrounds. I then turn to the Southern students, considering differences in their selection criteria, the context in which they made their choices, and the constraints they faced.

Choosing Yale: The "Standard Prestige Line-Up" and Other Routes

Instead of finding a common pathway among all Yale students, the interviews revealed several distinct routes to Yale. When asked why they had chosen Yale, students typically gave one of five reasons. Some students had long assumed that they would attend Yale or another Ivy League-type university without ever really making a decision. For others, Yale was a choice, either on the basis of its prestige or its match with particular characteristics. Some students were recruited through athletics, and at least a few of those would not otherwise have considered Yale. Finally, the arrival of some of the students at Yale could be characterized by chance, in the form of a sudden impulse or whim to apply or through the intercession of a teacher, guidance counselor, or parent. Further, this variation relates to social background. Almost all of the students who had their sights set on Yale or a similarly elite institution attended private high schools and came from the most privileged families, while those applying on a whim came from less advantaged circumstances and were much less likely to attend private high schools. Students in the other categories fell somewhere in between.

Eleven students (22%) explained that they had only considered a small number of Ivy League or similarly elite universities. To put this in context, the likelihood of attending an Ivy League is remote (less than 1% of four-year university students attend an Ivy League institution). However, these students had been on the path toward an Ivy League education as far back as they could remember and described their choice of Yale in the context of a range of options limited not just to the Ivy League and a few other top universities, but to the most prestigious institutions within that group.

> For me, the only schools that I would have considered would have included probably Yale, Brown, and Harvard.

> I've often explained it as if you thought you were gonna go to one of the Ivy League schools unless you did something wrong, and it was a question of which one.

These comments convey an extraordinarily high level of expectation and confidence. It is not simply that they aspired to attend the most elite institutions; rather, they planned on it.

> I applied to six schools total, but I really didn't know what I was gonna do if I didn't get in here. I didn't know where else I would have gone.

For these students, there was often little thought put into the decision; indeed, there was an absence of decision making in choosing Yale.

> I didn't have to make a decision [about Yale], because I was lucky in terms of getting into all my colleges. And then I knew from when I was eight years old where I wanted to go . . . And to me, when I was choosing schools, I couldn't even figure out what other ones I would possibly want to go to, because I didn't even think about . . . what really the benefits were logically [of Yale]. This was where I wanted to go.

Even though this student applied for admission to other colleges, she had her heart set on Yale since she was a child, and that desire was more important than logically weighing the advantages of different institutions. Thus, as a senior in high school, there was no decision to make.

Other students in this group made their selection among the Ivy League institutions on criteria that seem almost idiosyncratic. Perhaps because the universe of possibility for these students was limited to only three or four relatively

similar institutions, their individual preferences or subjective perceptions became key deciding factors.

> I mean, I guess in my mind I was looking seriously at Harvard, Yale, Princeton, and
> Amherst. I guess I eliminated Amherst 'cause I wanted a bigger school. And origi-
> nally I wanted to go to Princeton, largely because I was a big F. Scott Fitzgerald
> fan, and he went there and so, one of his books is about it. But I guess when I visited
> the schools, I just had the best feeling about Yale. I think it was because it seemed
> to have the friendliest environment . . . and struck me as the least competitive.

A second set of students (seven, or 14%) described choosing Yale because
it was the "best" institution to which they had been admitted. Compared with
the first group, these students applied to a wider range of institutions, including the Ivies, liberal arts colleges, and selective state universities. It is possible
that these students' academic records may not have been as solid as those in the
first group, reducing their certainty about being admitted to their top-choice
institution and obliging them to consider other options. These students ranked
institutions on the basis of quality or prestige and, after learning where they had
been accepted, simply enrolled in the best one.

> When it came down to it, I had a college advisor and I applied to a bunch of differ-
> ent schools, some of the caliber of Yale, some not quite up to that caliber, but my
> college advisor advised me on what he thought would be good choices and what
> wouldn't be . . . And then, as it turns out, [Yale] was really the best option I had
> once all the acceptance letters and rejection letters came, so I ended up here.

> Well, I applied to a bunch of colleges, of course, typical run-of-the-mill student,
> picked up applications from all the Ivy Leagues, sent them all in. And I came to Yale
> just because I thought it was the best I could do of all the colleges I applied to.

The students in this group employed a certain logic in their decision making,
with the objective of attending the most prestigious institution possible. These
students applied to a range of colleges, following the technique of including a
few "reaches" and a few "safeties," reasoning that if they were not admitted to
their top choices, they would have a fallback option. One student described this
approach among the students in his high school.

> I went through a high school where people were completely obsessed about get-
> ting into college . . . and people were just fighting as hard as they could . . . in
> order to get into the best college they could. And it was pretty much just a standard

prestige line-up. No one really deviated too much, did anything all that radical. They would just sort of go for the most prestigious thing they could get, so it just sort of churned along in that way.

A third group of students selected Yale on the basis of how well it matched some desired characteristic. This was the largest group, with fourteen students (28% of the sample). In some cases, these students were seeking a university that offered a particular field of study. For others, aspects of the campus environment or student body were important to them. Still others explained that Yale simply felt the best during their campus visit.

> I'm a science major, and I always knew I was interested in science, but I liked having a liberal arts, good liberal arts education. I liked the mixture of how, at Yale, there were so many other courses I could take besides science, and they were really good. There was a lot of different choices, as opposed to like MIT, where everybody's a science major.

> I chose Yale because it had an archeology major, and I figured out in high school that I wanted to major in archeology or that I was thinking about majoring in archeology. And I was looking at schools that were sort of small to medium-sized on the East Coast (I'm from the West Coast), and so Yale like fit those criteria and has an archeology major, and there are very few schools that have archeology majors that aren't combined with anthro[pology].

> Well, I visited it, I was visiting a lot of colleges, and I visited here and I really liked it . . . I liked the residential college system. I liked the fact that the people seemed nice and people seemed to really be having fun, and as much as, or more than anywhere else, they really seemed to enjoy life here.

> I visited and it felt right. It was kind of more instinctive than anything else . . . I guess I just saw a lot of people wandering around who seemed to be individuals and independent, and I was really attracted by that, and I didn't see that everywhere I went. I mean, I didn't want a place where it was sort of white baseball caps and flannel shirts.

These students had not always taken for granted that they would attend an Ivy League college and were more practical in their decisions. They began their college search with certain key characteristics in mind. In contrast to the standard prestige line-up, these students took into account the particular program strengths of different universities and other characteristics, such as their sizes and locations. In part these characteristics reflected the practicalities of career planning, of wanting institutions that offered degrees in their chosen field of employment. In part they pointed to individual preferences. There was probably some overlap with the previous category, in that these students may also have limited their search to the best or most prestigious institutions that met their criteria. They differed from the previous group, however, in that they offered a specific reason for selecting Yale over other institutions, rather than selecting Yale simply because it was the best.

Seven students (14%) came to Yale because they had been recruited through athletics.

> Yale was the only Ivy League school I applied to. I didn't really want to go to Ivy League. I didn't even know what it was, basically. I mean, I knew there were good schools up North, but . . . I knew the baseball coach, before he got a job at Yale . . . I'd met him earlier in my life. And so, I knew him, and then baseball helped me get into Yale. So that's how I, it kind of crawled in my lap, sort of.

> Well, it was basically through football. The team contacted me. They got my name from some list somewhere, and they asked me to send in a tape of my football highlights. And I did that and they got back to me and they flew me out here and I had a recruiting trip and liked it, and got in, and I couldn't turn it down. I wouldn't have applied here otherwise. I applied to like [University of] Michigan, Michigan State.

From these accounts, it is clear that some of these students would not otherwise have considered an elite institution. Some student-athletes also made it clear that their academic record alone would not have sufficed for admission.

> I could be pretty honest with you. I wouldn't, I'm not in the same level as the highest people here, but with hockey it kind of gave me that extra thing, whether, you know, some people have music or something like this, and the hockey was able to, I was able to use that to get me in here. I mean, if was just on my grades, I know that I, chances are, I wouldn't be able to get in.

In contrast, another student-athlete had been salutatorian of his graduating class and was deeply interested in history.

> Part of it was that I got recruited, and part of my decision to come to college was about soccer, and also the history department here looked very good, and so pretty much those two . . . And obviously the academic reputation was a big part of it,

too . . . One of the main reasons I came to Yale, actually on my recruiting visit for soccer, a big fan of the soccer team is Professor Kennedy. He wrote *Rise and Fall of the Great Powers*. And on that recruiting visit, I got an autographed copy of *The Rise and Fall of the Great Powers*. That was Yale's version of a recruiting violation . . . So one of the main reasons I came here was the history department.

Finally, for a fifth group of students, applying to Yale was due either to the intervention of a parent, teacher, or guidance counselor or to following a whim at the last minute. Choosing Yale was neither an easy assumption nor part of a careful process of choice, but rather one of chance.

Actually, at first, Yale wasn't like my first priority or my first choice. I almost didn't apply to Yale, and I applied on like one of the last days, and just randomly like typed an essay or whatever, because at first I thought everyone here was gonna be very snobby and not realistic and not down to earth.

I actually never really thought of Yale seriously. I didn't like Ivy League colleges because they were so prestigious and felt they were "all that," and I actually just applied. By the time I started applying, I had changed my mind and just applied to a whole bunch of different colleges, and I actually applied to Yale on a whim, just to see if I could get in.

For these students, even the consideration of Ivy League universities came late in their high school years. A few students explained that they had not known until then what the Ivy League was, such as one student who had moved with her family from Europe to the United States when she was a teenager.

I never really thought about really applying to Ivy League schools. I've only been in the country for like about six years now, and when I got here I wasn't really aware of Ivy League schools or anything. I didn't really know what that was all about. But, you know, I did well in school, and when I got to my junior year and started talking about going to college and looking at schools that I wanted to apply [to], and my guidance counselor actually was the one who pushed me to apply to Ivy League schools. And it was then that I kind of got familiarized with the whole idea of Ivy League. And I actually didn't want to apply to Yale, because I thought that I just wouldn't fit in here, but I ended up applying anyways.

Another student, whose parents were not supportive of her decision to attend college, cites the important role played by a teacher.

Well, I had, honestly, a teacher in sixth, seventh, and eighth grades who has been, I guess, the most influential person in my life. And she just constantly drilled into me that I need to go to college and that I would have a choice of the best to go to, so I should take advantage of it. So I just followed her advice and used her encouragement.

To understand if and how social background may be linked to these different patterns of choice, table 4.1 shows how characteristics of the students' family backgrounds related to their choice of Yale. The first part considers college choice by the highest level of education obtained by either parent, and the second part considers annual family income.

A strong majority of those students who had assumed they would attend an Ivy League-type institution came from the most privileged of families. Ten of these students came from families where at least one parent had a graduate or advanced degree; seven came from families with incomes in excess of $135,000. Students choosing Yale because it was a good match appear to be similarly well advantaged. Only one student came from a family with less than a graduate degree and none of the students came from families in the lowest income group. In contrast, those students choosing Yale on a whim or after outside intervention came from less privileged families. Six of the eleven came from families where neither parent had a college degree; four came from families with annual

Table 4.1   Yale students' college choice by family background and gender

	Elite only	Best	Best match	Athletic recruit	Whim or intervention
Parents' highest level of education					
Less than a college degree	1	1	0	3	6
College degree	0	1	1	1	2
Graduate degree	10	4	12	3	3
Annual family income*					
Less than $54,000	1	0	0	1	4
$54,000–$134,999	2	3	3	3	2
$135,000 or above	7	2	7	3	2
Gender					
Men	7	5	4	7	2
Women	4	2	10	0	9
Total	11	7	14	7	11

Note: N = 50; 2 missing cases for parents' education, 10 missing cases for family income.
*Dollar amounts are given in 2008 dollars.

incomes of less than $54,000. Students who were recruited as athletes are a more mixed group. While some came from highly educated and wealthy families, nearly half were first-generation students or came from low-income families. Finally, those students choosing Yale because it was the best tended to come from mid- to high-range families. Three of them had annual family incomes of $54,000–$134,999 and four of them had at least one parent with a graduate degree.

There are also gender differences in these students' college choice. Notably, none of the Yale women reported being recruited, in comparison with seven of the men. This finding parallels recent surveys showing that men are more likely than women to be recruited by Ivy League universities (Shulman and Bowen 2001). The women were far more likely to apply to Yale on a whim or because of an intervention. Because about half of both the athletic recruits and the students who applied on a whim were first-generation students, these findings suggest gendered routes for first-generation students. Women were also more likely than men to describe applying because of the match, but fewer women than men reported applying only to elite institutions or to the best institutions. Because Yale only opened its doors to women in 1969, the tradition of attending Yale extends much further down the male lines of families and may influence the way that families pass on expectations to attend Yale to their children. Sons may receive more encouragement to attend their father's and grandfather's alma mater than daughters.

Table 4.2 shows the relationship between high school type and the Yale students' choices. Almost all of the students who only considered Ivy League-type institutions attended private high schools. This is a high proportion, considering that just under half of the entire sample of fifty attended a private school. Conversely, all but one of those choosing Yale through a whim or because of an intervention graduated from a public or a Catholic high school. Students choosing because of the best match were equally divided between private and public schools, while a majority of those selecting Yale as the best institution attended a private school. Three of the athletic recruits went to public school, while only one attended a private school.

The students' routes to Yale varied in accordance with their family backgrounds and the kinds of high schools they attended. To better understand the circumstances and influences that contributed to their differences in decision making, I now turn to an exploration of these students' families, schools, and peers.

Table 4.2   Yale students' college choice by high school type

High school type	Elite only	Best	Best match	Athletic recruit	Whim or inter- vention	Total
Private	10	4	7	1	1	23
Public	1	2	7	3	8	21
Catholic	0	1	0	2	2	5

Note: N = 50; 1 missing case.

Families, Schools, and Peers

Three of the eleven students who assumed they would attend an Ivy League institution recounted instances in their childhoods where their families familiarized them with Yale. For some of these students, their father or their brothers had attended Yale, leaving a legacy that helped make Yale a natural choice.

> My dad was Yale class of '68, my brother was Yale class of '93. Not even just Yale, but it was never, it was always just the next step. I mean, it was like high school and middle school, there was never a thought of a year off. I don't think the thought ever crossed my mind. Just because I'd grown up with "For God, for country, and for Yale."

> My father went to Yale, and it was just kind of like, if that's another question about why I chose Yale, it was that I'd been exposed to it since I was eight years old.

These quotes reveal how the family's experience with Yale directly contributed to the formation of the student's own expectation of Yale as an appropriate and even probable destination. Even students who identified themselves as middle class still benefited from the powerful advantage of having a family member graduate from Yale.

> My father went here. I came from a middle-class family . . . In high school, at first . . . I always talked about going to either Princeton, Yale, or Harvard, and I used to say I wanted to go to Harvard, like against my father, and then I decided I wanted to go to Yale, like my father. As I became sixteen, seventeen, I applied early and I got in and I didn't have any real desire to apply anywhere else. I didn't know that much about Yale, really, but I knew that it was, you know, famous.

The powerful influence of his father's history came across in the way this student, even without knowing much about Yale, made his choice around being either "like" or "against" his father. In either case, his choice was limited to Harvard, Yale, or Princeton. Even when family members had not attended Yale themselves, some families explicitly conveyed the possibility of Yale to their children through their own knowledge of the university and its importance.

> Yale was a choice, actually, way back in about third grade . . . We passed by the school and my father said, "If you can go here, you have done well," and so I kind of made that my own little challenge.

Whether or not they had family members who attended Yale, what was consistent across these students' accounts was that their families successfully inculcated an aspiration, or taste, for the Ivy League. None of these students reported that their families overtly encouraged or pressured them in this direction. As one student explained, her father "hadn't actively but passively put the idea in my head so it just seemed like something I wanted to do." It was also not the case that all of the children of legacy families assumed that they would go to Yale. Four students whose fathers had graduated from Yale chose Yale for practical reasons or because it was the best institution to which they were admitted.

Family influences could also be found among the less advantaged Yale students. Here, however, choosing Yale, and even choosing to go to college, sometimes created tensions within families. The difficulties associated with going to college for working-class or first-generation students have been well documented. Lubrano (2004), for example, provides a richly detailed journalistic account of the transition from the working class to the middle class through the nexus of a college degree. Often the journey raises a painful set of identity and family issues, where individuals find themselves between two worlds, neither fully comfortable nor accepted in either. Working-class families, while proud of the accomplishments of their high-achieving children, may not always be completely supportive, sometimes out of a sense that family or class values are being betrayed. In a few cases in my own sample, family members were not familiar with Yale and did not understand its benefits. One student explained how she had to overcome her mother's reluctance for her to attend Yale because of its distance and expense, compared with the local colleges.

> My mother is very supportive in anything I do. However, she's just, she didn't know what Yale was when I got in. At first she was like, "Hmm, why can't you just go to the local college, because then I won't have to pay anything, and then you can just go for free." And I was just like, "Well, no, no, no, no."

Other families not only disapproved of their child leaving home to attend college, but also questioned the basic decision to go to college.

> I'm the first person in my family to go to college, so I've had to do a lot of fighting, I guess, to make my parents understand why it's important . . . I think they would have preferred had I just stayed in my home town . . . After they accepted the fact that I wanted to go to school, they didn't like that I chose Yale. They wanted me to go to a school in Ohio, which is closer. So . . . this next year, I'm taking off for a year to work, because my parents won't cosign a loan for me, to pay my tuition. That's how much they don't want me here.

These examples highlight the obstacles faced by some low-SES students. In contrast to the close correspondence of values and expectations experienced by more privileged students and their families, these students contended with sharp differences and even disapproval from their parents. Rather than benefiting from family support, these students faced the burden of convincing their parents to accept their choices.

The figures presented in table 4.2 demonstrate a relationship between attending a private high school and the kind of decision making that led to the students' arrival at Yale. Almost all of the students who assumed they would attend an Ivy League university attended a private high school. Because privileged families are more likely to send their children to private high schools, the influences of high school are also those of family background. The privileged families who invested in their children's education long before beginning to pay Yale's tuition gave their children a tremendous advantage. Besides the academic benefits, high school environments and peer groups also help shape students' aspirations for particular types of colleges, as well as facilitate the application process.

Many private college-prep high schools now market themselves to parents on the basis of their track records in the matriculation rates of their graduates at top colleges and universities. Perhaps for this reason, many students were knowledgeable about the current rates at their own high schools, recounting the exact numbers of students from their high school class attending Yale and the other Ivies.

> I had a graduating class of sixty-two and seven are here. I think over a third of my class went to the Ivies.

> I had the luxury of, at Deerfield, where I went to boarding school . . . there are nine kids from my class who are here. There are twelve who are at Princeton.

[Handwritten margin notes: "Family Background ↓ Better HS ↓ Iv League"]

The emphasis of these high schools in placing graduates at Ivy League or other prestigious colleges and universities created an atmosphere among the students that promoted this expectation.

> I'd say [my high school was] private, very self-assured, college obsessed, and probably considered itself to be the best high school in the country, at least in terms of day schools . . . And it probably thinks that because outside of places like Exeter and Andover, as far as day schools go, it probably has the best numbers for getting people into colleges of any high school.

> I went to a top private school where everyone goes to college and where most people go to top colleges. So, I mean, from that sense it's something everyone does.

> There was sort of this Harvard, Princeton, Yale thing at my school, where you would sort of specify which one you really liked and then they would sort of pull for you, and everyone else was like Harvard, Princeton, so I was like, "Okay, there's no one in the Yale category."

As the quote above shows, some students chose *which* Ivy League to push for on the basis of their peers. In one case, a student chose Yale, after originally aiming for Princeton, because of his high school friends that also planned to attend Yale. Part of choosing Yale became choosing with which friends he wanted to spend four more years.

> Like freshman year, we, for an English class, we had to write letters to ourselves our freshman year that the teacher then gave back to us senior year. Freshman year, I was like, "I know I'm going to Princeton, blah, blah, blah," because that's where everybody who I kind of looked up to, my captains, and everything, a lot of them were going to Princeton, or different places like that. [Later], just the kids that I saw from Deerfield who came [to Yale], it wasn't necessarily my best friends, but it was the people that I wanted to spend four years of my life with . . . And I just decided, "No, I want to spend four years of my life with those people."

Thus choosing an Ivy League college became a normalized part of these students' high school experiences. By explicitly working toward preparing and sending their graduates to top colleges, these schools helped instill a set of high expectations in their students. These expectations then carried over to the peer culture, and decisions about which Ivy League institution to aim for often became a decision made among friends.

In addition to these advantages, students attending private high schools also benefited from professional guidance during the college application process. Private schools, and some well-funded public ones, employ college counselors trained to carefully orchestrate every step of the college application process for each student, assisting in selecting potential colleges, managing the myriad clerical tasks of the application itself, and writing letters of recommendation.

> My college counselor was insistent on a rigorous routine, which was you have to have two to three "reaches," you have to have two to three "mids," and you have to have two to three "safeties" . . . The policy of the school was that you're only allowed to apply to two Ivy League or Ivy League–type schools. We finally settled on MIT, Harvard, and Yale.

In his fuller description, this private high school student explained that his college counselor coordinated the entire college application process: guiding the final selection of institutions, requesting letters of recommendation from his teachers, editing the essay portions of the application, checking all the required forms, and ensuring that everything was mailed before the deadlines. This kind of in-depth assistance was absent for students attending most public and parochial schools. The students with parents wealthy and savvy enough to select private high schools for their children gained a number of advantages, including having the educational aspirations fostered in their families reinforced and refined, and receiving intensive, individualized assistance with the college application process.

In contrast to the experiences of the students attending private schools, many public school students at Yale came from peer groups where college itself was not taken for granted as the next step, much less an elite college. A student whose mother "forced" her to apply to Yale attended a public high school where only half of her peers went on to college. Another student who credited an influential teacher with her decision to apply to Yale explained that most of her high school classmates went right from high school into jobs and that many of them were already married with children. Without the high expectations instilled by one's school and reinforced by peers, it becomes clear why intercessions played a critical role in these students' decisions to apply to Yale. Without them, it seems likely they never would have applied.

Occasionally, peer groups may develop preferences for types of institutions seemingly independent of their high schools. Several students reported being the first in their high schools to apply to Ivy League institutions. One recruited student-athlete explained that he had not initially considered Yale, in part "because no one really goes to Ivy. I mean, it's rare. I think in the Midwest in general, but especially from my town. I don't think anyone else has gone to an Ivy League school . . . I mean, because everyone considers Michigan the really good school." Another student described how a group of students the year before her had started a new trend in college applications, and how that influenced her own decision.

> I always thought that I would actually go to the University of Texas. I'm from Austin, and so most of my family either went there or went to the University of Houston, and so I always knew that I'd just end up in college there. It was kind of the natural thing to do for a lot of kids around there. But the year before my senior year, there were a group of kids who decided to apply outside of the state, and so two of them ended up going to Harvard. And so then my year, some of us thought, we were friends, and we were like, "Well, maybe we should try and see what happens." And so then we applied, and, you know, I ended up at Yale and a friend of mine ended up at Stanford and another one got into Cornell but decided not to go. And so, the year before us, they sort of started a trend of trying to see, 'cause for our school most people like, either they don't go to college, or 75 percent of them go to a University of Texas school or Texas A&M or something. So that's why I applied.

This account demonstrates how "natural" choices may shift over time, as student peer groups expand their sense of potential institutions, in this case apparently on their own initiative.

Families, schools, and peers all contribute toward naturalizing or inhibiting the choice of an Ivy League institution. Their cumulative influence can be seen in the students' subjective evaluations of their likely fit at Yale; those who came from more privileged families and had attended private college-prep high schools were much more likely to feel a sense of belonging.

> I interviewed at fifteen, twenty schools and came down here for my interview and stepped on the campus and loved it. And it was just a feeling inside of me that I knew that it was right for me and that I belonged here.

> I feel very much at home . . . I really feel like this is where I belong.

On the other hand, students from less advantaged circumstances did not expect to feel comfortable at Yale. A number of them mentioned having concerns about not fitting in or worries about snobbery. One noted, "I actually didn't want to apply to Yale, because I thought that I just wouldn't fit in here." A student-athlete who was recruited mentioned how he had originally discarded the idea of Yale because of these concerns.

> I guess my sophomore or junior year somebody mentioned, "Maybe you might want to think about going to Yale," and I was just like, "Everybody that goes there is snobs [*sic*], and they're too smart, and brainy, and I'm just not like that," and so I never thought about it.

This disinclination appears even for students from middle-class families. Another student, whose father was a veterinarian and whose mother had a college degree, described her initial reluctance.

> And Yale wasn't really one that I was considering, at least junior year. And then my grandmother lives [nearby], and I think I was visiting her, and I thought, "Oh, well, while I'm here, maybe I'll just go check it out and see what it looks like." And I really didn't think it was going to be anything that I liked, just because it's, you know, your stereotypic image of Yale as being like real snobby and very elite and not what I would want.

While it is difficult to untangle the various factors contributing to students' predictions of whether they would feel comfortable at a place like Yale, the students did show a consistent variation by social background, with low- and middle-SES students much more likely to express initial reservations about fitting in at Yale. While these students expressed their concerns as being class based, it is more than likely that racial and ethnic minority students also held reservations about attending a predominantly white institution, given the myriad difficulties faced by minority students in white universities (Feagin, Vera, and Imani 1996). These concerns, and the feelings of belonging expressed by the more privileged students, provide a reflection of the students' habitus, a disposition toward a certain choice expressed as the likelihood of fitting in. For many, these concerns were enough to eliminate Yale as a possible option until outside forces intervened, either in the form of a campus visit or the efforts of athletic recruiters.

The different routes to Yale described above illuminate the advantages of social background, beginning with the role played by the kinds of educational expectations families pass on to their children. The students for whom going to college was synonymous with attending an Ivy League institution came predominantly from wealthy and highly educated families. Those who had not initially considered Yale but applied unexpectedly tended to come from families with much less higher educational experience and with fewer economic resources. Families transmit educational advantages to their children in three important ways. First, families with knowledge of the Ivy League communicate the importance of attending one of these institutions to their children, often at an early age. Rather than applying active pressure, these parents successfully inculcate expectations in their children such that the children perceive them as their own. Second, through their knowledge and sometimes their personal experience with an elite education, these families help convey to their children that Ivy League institutions are appropriate destinations. Students then expect to feel at home, rather than harboring concerns about feeling out of place. Third, these results underscore the role of private college-prep high schools. Enrolling one's children in private high schools becomes an important way high-SES families successfully reproduce their class position through education. By selecting such high schools for their offspring (and having the economic resources to pay for them), these families ensure that their children spend four years in an environment that helps inculcate prestigious colleges as the norm and provides concrete resources to facilitate their eventual application to and enrollment in these types of institutions. Moreover, these high schools pave the way for a smooth transition to elite liberal arts schools by generating in their students the requisite academic skills and the liberal arts attitudes that align with these colleges. Taken together, these findings show that privileged families provide their children with a potent bundling of advantages. The expectations instilled by the family and then reinforced through private schooling or top public schools collude in developing strong predilections for elite institutions. Given the abundance of social and academic resources available to them, it is no wonder that these students take for granted their eventual enrollment in an Ivy League or other top university.

In the absence of such resources, it is not surprising that less privileged students are not as likely to develop preferences for elite institutions. What stands out in these students' accounts is how commonly Ivy League institutions were initially not even considered as possible college destinations. These students' descriptions of applying impulsively or just to see if they could get in suggest how the students placed these institutions outside the realm of the possible. For some, if the choice had been left solely to them, they never would have even applied. The interviews also revealed a striking disinclination to attend elite universities among some of the less advantaged students, because instead of imagining feeling at home, these students anticipated the discomfort of not fitting in, paralleling recent findings in Britain (Ball et al. 2002; Power et al. 2003).

Choosing Southern: Cost and Convenience

For the Southern students, selecting and applying to college was an equally complex process, but in almost entirely different ways. First, almost half of these students attended another institution before coming to Southern. Some started at two-year colleges, some transferred from another four-year institution, and some even attended a two-year institution *and* another four-year institution before coming to Southern. Unlike the Yale students, the Southern students often selected more than one institution and also chose between types of institutions. Second, whereas nearly every student at Yale begins their college education in the September following high school graduation and then studies full-time at Yale for four continuous years until graduation, Southern students often take less direct routes toward their degrees. In the sample of students from Southern, twelve had either worked for a while before starting college or had taken some time out after beginning their college education, either to work or to have a child. In these ways, the Southern students more closely resembled the national norm. Students who enter a four-year college directly after high school and then earn a degree while studying full-time at just one institution are now in the minority. Nationally, a third of all students delay their entry into postsecondary education for more than a year following high school. About half of all students begin their postsecondary education at a two-year institution. Less than half of all students attend college full time, and a third take time off at some point. In addition, about a quarter of all students beginning at four-year institutions transfer to other institutions (Berkner, He, and Cataldi 2002). All of these trends relate to social background. Family income is a strong predictor of the initial type of institution (two-year versus four-year and private versus public), as well as the likelihood of both transfers and full-time, continuous attendance.

At Southern, these patterns also fell along the lines of social background. While first-generation and non-first-generation students were just as likely to transfer from another institution, the first-generation students were much more likely to begin their college careers at a two-year institution (see table 4.3). Ten of the first-generation students, compared with only four of the non-first-generation students, started at a two-year institution. The non-first-generation students were much more prone to begin at another four-year institution and then transfer to Southern after either financial or academic difficulties (or, in a few cases, serious health issues). In addition, five of the first-generation students stated that Southern was not their first-choice institution, compared with nine of the non-first-generation students. This suggests that students from better-educated families have a wider range of options under consideration.

Like the Yale students, the kinds of high schools attended by the Southern students also related to their choice of college. Students who had attended public high schools were far more likely to begin their postsecondary education at a two-year college; they were also more likely to have transferred from another four-year institution. In comparison, students who graduated from Catholic high schools tended to enroll directly in Southern. Men were more likely than women to start at a two-year college and slightly less likely to have transferred from another four-year institution.

These transfer patterns resulted in part from two types of constraints faced by many of the Southern students, but not by the students at Yale. Economic realities worked to limit their options when they could not afford to attend or to stay at their preferred institution. In addition, many students were restricted by a lack of academic preparation. In some cases, they were not accepted at their first-choice institution because of their high school grades and test scores. In other instances, they were not able to stay at their first-choice institution because of failing marks. Finally, some started at Southern, planning to soon transfer to another institution, but they were unable to do so because of their low grade point averages.

Whether or not they had transferred or taken a break from their education, the Southern students evaluated colleges on a different set of criteria than the Yale students. The most important college characteristics for these students were cost and convenience. In addition, because some students had already selected their future occupations before beginning college, they sought institutions offering their planned fields of study. Interestingly, there were no differences between first-generation and non-first-generation students in prioritizing these features. The salient characteristics in their decision making suggested a different kind of logic at work: whereas the Yale students tended to prize prestige and fit, the Southern students looked for low-cost institutions within a convenient commuting distance that offered programs in their chosen fields. Theirs was a logic of efficiency, based on completing a degree with the least expense and interruption to their lives.

Table 4.3   Southern students' college transfer patterns by family background, high school type, and gender

	All students	Attended two-year	Attended other four-year
Parents' highest level of education			
Less than a college degree	26	10	5
College or graduate degree	24	4	9
Annual family income*			
Less than $54,000	11	3	4
$54,000–$134,999	33	9	7
$135,000 or above	5	2	3
High school type			
Public	42	13	11
Catholic	8	1	3
Gender			
Men	25	10	6
Women	25	4	8

Note: The categories are not mutually exclusive, as some students may have started at a two-year institution and also attended another four-year institution before transferring to Southern. N = 50; 1 missing case for family income.
   *Dollar amounts are given in 2008 dollars.

When I asked the Southern students how they had selected Southern, nearly all of them (forty-five out of fifty) mentioned cost, convenience, or program offerings as their primary reasons. In comparison, not a single Yale student mentioned cost or convenience, and only seven mentioned that Yale offered the programs that interested them. Cost concerns for the Southern students included tuition and location, as many of them could not afford paying for on-campus housing and thus needed their college to be within commuting distance from their homes. Convenience was also often a factor in selecting location, because many students were fitting in their college courses between jobs and/or family obligations. For these reasons, proximity was an important consideration.

> I did a few applications within the state and got accepted, and the one that was closest I just chose it, the closest one.

> I knew that I wanted to stay home, or to live home and commute, and this was something that was close.

> It was close, nearby, it wasn't that expensive.

While the quotes from the three students above reveal the importance of both cost and convenience, for many students cost was the sole concern. Some of these students described a process of comparison shopping where cost was, of necessity, the most important point of consideration.

> It was the money at the time. I applied to other schools around the state, but Southern was the cheapest. That was how I chose it.
>
> *And you wanted to stay in the state?*
>
> It was more like I knew I had to stay in-state because of money, and then since I had really little money, then I had to go to Southern, because I'm local, so it was the cheapest to do that.

Prestige, or even perceived quality, is one characteristic that was notably absent from the considerations of the Southern students. Unlike the Yale students' heavy emphasis on the standard prestige line-up, Southern students remained remarkably unconcerned with an institution's perceived status or quality. There was no mention of trying to get into the best college or a ranking of some colleges as better than others. In these students' decision making, cost not only trumped status, but status appeared to be entirely insignificant in the face of cost considerations. This became clear when students had applied and been admitted to several institutions and then chose Southern.

> What actually made me come to Southern was the price, 'cause I applied to a bunch of schools and it was down to Sacred Heart and this school. And I was working at UPS [United Parcel Service], so they were helping me with tuition, plus I was making decent money, not good, but it was decent. And what I did was I averaged out how much it would cost me to go to Sacred Heart with the scholarship they would give me and how much it would cost to come here. And Southern was a lot cheaper, I guess, than Sacred Heart. So that's why I originally decided to come here.
>
> I applied to Hofstra, URI [University of Rhode Island], UConn [University of Connecticut] . . . I got into all of them, but the cost was better here and I didn't get any scholarships. I think [the reason was] I was a white student, who went to school in New Haven, and that just doesn't work out as far as getting scholarships goes.

In both of these instances, the students were admitted to more prestigious universities and then chose Southern on the basis of cost. As is evident in both examples, the students did not apply a metric of weighing cost against status; rather, cost was the sole deciding factor.

Several students who had transferred to Southern also cited cost as key in their decision. In some cases, the students had transferred from more expensive four-year institutions; in other cases, the students began at two-year institutions, hoping to save money before coming to Southern.

Well, I originally didn't pick Southern. I was out in Missouri for a couple years. I was at a school there, a private school, and that kind of got expensive 'cause I'm paying for it myself, so I was like, "Well, you know, I'll go back to Southern. Southern's a pretty good program. I'll kind of regroup." I took a semester off, I switched majors, went into education, and I figured Southern was really good for that.

Actually, I transferred here. I went to UConn originally. To be honest, I came here 'cause my grades weren't great at UConn, and I had to come here 'cause my parents didn't want to pay for it anymore, 'cause it's really expensive.

There was just no money left [after my parents divorced], so I worked for a semester and then I started at Gateway [a local community college], just to take the core requirements that I needed, so I didn't really want to start with the loans right away. So when I moved here, I started with the loans and now the loans are through the roof. And now I need a college degree to pay off the loans [laughs]!

For some students, it was not just the cost of more prestigious institutions that dissuaded them; they also had to contend with class dynamics. One student began her college career at Quinnipiac University, a small, private institution in New Haven. She left after one year because she found it "a little unfriendly, I guess. There was [*sic*] a lot of people that were richer and they have the attitude that, you know, if you don't have a BMW . . ." While only a few students discussed this kind of class-based social discomfort as a reason for rejecting certain institutions, it is easy to imagine that it may have played a role. Likewise, a few students noted choosing Southern because of the fit with their own background and a sense of belonging.

This place is diverse and that's why I felt I belonged here, because it reminded me of my high school. There's a little bit of everything here, so I enjoy that. I don't think I could have gone to an Ivy League school like a Yale.

Why not?

Nah, nah, I don't, I relate better to people from my own background, I think. There's some people here that come here that have money, but then there are others like me that come here and it's almost like a quest, you know, to better yourself, and there's nothing easy about that, so you work hard towards that. And I'm not saying that kids that go to Yale have it any easier than me, but I know that most of them come from substantially more, they have more resources than I ever did, and that definitely can be attributed to the reason they're there. And, you know, whatever, a whole bunch of other factors. So I would rather come to a state school, because this is my people, this is the kind of people I feel most comfortable with. I don't deal really well with wealthy snooty people at all. I'm a social creature, but there's certain kinds of people that I don't level well with, and the people here, I definitely, I feel this is the kind of school I belong.

While institutional status is rarely salient in the students' choices, program offerings are often of critical importance. Many of these students first selected their future occupation and then entered college to earn a degree related to their chosen field. Thus whether a college offered a program in this field, and, if so, the quality of the program, became key factors in their choice.

I'd heard a lot of great things about the education department and . . . it was convenient and it was inexpensive.

I knew that I wanted to do communication disorders or speech language pathology . . . and I knew that I wanted to stay home, or to live home and commute.

They have a good social work department. That's basically how.

I thought I wanted to be an elementary school teacher. And I heard that Southern had the best program in the state and I wanted to stay in the state. So that's why I came to Southern.

In each of these accounts, the students emphasized the programs available at Southern as deciding factors. At the same time, most of them combined program considerations with concerns about cost and convenience. An ideal institution was one that offered their chosen field, was close to home, and charged a low tuition. Some of these students also commented on the quality of Southern's programs, particularly education. It is difficult, however, to know how students might have rated program quality against cost and convenience, because none of the students noted prioritizing one over the other.

Constraints

Clearly, the Southern and the Yale students prioritized and selected institutions on very different characteristics. Whereas quality or prestige held prime importance for many of the Yale students, the Southern students selected institutions on the basis of cost, convenience, and program offerings. It is also useful to compare the kinds of information these two groups of students brought to bear on their decision making. The Yale students tended to be knowledgeable about quite a number of institutions throughout the country; they could compare institutions across a range of factors, such as size, liberal arts focus, types of students, and campus environment. Many of them even visited several different campuses before making their decision. While the Yale students invested in informing themselves, their task was made easier because they could draw on the extensive knowledge base of their immediate families, relatives, guidance counselors, teachers, and friends. The Southern students, on the other hand, worked with a more limited knowledge framework. Many of their parents and relatives had not attended college, and their high schools often did not offer much in the way of guidance. Perhaps because of this, the Southern students often relied on their friends and sometimes their siblings.

> I had a friend who went here. Actually I had two friends who went here, and one of the friends was a regular education major, so she had a lot of information for me.

> I had worked with someone who graduated from Southern and got her master's here, so she kind of introduced it to me as one option.

> Well, my sister came here. She graduated, she was also an education major, so I knew that the school was good for education and especially special ed., 'cause that's my major, so I applied.

What stands out in these quotes is the extent to which these students' choices could be greatly influenced by contact with just one or two people. Many of these students relied on their social networks to provide information about college; however, these networks were often small. Further, while some of the Yale students, particularly those applying after a teacher's intervention, also depended on only one or two individuals for information, their contacts were knowledgeable and well informed. The Southern students were more likely to receive limited or mistaken information. For example, when one student mentioned having applied to colleges around the state, I asked whether he had applied to Yale.

> Yale never really interested me. To me Yale has always been not only a very preppy school, but it was also very towards medical. If I was going into medicine, I would definitely have applied there, but otherwise it didn't really interest me. Besides the point that it was twice as much as the other schools.

His remarks revealed not only a mistaken impression of the Yale undergraduate program, but also likely misperceptions about the availability of financial aid. The comments of this student, as well as many others, suggested that cost comparisons were made on the basis of each university's full tuition rate, without taking into account the possibility of need-based financial aid. Thus, while certainly most of the students attending Southern came from families with much more limited economic resources than the Yale students, they also came from families with more limited information resources. Their decisions to restrict their applications to "affordable" colleges and to live with their families sprang in part from real financial constraints and in part from imagined constraints due to their lack of knowledge about true tuition costs and financial aid options.

Beyond the limitations of their knowledge, the Southern students' options were sometimes curtailed by their academic qualifications. Some students came to Southern after not being admitted into their first-choice institutions. Others started at Southern with the hope of transferring to another institution, only to end up revising those plans when their grade point averages were not high enough.

> I was kind of just really gonna go here, just for a year, and transfer out, but that didn't happen because freshman year I didn't do too well here.
>
> *Where did you want to transfer to?*
>
> University of Maryland. That was my first choice. I went there and I was just completely awed by it. I just wanted to go there so bad, but I didn't get in. So then I was thinking, you know, "I'll go to Southern for a year, it's close to home," 'cause I'm very like, a homebody, and, you know, I was just gonna transfer after a year.

> I was supposed to go to a school around here for about a year, two years, and then I was gonna transfer, you know, save some money and then transfer. And, well, I can't do that, because I have a very low grade point average now.

Overall, the Yale and the Southern students went about selecting colleges in fundamentally different ways. The prestige of an institution, the all-important quality for many of the Yale students, carried little relevance for the Southern students, and concerns about campus life rarely made it onto their list of priorities. Their selection process was narrowed by their lack of social, financial, and academic resources. The Southern students rarely had a team of savvy supporters helping them throughout the process; rather, they drew on limited information provided by one or two friends, a family member, or perhaps what they had gleaned from a college fair at their high school. Economic constraints weighed heavily, and tuition became a key deciding factor. Living on campus would be out of the question for many students, thus limiting their choice to colleges within commuting distance from their parents' homes. Only rarely did these students contemplate out-of-state colleges. Finally, many had neither the high school grades nor the test scores to be competitive at even the best in-state colleges and universities. Some of them were rejected from their first-choice institution, some of them failed or dropped out after a semester or two, and many chose to begin their college careers at community colleges. All of these factors taken together meant that the Southern students made their selection from a much more limited set of institutions than the Yale students.

It is possible that additional considerations lay hidden underneath the narratives the Southern students provided about their college choice. While these students expressed their desire to live at home as having to do with cost, it may have also been that this choice was related to the importance of maintaining close family ties and an ability to draw on families for support. This may have been particularly relevant for first-generation students in making the transition into college. In fact, national surveys show that half of all high school seniors have parents who think it is important for their children to live at home while attending college, and that parents with lower levels of education are the most likely to hold these views. Moreover, these parents' attitudes influence the application strategies of their children (Turley 2006). The students I interviewed may have taken it for granted that living at or near home was important and consequently not mentioned it. Second, I wondered about the process through which the Southern students excluded institutions on the basis of their own academic credentials. It is possible that the Southern students underestimated their own academic abilities, particularly when their families and teachers were less involved in their academic progress. It is also possible that the Southern students framed their decisions not to apply to some institutions on the basis of their perceived academic abilities when, consciously or not, the real reason had more to do with their expected level of social comfort. This same dynamic may have also been present in their considerations of cost. Because tuition increases as the prestige of an institution increases, concerns about tuition may parallel concerns about fitting in, but it is likely more comfortable for these students to discuss financial concerns than social concerns in an interview. It is impossible to know whether, in fact, these dynamics occurred in the interviews; however, if they did play a role, then they may have also skewed earlier survey-based studies.

• • •

Comparing the selection processes of the Yale and the Southern students brings to light the effects of the great disparities in the material, social, and cultural assets available to these two groups of students. With some exceptions, the Yale students mobilized a remarkable set of resources in choosing their future colleges: a team of supporting players providing assistance at each step of the process; the collective knowledge of a large and well-informed network related to both the process itself and to the features of different colleges and universities; and, not least, sufficient funds to cover trips to various campuses, exam-preparation courses, and the applications themselves, which can range from ten to seventy-five dollars apiece. The Southern students often made the journey on their own, and they made do with more limited information and fewer financial resources. Thus the Southern students faced constraints on both their range of options and the information available for their decision making. From the start, their lower high school academic performances foreclosed many college options. In addition, their families' more modest economic means further restricted the available choices. Finally, their sources of knowledge about the higher educational arena were much more limited than for most of the Yale students.

These findings support earlier studies by showing how families, schools, friendships, and financial considerations influence college choice. They also highlight the contrast between those with optimal resources and those without. The privileged position of most of the Yale students opened the door to a much wider range of college possibilities and also gave them a substantial boost in their pursuit of entrance into the top colleges and universities in the country. The disadvantages of the Southern students meant that their choices would be largely limited to the least expensive local colleges.

Social background also relates to differences within each institution. At Yale, the most privileged students were those most likely to have taken their eventual enrollment at an elite institution for granted. Those who were recruited through athletics or applied on a whim tended to come from more modest social origins. At Southern, those students who worked up to Southern after starting at two-year colleges were more often first-generation students. Those who ended up settling for Southern after an unsuccessful experience at another four-year institution commonly had college-educated parents.

For both the Yale and the Southern students, an important selection factor was choosing institutions in which they felt a sense of belonging, which varied with their social positions. Some of the Yale students chose Yale because it "felt right." Others more unexpectedly chose it despite their concerns about "snobs." Likewise, some of the Southern students made the choice to go to college with the kind of people with whom they felt comfortable. These remarks reflected the students' habitus in their perceptions of the possible and the sense of one's place (Bourdieu 1984). In this manner, the students often excluded themselves from the institutions that probably would have rejected them. Or, in the case of some others, they nearly preemptively excluded themselves from institutions that did accept them.

The portraits presented here of the decision-making processes of these two groups of students suggest limitations in the higher education research that attempts to model college choice (e.g., Chapman 1984; Hossler and Gallagher 1987). While these models do take family-background variables into account, they tend to treat the choice process as if it were relatively uniform across all students, that is, as if the students differed only in their preferences. Perhaps the modeling approach could be fruitfully extended if different models were constructed for different groups of students (McDonough, Antonio, and Horvat 1996; Tinto and Wallace 1985). Further, most of the modeling approaches have not taken into account differences in educational values and strategies. College decision making is not only about how students choose institutions according to differing criteria, but also about how that choice relates to their rationale for going to college in the first place.

Different kinds of logic are at work in the evaluation and prioritization of college characteristics, giving us a glimpse into the kinds of values students attach to their education. Most of the Yale students evaluated institutions, to some extent, on their perceived level of prestige. That, along with other characteristics, such as size and program offerings, helped determine their choice. For the Southern students, though their journeys had more stops and starts, the selection process seemed much simpler. The college characteristics they considered salient were almost completely different; status and campus life barely mattered to the Southern students. Instead, they employed a logic of efficiency, concerning themselves with cost, convenience, and program offerings. Because of both financial constraints and a lack of interest, few of these students thought about out-of-state colleges. Status, it turned out, was not one of their considerations.

The disparate processes of the Yale and the Southern students in selecting college destinations also provided a glimpse into the educational strategies employed by these students. Unlike most of the Yale students, the Southern students entered college to acquire the skills and credentials that would allow them to find a job in their selected occupation; their intentions were pragmatic. While real economic constraints certainly played a role in shaping these decisions, we also saw something of the way the Southern students valued their college education. Many of the students made an institution's proximity the most important criterion for selection. As one student said, "the only reason that I picked Southern, 'cause it was like the closest to my house. It was like right down the street." This suggests that convenience mattered more than either the quality of the education or the experience, even the enjoyment, of attending college. They intended, as much as possible, to simply fit college in around their existing lives. Indeed, it is striking how few of the Southern students mentioned anything about the overall quality of the university; where concerns about quality were made, they related to programs of study. The quality of the general education they would receive appeared to be of little importance. These students also did not attach much importance to campus life or to the student body, suggesting that they did not expect these factors to play a major role in their college experience. Indeed, college as an experience, either socially or intellectually, did not seem to be the way most Southern students thought about their education. They were not expecting to form meaningful friendships or to develop their intellectual repertoires. These students had set their sights on the training and credentials that would allow them to find a good job. College had little value beyond this.

Unquestionably, the resources available to most of the Yale students opened a wider range of options. Yet we also see the Yale students ascribing a different importance to their education than the Southern students did. First, the Yalies were more than willing to move to another city in another part of the country to pursue their education. These students did not limit their searches to colleges and universities near their homes, even when they lived in cities with prestigious local institutions. The Yale students, unlike the Southern ones, did not try to fit college in around their existing lives; rather, going to college became their new life. Second, the concern the Yale students showed for nonacademic characteristics—such as the student body, the physical attributes of the campus, and their subjective fit with the institution—suggested that they considered the college experience to be an important part of how they would spend their four years. Thus their focus on going to college was far broader. This approach suggests that for them, college was not just about acquiring a high-status credential or being trained in a particular field; rather, going to college was an important part of the process in becoming the type of person they wanted to become.

The students at Yale and at Southern had little in common in the ways that they went about choosing colleges. Further, while the students regarded their decisions as their own choices, in a sense conceiving of this process as an individual choice is problematic. Instead, well before a student made his or her "choice," the range of options had been either kept open or narrowed down by the resources related to that student's social background. The students' choices differed just as much as the contexts in which they made those choices. Their varied options revealed the social distance between the two groups. The fact that not one Southern student had applied to Yale, and that not one Yale student even mentioned Southern or any other local university, let alone applied to any of them, plainly exemplifies the gap between their worlds. Yale was as much out of the realm of possibility for the Southern students as Southern was never a consideration for the Yale students.

CHAPTER FIVE

Going to College

"College is the best four years of your life," goes the popular saying. Within this discourse, going to college is seen as an important life experience, one that entails much more than taking courses. It's about being on one's own for the first time, immersing oneself in a campus environment, making friends, and having a range of new experiences. It's a time for becoming independent, growing, maturing, and finding oneself. In this way, college can be considered a rite of passage, marking the transition from adolescence to adulthood. If uncertain about how to best proceed into this new life, students may draw on a host of guidebooks offering advice on the college experience. *Living the College Life, A Girl's Guide to College*, and *Navigating Your Freshmen Year* (Maynigo 2003; Paulsen 2005; Students Helping Students 2005), for example, all promise to help students smoothly transition into their new life on campus, both inside and outside the classroom, and show them how to make the most of their college years.

There is, however, a contrasting discourse about going to college, one with a more pragmatic emphasis on getting an education or getting a degree. The rhetoric shifts from the *college experience* to going to college to gain the knowledge, skills, and credentials that lead to good job opportunities. There are no popular guidebooks to advise students here, probably because they are not needed. Once a student has enrolled, college means taking the series of courses and fulfilling the university requirements that lead to a degree. It does not involve college life.

These two approaches can be seen as modern variants on the liberal arts and vocational educational ideals. They also correspond to class-based approaches to higher education. At a material level, college as an *experience* makes sense if students live on campus, preferably in a city away from their families, attend college full time, and graduate in four or five years. Students from middle- and upper-class families are much more likely than less privileged students to attend college in this way. College as a means to a *degree* makes sense for students striving to get ahead, to go beyond the kinds of work and salary levels available to their parents. To what extent do the popular discourses on higher education sketched above capture the Yale and the Southern students' experiences? How did the two groups of students go about their college years? Did they come to college for the experience, or were they mostly focused on getting their degrees? In either case, how did they choose to spend their time, and what became most important or meaningful to them?

Before turning to these questions, it is helpful to consider two key differences in college going that not only separate the two groups of students in this study, but connect to class differences nationwide. The first is living on campus (or off campus with fellow students) versus living at home. Almost all Yale students (about 84% at the time of this study) live on campus in one of twelve residential colleges. In fact, freshmen and sophomores are required to live in the residential colleges and may only choose to live off campus in their final two years. Students living off campus rent nearby apartments either alone or with other students. None of the Yale students interviewed for this study lived at home with their families (not surprisingly, since less than 2% of Yale's students come from Connecticut). Conversely, 93 percent of the Southern students came from Connecticut and only about a third of them lived on campus. A few of the remaining two-thirds shared apartments off campus with friends, but most of them continued to live with their parents. These figures are much closer to the national norm than are Yale's. Nationwide, in 2000, 85 percent of first-time undergraduate students attended an institution in their home state of residence (Knapp et al. 2002), and 31 percent of young, full-time undergraduate students lived with their parents (Choy and Berker 2003). This latter figure varies by both annual family income and institutional type. Choy and Berker found that at public nondoctoral institutions, such as Southern, about 40 percent of the students from families with incomes of less than $45,000 live at home, compared with 25 percent or less of those from families with incomes of $75,000 and above. At private, not-for-profit, doctoral-granting institutions such as Yale, only 11 percent of the students live at home, and this figure shrinks to 8 percent for those from high-income families.

A second key difference relates to working while going to college. Southern students are more likely to hold jobs during college and more likely to spend more hours working in those jobs than Yale students. Three-quarters of the Southern students I interviewed mentioned working during college, at an average of 23 hours a week. In contrast, a survey of all Yale undergraduates conducted in the spring of 2003 shows that only about 55 percent of the students spent some time working for pay during that academic year, with most of those (81%) working less than ten hours per week.* Only three of the Yale students I interviewed for my study mentioned working, probably because the small number of hours per week they spent at their jobs made it a relatively insignificant activity. These figures parallel those reported in nationwide surveys. Overall, in 2000, a full 76 percent of young, full-time undergraduate students worked while enrolled. However, students from low- and middle-income families were more likely to work, and to work more hours per week, than students from upper-middle- and high-income families (Choy and Berker 2003).

Both of these factors are strongly linked to students' economic resources. Even after taking into account grant and loan programs, students from low-income families face a steep gap between the remaining costs of attending college (regardless of the type of institution) and government estimates of expected family contributions (Choy and Berker 2003). This unmet need is often filled by working during college. Thus, while discussing the students' approaches to their college years, it is important to remember that choices to live on campus and to work while going to college are partly determined by economic need. Further, these factors influence the amount of time the students have available for new friendships and organized campus activities.

Going to College for Yalies: The College Experience

Going to college for the Yale students involved much more than just attending courses and studying. They also joined clubs, fraternities, and sororities;

---

* E-mail correspondence with Rebecca Friedkin, Office of Institutional Research, Yale University, March 12, 2007.

volunteered their time to community-service and local charity organizations; played intramural or varsity sports; participated in music, theater, and dance groups; and spent a fair amount of time making friends and socializing. Indeed, Yale offers a wealth of activities for undergraduate students, and part of the students' task as freshmen was in identifying and selecting those they found most interesting.

> There are so many opportunities to be involved and be good at anything, anything that could appeal to a person. Sports, organizing, you know, community service, just everything's here.

This approach to college going has been common to upper-middle-class students since at least the late eighteenth century. Indeed, during the 1920s one observer conjectured that an average student spent only 10 percent of his time on academics, with the remaining 90 percent devoted to involvement in various organizations, clubs, sports, and social activities (Horowitz 1987; Levine 1986). The logic behind this approach reveals an important element in how students perceive the real purpose of going to college. Students do not seek out these activities just for fun or relaxation. Rather, far from being simple diversions, students select a program of social and extracurricular involvements in order to create a successful college experience.

College as an experience suggests that the value of four years of college comes not just from the academic learning that goes on, or from the degree received at the end of it, but from the full spectrum of experiences, both inside and outside the classroom. Further, a careful look at the students' descriptions reveals an assumption that the cumulation of college experiences would change them. They expected to leave college as different people from where they started.

> Over four years there's no question that I've grown up a lot. Just looking back to the kid who first got here is just, the difference is amazing. It's a completely different person.

> You know, I've learned a lot academically, but I've just, I was a very different person when I came here three-and-a-half years ago. I mean, I think I've matured a lot, just socially as well as intellectually. And I've had a lot of friends, I've gone through a lot of things with other people and by myself and I've just, hopefully I've learned a little better how to, you know, just interact, to be a good person, a quality human being.

This planned transformation occurs at multiple levels. In terms of the self, the students worked toward developing inner qualities, such as maturity and confidence. Relational qualities were a second important arena of change, as the students expanded their capacities to understand and communicate with others. Finally, the Yalies expected that what they learned—from their peers, in the class-room, and in their own outside reading—would change not just what they knew, but also how they thought. In each of these three arenas, all aspects of the college experience (friendships, organized activities, and courses) contributed to growth. The cumulative effect produced broad overall changes in the individual.

Friendships

For the Yale students, friendships formed a central part of their college ex-perience. Developing close friendships became almost inevitable, as most of the students were living away from home for the first time and sharing dorm rooms or apartments with other students. Far from their families and childhood friends, surrounded by people of their own age, and housed together, the stu-dents quickly formed strong friendships, along with a wider social circle. This blossoming of new friendships was not merely the result of circumstance. Yale students expected friendships to be an important part of their college years.

This centrality of friendships came across most strongly in the students' an-swers to the question of what would stay with them most about Yale. Again and again, the students cited their friendships, above and beyond academics and other activities.

> More than anything else, the friendships.

> Definitely my friendships. I think that's definitely a really, really big thing.

> I'd say four or five specific friends . . . I've always appreciated them but now it's really kind of hit home, and that's what I'm gonna take from school, not what did I learn in Introduction to International Relations, or anything like that.

The students elaborated on the closeness of these bonds, the good times they shared, and the support proffered through difficult times.

Friendships also provided an important source of learning. Students fre-quently commented on how much they had learned from and been changed by their experiences with friends. Interactions with peers facilitated the students' abilities to communicate, better understand people from diverse backgrounds, and generally get along better with other people. As one student explained,

"I definitely learned how to live with people here in a way that I'd never had to deal with before in these situations and that's been terrific."

Part of what the students learned was an improved set of social skills. As one student described it, "I'm a lot more like, in terms of the way I interact with people, I'm less nervous around people I don't know and like I feel more self-possessed." Other students echoed this sentiment, describing becoming less insecure and more confident. Several students mentioned initially feeling intimidated by their peers. Although most had been at the top of their high school classes, at Yale they were no longer a big fish in a little pond, but just one of many equally talented students. Developing the ability to hold one's own in this new milieu became an important new skill.

The Yale students also learned a great deal about interacting with people from divergent backgrounds. For many, coming from homogeneous neighborhoods and high schools, it was the first time that they had encountered people who were different from themselves. They also began to gain an awareness of how essential getting along with a wide range of people would be for their futures.

> I definitely see that there's, you know, there's a lot of different people out there now, there's a really broad spectrum. Like back in high school, everybody was like, they pretty much fit the same mold, everybody was really the same . . . I guess the kids that I went to high school with, they were really from an upscale neighborhood and stuff like that so they all, they're all pretty much the same. But out here it's like everybody's different, and you just got to realize once you're out of here, it's like, it's not gonna be like, everybody's just gonna be different. It's like, you can't, you don't know what to expect anymore. And you have to learn that you have to get along with all these people, too, you have to learn how to deal. Everybody has their definitions.

> I think I've learned a lot more compassion . . . for other people . . . or just . . . how important it is to try and understand, to try and see or understand the point of view of people around you, people around you in the room, people around you on the block, people around you in the country, people around you in the world, just trying to understand people. That's something that I've learned a lot more about.

One student even identified this factor as what had been the most helpful about being at Yale.

> Maybe just the opportunities that are available here . . . just in terms of like the different types of people that are here. It's very interesting to interact with people from different cultures, from different countries, seeing different viewpoints. Even

if people are like from the same area, it's different to see people from different economical structures, people from different parts of a state.

Another important kind of learning from friends came from discussing ideas and sharing knowledge. This idea of learning from one's peers was much more common at Yale than at Southern, with three times as many of the Yale as the Southern students noting its importance. The Yale students emphasized how much they had gained from their peers: in casual conversations in their dorm rooms, over dinner, and after classes. For many, this kind of learning formed part of the ideal of a college education.

> Education, especially at a university where you're with so many bright people, like so much of your education should be what you get from each other, too, you know, and working together and putting two minds together that are smart minds.

Another student made the same point in discussing what had been most helpful about being at Yale.

> I would say that having access to really smart people . . . just being able to discuss some really critical topic in a serious manner with my roommates.

Two other students described the value of learning from their peers.

> People are always coming up with things. That's the thing about this place, is that people talk all the time and they throw things out all the time that make you think, and that's interesting, which I think a lot of schools don't offer. And it's more the students doing it than the professors, I think. Sometimes the professors are, like, they provide the impetus to like think about one subject, but the students are the ones who just kind of go off on these different little tangents, whether they be right or wrong. And then sitting down and talking to my roommates or whoever about these things. It's a really good deal 'cause it's kind of cool.

> I found that there was a lot of information and a lot of learning that went on outside of the classroom, which was not something that I really had the opportunity to do in high school.

These kinds of conversations offered students a chance not only to learn from their peers by sharing ideas and knowledge, but also to hone the ability to express themselves and to debate. Some of the Yale students had adopted an appreciation of this kind of learning from their parents, who had conveyed the value of developing these verbal skills during college.

As my father use to call it, it's the "quality bullshit," like, it's the meeting people and talking to different people and just the academic banter that goes back and forth more than, I mean, I'll take just the ability to think, and having to argue and support your views against your peers, as opposed to against your professors or in your classes, like defending yourself against your fellow students. Like I've probably grown the most, you know, from roommates and dining room conversations and fraternity conversations and just, people out at bars or whatever. I think it's the interaction with the rest of the student body that's been the most valuable for me.

What stands out in this passage is how this student highlighted academic banter as what had helped him grow the most during college and what had been most valuable. His comments reflected the importance this student attributed to *growing* and to his ability to converse with his peers, which he ranked as more important than classroom learning.

One final component of the Yale students' interactions with their peers during their college years centered on making connections. Elite institutions purportedly provide their students with important contacts that help facilitate their later career successes. Some of the students mentioned this as an element in making friends at Yale, such as the student who aspired to become a Navy Seal.

Again, it's the people . . . It's more than my friends, it's the acquaintances. I've been fortunate to meet, you know, all kinds of different people. I met a guy who's a partner at Andersen Consulting and I've got an offer from there as well, and because I met this guy, he helped me get a job, so I've made that connection. There's a kid here who . . . was in the Seals for I think six years, so I've met him, so I've finally gotten to know him. There's a couple other guys in the Seals program that have graduated from Yale, and because they've come from Yale, and they've been successful, that helps, that's been a great help . . . So you make a thousand different connections and it's a great stepping stone into whatever you want to do, you know, whether you want to go into consulting or marketing, you meet people here that can help you. And so, your opportunities are basically, if you look for 'em, are limitless, and that's nice.

His comments showed just how instrumental contacts made at Yale could be. However, not all of the students enjoyed the same easy access to connections. Several of them commented on the ease with which elite students drew on their existing networks, using them to arrange summer internships and jobs, while

these other students had learned that their own expectations of quickly developing contacts required more time and work than they had imagined.

> A lot of my friends are legacies, you know, their father and grandfather and great-
> grandfather and whatever came here, and they have like a built-in connection
> network. And I think a lot of people come here expecting to make connections
> and stuff like that, and just have that Yale name be the key to the open door to the
> life of luxury and security but it's definitely not . . . [My roommate] freshman year,
> he's had family since the third graduating class of Yale, and if he needed a summer
> internship he could always call on, maybe not one of his relatives but somebody
> who his relatives know, and he had this vast, vast network of family and family
> friends. I wasn't born here . . . you know, so I don't have that network. I mean, my
> [high school] friends always joke that "I can't wait until I'm old and my kids need a
> job or something because I'll call you up, you know. I'll call you for an internship."
> Well, I think my friends don't really realize that you don't get instant connections
> here, that you have to go out and make 'em, and stuff like that, but there's still an
> aura in my circle of friends about me going to Yale.

In this set of remarks, the student pointed out that valuable connections did not
come simply from being at Yale; indeed, those with the kinds of connections
imagined by his high school friends were the elite students with long family
histories at Yale. Moreover, their connections came not from being at Yale, but
from their existing networks of family and friends. Students without those kinds
of family-based networks might still benefit from being at Yale, but only if they
made an effort to cultivate connections.

Extracurriculars 🏊

Next to friendships, extracurricular and volunteer activities figured most promi-
nently in the Yalies' accounts of their college life. Nearly every student was
involved in some organized activity, and most students partook of two or three,
usually selecting a mix of athletic, club, artistic, and volunteer activities. Some of
the motivation for these pursuits most likely came from seeking to build strong
résumés for future job or graduate program applications. However, the students'
descriptions also revealed the ways in which these involvements helped shape
them as people, in part by developing their artistic, athletic, or organizational
talents and in part by developing their personal qualities. For example, two different male students, when asked what would most stay with them about their
experiences at Yale, cited their participation in athletics.

There's a lot of competition on the team, so you kind of get out of that competitiveness, and then if you actually do well, you feel very confident and very good about yourself.

Just the feeling of being able to try or become excellent in one thing, you know, not necessarily excellent compared to other people, but as excellent as you could be at that one thing. It's the kind of sport, like, where you get as much out of it as you try. There's a little bit of talent involved, but not really. I mean, you can become, you put in everything you have into the sport and then you reap the rewards of that hard work.

These accounts showed how the students' involvement in sports contributed to the development of their characters. Pursuing excellence, developing talents through hard work, and engaging in competition through sports are all considered character building.

One of the most commonly cited qualities the students actively honed through their athletic and other extracurricular activities was leadership.

I guess I feel a lot more importance, I guess, being part of a team like that, 'cause I row stroke seat in the boat and everyone follows me, like I set the rhythm and that kind of thing, so [it] makes me kind of feel like a leader, and every day it's up to you to keep the same kind of thing going. So there's a lot of pressure, but I think that I like it. So if you're doing something wrong, the whole boat's gonna do something wrong.

Another student characterized her involvement in several campus organizations as actively seeking out opportunities to be a leader: "I think it's been more me exploring new things and trying to be a leader more."

The Yale students may also have taken advantage of these opportunities to explore and define their future career interests. Two students mentioned this in describing their involvement in campus clubs.

As I said, I came in thinking I was on sort of a poli[tical] sci[ence]/econ[omics] track or something. So my first semester I took a lot of those types of classes, and I was involved in political clubs.

I am so fascinated with corporations on Wall Street these days. Yeah, part of my being the treasurer [of a student organization] is I have a tendency to imagine things. So right now I'm imagining this is my company. I had to get it, us, out of debt to raise the value of our stock. I tend to think of things along those lines, so it gives a sense of excitement to my life. But right now I'm really, really interested in just investment banking in general.

Finally, the Yale students also described their volunteer activities as growth experiences. The following student spoke about nearing the completion of the requirements for her major in political science after her second year and "feeling that there was nothing else in political science for me . . . and I felt like I needed to do something different." She chose volunteer work, describing her involvement as an experience that helped raise her awareness about social issues.

> I've been involved with this program, I Have a Dream New Haven, for about two years now. And I also used to work with kids before. And just working with I Have a Dream, and also as part of the AmeriCorps, a national service program . . . that was something that has been like such a great experience, just because you're just, like, the awareness just about, like, what goes on in the world, you know, 'cause the whole purpose of the program basically is for you to serve the community where you live in, and whatever, and we do a lot of training about a lot of different things.

The Yalies' dedication to extracurricular activities represented far more than a means of distraction from the real business of going to college or a calculated strategy of résumé building (though both of these factors did play some part). Rather, the Yale students regarded their extracurricular activities as an important component of their education. First, they saw these activities as a way to develop their characters, to become leaders, and to learn to interact in competitive environments. Second, they employed them to explore and develop new interests. Third, they used them to enhance their college experiences and broaden their learning. Taken together, the Yale students engaged in these activities to further develop themselves as people. One student reflected on how his activities contributed toward making him a better person.

> I guess what I do is, you know . . . like what kind of person do I want to be, you know, and is how I'm acting consistent with that person . . . just 'cause I do things that I think will make me a better person, you know. I think, like the rock climbing for example, you know, it's kind of facing a certain fear and I think, you know, that makes me a better person.

Learning and Intellectual Development

The Yale students harnessed both social experiences and organized activities to further their own learning and intellectual development. By and large, they took their learning, both inside and outside of the classroom, quite seriously. For many of these students, their intellectual development became a project that was much broader than their formal course of study (some of the exceptions to this general trend will be discussed later). Some students conceived of this as a process of attaining intellectual maturity.

> I'll look back mostly at these two years, my junior and senior years, and I'll look at them as the real point where, like, the first two years of my intellectual maturity or something like that.

Many students reached this point by developing autonomy in their learning, a process described, in varying degrees, by two-thirds of the Yale students. One sign of this trend was that grades became less and less important, replaced by the students' own sense of what they were learning and the value of their efforts, independent of a professor's opinion. Second, the students more actively chose where to direct their efforts, focusing more intensely on the learning opportunities that were most meaningful to them and largely divesting their efforts from courses that turned out to be of less interest or importance to them.

> Yeah, I'd say that for the first couple of years I was still sort of the same [as in high school], just learning and cramming . . . and, you know, taking things that I thought I was supposed to take. And then, I think lately I'm more focused, and I know what I'm interested in and I know why I want to learn it, and I don't feel scared to take anything. I used to be scared to take certain classes, because I thought they were too advanced and I would fall behind, and I'm not like that anymore. I'll take whatever I think I should take, because I want to learn it. And in terms of, like, studying style, I would say I don't cram as much anymore, because I really want to learn what I'm learning and so I'm not as much of a crammer.

Some students began doing more reading outside of their classes. As one student reported, "I got interested in a lot of philosophy here and I do a lot of reading on my own. And I also find that the reading on my own I often take to be more important than the reading I'm doing for my classes." Students also began to select their courses more carefully once they had finished many of the required courses. Some students tried to choose courses that were, in some way, linked, in order to create better-integrated learning experiences.

> Because the thing is with me now is that, like, the courses I take always have to be related to each other somehow. So, like, I'm taking Politics of Food and Hunger, and this Power and Resistance, and Child Studies, and Social Policy, and what else,

Colonial Empires, and Women's History. And somehow, I don't know how, I'm able to like find some way of putting them all into this, like, whole. I feel like now to me like things have to kind of make sense and make sense together, so although you might think that Colonial Empires has nothing to do with Child Studies, I feel like in some way you can find some sort of way to connect the two together.

I don't think of my courses as courses, the way I used to think of it as like class. I think of it as like a project. And I pursue it with as much strength and imagination as I can muster. For every course I kind of make my own syllabus, my own project. And I try, I take almost all literature courses, right, so most of the work involves writing papers, critical essays, and I try and always, I've only been doing this for one year really, but with all the courses I've taken, I've tried to tie what I'm working on into some issue that I'm interested in my own life, which means in my own poetry, and to use other texts from other places in my life that I'm interested [in], other issues, and apply them to whatever I'm working on in the course.

The students sometimes began to move away from allowing their courses to predominately define their education and instead began to prioritize their own outside learning. One student described how he had started taking easier courses in order to allow time for independent learning and reading.

I'm taking pretty easy courses . . . because I guess I'm more interested in like learning about computers now, and just doing like my own reading, and just like, I don't know, even just pursuing leisure, than I am in like studying for courses . . . I guess like I don't like learning in such a way that like someone's always breathing down your neck, and evaluating everything you do, and like asking you to turn in weekly evaluations of the reading, and like I don't like being held under constant scrutiny like that. And so I'd rather just like pursue like my extracurricular activities, and like write for the *Yale Daily News Insider's Guide*, and do my computing assistant work, and not work so hard in classes.

Overall, many students described a broad pattern of developing a sense of autonomy, through setting their own priorities for learning and choosing to concentrate their efforts in only select courses and activities. Of course, this did not apply equally to all. One exception was the medical students. Perhaps because admission to medical schools is exceptionally competitive, these students felt as though they had little freedom to take charge of their own education and instead worked to maintain the highest grade point average possible, particularly in the required courses. Some of the student-athletes did not fall into this category, either. However, for the many students who did follow this route, one outgrowth of their efforts was a change in not just what they knew, but also in how they thought. The students often described their evolving philosophical, political, and moral viewpoints. One student, for example, elaborated on how his education had affected the very manner of his thinking.

> One way that Yale's changed me is that I now have a little voice in my head, besides whatever else I'm thinking about, that kind of, and this is not just one way that Yale's changed me, one way that being a student of history of art, literature, and philosophy has changed me, is that I now have a little voice in my head, that whenever I'm speaking, thinking, almost always . . . I have a little voice that tags my ideas historically. It's like, "Oh, that's an aesthetic viewpoint related to Oscar Wilde and Pater; oh, that's a philosophical idea coming from the Socratic through Montaigne; oh, that's an . . ." And then I have my taste, which either appreciates, thinks it's a good thing, or revolts against it. And I have this funny high/low thing that goes on, where I don't want to have a way of thinking, speaking, feeling that is too much of the aristocratic thing nor do I want to fall too much into like a campy, pop, childish thing, and this all has to do with my identity as an artist. And that's one way that Yale's really changed me.

This student expounded on how Yale had changed him as a person, repeating the theme that appeared in other students' descriptions of their social and extracurricular pursuits. In his case, the change came in his heightened awareness and ability to categorize his thoughts and ideas and extended even to the way he chose to speak.

In sum, the students differed in their investment in coursework, in the kinds of social and extracurricular activities they preferred, and in the types of change and growth they envisioned as most beneficial. But what remained constant across the accounts of the majority of these students was an expectation that their college experience would effect a powerful change on their very selves, that they would emerge after four years as a different person from whom they were when they entered Yale. Part of this change arose from the students coming to know themselves more deeply. As one student summed up about his education, "all of this in the end has to do with knowing myself, and that is, I think, at the core of my education."

Some students explicitly discussed how the process of knowing oneself was one that occurred not just through books, but through the whole range of college experiences.

Really, the classes are here for a reason, but a large reason of why I'm here is to figure out, kinda in the cheesiest sense of "who I am." I get really upset at people who are total, just little book havens who do absolutely nothing but their work, and, I mean, maybe that's them and that's who they want to be, but I think most of what I'm getting out of classes, getting out of trying different things, is just kind of figuring out what it is that makes me happy. Because, I mean, that's basically what I want to find out, 'cause that's what I want to do the rest of my life, is to do what makes me happy . . . And so I kind of look at myself as somebody who's sitting here just using Yale to kind of figure out what I want.

In the quote above, the student linked the process of self-discovery to one that occurred not just in the classroom, but in trying out different activities. He also saw the principal value of courses as not about the material he was learning, but about what he learned about himself in the process. The value of attending Yale, for him, was all about discovering what would fulfill him as a person.

Other students, in describing how they had changed or how they hoped to change, employed the notion of becoming a fuller, or richer, person, and directly linked that to their time in college, to the people they met and the activities they engaged in. College was not just about learning or preparing for a job, but about having experiences that made one a better person.

I really want to have had good experiences while I'm here. I'm very aware that they're just things I want to do, and people I want to talk to. And it sounds a little bit silly, but it's really important to being a full person.

I mean, I've learned like a lot more about myself, and I think I've developed a little bit socially, and I think I have like a better and saner perspective on the world now.

For many students, these views were handed down from their families. The following woman recounted her father's advice about college, which suggested maintaining a certain distance from grades and instead focusing on the value of experiences.

My father's always been really good about telling me that the grades don't matter that much and bad experiences don't matter that much. It's what I take away from it. So I think that even if something was bad, I learned from it.

Other parents advised their children on the importance of friendships and social experiences, valuing them on a par with academics.

My parents told me before I went to college that, you know, college is 50 percent academic and 50 percent social, or maybe more, of what you learn and what you get out of it. And I think they're definitely right on there, like, that's totally what it is.

A history major described how his parents passed on their liberal arts approach to education.

My parents always said, you know, "You don't go to undergraduate to get a job. You go to undergraduate to kind of make yourself a more educated person in a sense, a richer person."

Each of these accounts reveals how parents oriented their children to a particular way of going to college. By emphasizing college as an experience, the social aspects of college, and the goal of becoming educated rather than being trained for a particular job, parents passed down the liberal-educational philosophy. By preparing their children with these attitudes, these parents facilitated their children's smooth transition to and success at Yale. Similar to the way parents may instill tastes for elite colleges in their children, this kind of coaching by parents who themselves have a liberal arts education becomes another channel through which social advantages may be transmitted.

The Pre-Med World

Overall, the Yale students differed significantly from the Southern students in their pursuit of a full college experience. Yet even at Yale, the students varied in terms of how much they prioritized the social, academic, and extracurricular realms. Some of the students invested themselves more heavily in their creative and artistic pursuits, while others devoted more of their time to friendships. Similarly, while almost all of the students described a degree of intellectual engagement with at least some of their courses, its intensity varied considerably among them. In addition, some of the students' commitment to academics began to stem more from their plans to apply to graduate school than from a genuine interest in their courses. For example, the following student explained how her studying was currently geared toward maintaining her grade point average at an appropriate level for graduate school.

Right now everything is geared towards the GRE [Graduate Record Examination], which is coming up in two weeks, so I've been studying for that and basically trying to keep my GPA at a 3.6, 3.7, because I'm starting to look at graduate schools now.

Amid the variation among the Yalies, the students intending to enter medical school stood out. About one-quarter of the students in my sample had planned (at least at some point) to enter medical school and were fulfilling the medical school, or pre-med, requirements. Most of these students chose majors in biology, although a few majored in social science fields while also completing the pre-med requirements, which included one year each of inorganic chemistry, organic chemistry, biology, physics, English, and math.

The students on the medical school track confronted a high level of competitiveness, one not encountered by the students in any other field. Two factors drive this. First, admission into medical school is extremely, and increasingly, competitive. Second, most science courses at Yale are graded on a curve, meaning that grades are assigned to students based on their *relative* performance in comparison with their classmates. Under this grading scheme, even a high percentage score on a test may mean a low grade if the overall performance of the class is high. Likewise, because the curve is based on a set distribution of grades, only a certain percentage of the students will be awarded As. This grading practice created competition among students and increased the emphasis on grades.

> It's made grades a lot more important to me than they were before. [In high school] it was just sort of, like, do your work . . . and you do well. Here you're a lot more like concerned about, like, the mean and like being above the mean . . . so that makes it a lot more like stressful. I've become a lot more stressed being here than before . . . It's a lot harder because you're competing with, like, I mean, even if you get like a 90 on the test, and the mean is like a 95 and you have a B, or if the mean is like, if you get an 80 or something, you have a D or something like that, so the mean can make a big difference. Regardless of how you do, you're still up against your peers.

> You go into Intro[duction to] Bio[logy] and you have to fight with people that are really intense about Intro Bio and getting their grades for medical school.

> I think people here are a lot more intense and a lot more, like, grade grubbing and a lot more concerned about . . . I think it's because of the track [pre-med] that I'm in. People are just very like anal, and very, like, have to be at the very top. And I think sometimes they can get lost in the race, so that's a negative experience.

The pre-med students complained about the degree of competitiveness and the intensity of the emphasis on grades among their peers. Rather than describing instances of relying on peers for help with coursework or for the exchange of ideas, pre-med students more commonly recounted the unhelpful, aggressive, and even hostile behavior of their classmates.

> Last semester, in one particular biology course, I remember they had some hand-outs and literally right when the bell rang, or the professor dismissed class, I was being pushed out of the way by people because they were so desperate to get these handouts, because at times, you know, they run out, or they didn't make enough copies, especially at the beginning of the year when they're not sure what the class size is. And I couldn't believe it . . . just pushing other people out of the way, really being like "Give me that handout!" So just focused and driven that they don't have any time really.

> [Pre-med students] can be very competitive and very nasty, I think, at times. Obviously not all of them, some of them are very nice people, but I've run into people, pre-med students who are very competitive. They won't help you, they won't study with you, or if you ask them a question, they're just as likely to tell you the wrong answer, you know.

> There's some very, very intense people here and I think that, yeah, in the pre-med world you'll find most of them . . . I know someone who would just use people for the sake of, you know, but then they'd be open about it, it would be like, "Oh, so-and-so does good in Organic [Chemistry], so I'm gonna be friends with this person." I can't even conceive of why people would do that. And I think like even my roommates, my roommates are my best friends and they always think I'm kind of strange, because neither of them are pre-med, and I don't think, they think that I don't really fit that mold, which makes me feel kind of good, because, you know, it's kind of a scary group.

In this last quote, the student's reference to the "pre-med world" shows the extent to which this group is set off from other students at Yale. While almost all of the pre-med students in my sample attributed these kinds of behaviors to other students, a few acknowledged using these practices themselves, sometimes in response to negative experiences with other students.

> I came here hard-core pre-med, again with that competitive streak and that extremely cutthroat attitude. Like chemistry class, we get our tests back, it's like, "What did he get?" that, you know, you use peripheral vision a lot.

> I don't want to tell anyone anything, like even those who I work with. They ask me a question like, "Can you help me with this?" I'm really, for some reason,

instinctively I don't want to help them and I say "I don't know" or I give them a roundabout answer . . . Just 'cause I guess my first year I realized people use you, you know. They'll ask you for help with their work and then they won't return the favor later, that sort of thing, you know? They'll ask you for your problem set, and what they do is just end up copying it versus checking answers like they said they would.

Whether because of the intense requirements and a grading structure that promotes competitiveness, or because the pre-med students came to Yale with a singular focus on gaining admission to medical school, these students approached their education in more instrumental and less intellectual ways than the students in other fields. A student majoring in biology, but not planning to attend medical school, described these attitudes among pre-meds.

I didn't like the way other students, who basically are majoring in biology because they were going to medical school, or some of them aren't even majoring in biology, but these people whose main goal is to get into medical school. The way they approach it is exactly the way it's most easily fed to them, [which] is that, "Just tell me what I need to know. Not why or what it means, just what do I need to know?" And that's really bothered me . . . I kind of get annoyed when people do that, because I'd rather remember something because I thought about why it works and what it is. And they're very, very stressed about it, too.

Do you think they're not that interested in the subject but more interested in being doctors?

It depends on the person. But yeah, I mean, you can hear about people walking into Orgo [Organic Chemistry] tests, just being like, "Well, this all isn't gonna matter because you're gonna make so much money once you get your medical degree." It's so disturbing, especially 'cause it's not true anymore . . . And just people sitting in review sessions, and the TA [teaching assistant] will kind of go into something because they're interested in it, and they'll be like, "But yeah, what do we need to know?" They'll be like, "Yeah, well, what do we need to write down?" you know?

These observations were borne out by the interviews. The pre-med students were significantly less likely than the other students to mention the ways in which their education had enriched them or increased their maturity; they were less likely to comment on autonomy in learning or instances of critical thinking; and, indeed, they were more likely than the other students to mention the importance of grades. They were also more likely than the other students to be involved in volunteer work, though this seemed to stem from the goal of building a strong résumé for medical school applications rather than from higher levels of altruism.

Athletes

Of the seven students who discussed being recruited as a central reason for coming to Yale, only one resembled the students described in the first part of this chapter, while four of them differed notably and two others could be characterized as somewhere in between. These latter six students prioritized their athletic involvement at Yale. To varying degrees, their schedules, friendships, and social activities revolved around athletics. Academics not only took second place, but these students also showed a striking level of disinterest in their academic courses. A few of them aspired to be professional athletes, at least for a while; all of them preferred applied fields of study; and most of them considered going into business at some point. Most of them also noted their difficulties with Yale's liberal environment. Perhaps because their status was on the margin, they held particularly interesting insights into the value of a Yale degree.

The principal characteristic distinguishing the student-athletes from the other Yale students was the importance they placed on athletics, above and beyond academics or the college experience. For example, one of these students referred to football as "*the* biggest accomplishment of my life." Another student, when asked what would most stay with him about his experiences at Yale, explained that his primary reason for being at Yale was baseball.

> Baseball is the entire reason I'm here, pretty much. Obviously to get a good education, but I got in because of baseball and to come play baseball here. I mean, if they didn't have a baseball team I wouldn't be here, so, I mean, but baseball, that's pretty much all my friends on campus is [*sic*] the baseball team. We pretty much do our own thing. I mean, I have other friends and stuff, I don't room with any baseball players. But that's, the baseball experience will probably stick with me the most.

Similarly, a hockey player explained how important his sport was to him and how it shaped his time and friendships.

> I mean, hockey's pretty much the biggest thing in my life, for the most part . . . I mean, I spend every day with the guys on my team, basically all year round, so that's a big aspect of it. I just, I mean, I live off campus and I've never gotten a chance to live in [a college]. I moved off after my freshman year, so I never really

made real close friends, just in my college my freshman year 'cause I was always
. . . I had three roommates and two of us are varsity athletes, so in the afternoon
we were away practicing. Everybody else was making friends and stuff in the afternoon, you know, maybe doing their work at home. We'd be away all afternoon,
we'd come home and do work. So I just never, so, it was better for me to live off
campus . . . especially with hockey, and weird practice times.

The interests of this last student and the required dedication to practice
seemed to have precluded his opportunities to make friends. In other cases, it
was clear that the student-athletes experienced frustration with intensive practice schedules that prevented them from exploring other interests.

I guess one thing is possibly playing a varsity sport made it difficult to . . . I like to
write, and I was interested in journalism, but I wasn't able to put in the full-time
commitment to the *Daily News* or the *Herald* [student newspapers] or something,
just because of the time it took to do soccer.

And a member of the crew team explained that the all-year-round, six-days-a-
week practice schedule meant that he hadn't "taken in the whole, what's available at Yale, like artwise and that kind of thing," because he simply did not have
the time.

The student-athletes also differed from the other students in their lack of
enthusiasm for learning, either inside or outside of the classroom.

I've found that . . . it's tough to find a class that you're really interested in, completely. Just because there's so many requirements you have to fulfill . . . and all
these different things that you really don't like . . . And so often I think professors
can make or break a course, so if you find a class that you think will be interesting,
the professor's gonna ruin it anyway.

It was unusual for these students to describe any degree of serious intellectual
engagement with their courses. Some of them found discussion sections one
of the most onerous aspects of their college experience. Discussion sections at
Yale are designed to complement the professor's lectures and typically consist
of a group of eighteen students who meet once a week for an hour to discuss
the lectures and readings under the guidance of a graduate student teaching
assistant. Discussion sections form an important part of liberal arts learning,
providing students with a chance to engage more deeply with the course material and to develop critical thinking and verbal communication skills. While the

other students described discussion sections as a productive venue for learning from their peers, some of the athletes held a different view.

> I don't like all the discussion sections, because a lot of times I feel it's a waste of time. I feel like people just kind of go in there and try to be smart and articulate, and it's just annoying. And really all they're doing is just talking about what the . . . re-saying what the book has said. And it's just a waste of an hour.

> And I don't really like seminars . . . There's twelve of you only in the class. I mean, you have to talk, you have to read, and you have to be prepared, and last semester I didn't like the teacher, so I just, I didn't prepare, I didn't read, and I just sat with my head down in seminar for two hours and that's kind of hard in itself, staying awake and stuff.

As far as developing an autonomous sense of their own learning, the athletes were generally more concerned with simply getting through their courses and graduating. In one of the more extreme examples, one student-athlete described his philosophy about his college education.

> I skate by a lot, and I mean, it's the only way I know how. I mean, like I always think, you know, I'm gonna graduate from here anyway, and once I get out there I'm not gonna look back at GPA or major or anything. I mean, it's, Yale is Yale. I'm gonna have fun while I'm here and I basically live my life according to having fun. I mean, baseball's fun, the team's fun, hanging out with them and stuff. I mean, when it comes down to it, I'm a good student, but I don't, you know, I never pull all-nighters. I'd rather go to sleep and get a C than stay up all night and get a B, stuff like that . . . I don't see the difference, graduating from here with a like, I'm right at 3.0, but I don't see the difference between a 2.7 and a 3.3. I mean, if you were gonna graduate [with] a 3.8 and just work every single night that's one thing, but, I mean, if I'm not gonna graduate with a 3.5, I mean, I'm not gonna go lower than like a 2.8 or 2.9, I don't think anyway, so what's the difference between a 3.1 and a 2.8? There's nothing to me, so, I mean, to me, that's just, I just didn't put in as much work to get a 3.1 as I could have or whatever. It's not a big deal.

His academic experience was essentially reduced to his grade point average. Knowing that regardless of his grades, he would graduate with a Yale degree, he chose not to invest unnecessary time in studying. He went on to explain that he did not know if he had gotten "anything like life lessons out of any of my classes or anything." This was evident in his response to a question about whether he had changed during college.

> Not really. I mean, I live, you know, pretty much according to the way I was raised, you know. I mean, definitely always try to be classy, stuff like that. So, I mean, Yale hasn't changed me, according to the way I think I should live, anyway.

Part of the explanation for the difference in this student's focus during college can be found in his view about what going to Yale meant to him. While he intended to become a professional sports player, he also stated, quite practically, that "if it doesn't work out for me, then I graduated from Yale and hopefully I'll have a good job somewhere." His emphasis was clearly not on self-development during college.

Class and Color

Many first-generation college students, and some middle-class students, noted their reluctance to apply to Yale because of concerns about snobbery and not fitting in. For some of these students, their apprehensions were alleviated during their initial campus visits or during their first semester.

> I came down for my visit. But I liked the people here. They weren't, I guess it was going from expecting them to be real brainy, intellectual snobs to, you know, meeting a lot of people that were just like me. It was nice, so I seemed to fit in well here and with the people I met.

For several other students, their concerns and discomfort continued into their freshman year and beyond:

> When I came as a freshman, I was extremely, extremely intimidated by just about everybody I met because of their backgrounds and, you know, the things I heard about them and whatever. But I think that's one of the things that makes you grow. You come here and you deal with that. You deal with being, you know, leveled with everyone else, and then you just decide to focus on what interests you, and I think that's one of the things that helped me a lot.

> I've been raised, you know, like lower middle class . . . Sometimes I find the elitism here very annoying and stifling.

> If I could do it over again, I don't know if I'd come back to Yale, actually.
>
> *Why is that?*

I don't know. It's just a different crowd, I guess. Everybody's just . . . it just doesn't seem like a school for me, you know. I don't know, everybody's into like different things, and I'm not really, I really don't like things that go on here . . . It's just like everybody's really into themselves, I find, and everybody's really pretentious, and, I don't know, I just . . . Then, the frats, the things like the social life here, I don't really like that much also . . . I tend to have a lot more friends around from other schools, like neighboring schools. I feel like I fit in more, and I get along with people around there more.

Many of the students also contended with their racial or ethnic minority status in a predominantly white university. The discomfort they experienced along racial lines seemed even more intense than that along class lines. Students of color grew tired of having to serve as spokespersons for their race and constantly having to "educate" students who had grown up in almost exclusively white environments. These situations are not unique to the students at Yale, but are shared by students of color on many other campuses.

The difficulties encountered by minority students, particularly black students, in a predominantly white university have been well documented. Black and Hispanic students confront a host of issues, ranging from blatant racial discrimination to stereotyping and hostility (Feagin, Vera, and Imani 1996). African-American and Hispanic faculty are underrepresented across institutions of higher education, and are particularly scarce in elite institutions. It is often difficult to interact with or take as role models white faculty members who may be racially insensitive or prejudiced. Racial barriers may impede friendships, as well, and usually the onus is placed on minority students to bridge the divide by initiating interactions. In addition, physical spaces may become racialized, creating an unwelcome climate for students of color. In my study, while there were no specific questions about race dynamics in the interviews, nearly all of the African-American students commented on it.

There are a lot of racial incidents here that are unnecessary. A lot of people haven't been exposed to like African-Americans, and it just gets like very tedious after a while, when people are like asking ridiculous questions and always like trying to ask you to represent an entire black community and stuff like that. It just gets very frustrating, so . . . very redundant and frustrating . . . Just the way people like perceive you, as an African-American, is just very like frustrating, constantly frustrating . . . But, I mean, I think that would be that way anywhere, except like a historically black school, so I just take it with the territory.

Sometimes there is a level of ignorance amongst the student body and, to a certain degree, amongst the faculty, just in terms of, you know, cultural sensitivity and that affects the potential and it may even reflect on grading. That's why, you know, I don't think too much upon grading patterns. As well as, you know, well, that's the most disappointing, when you go to a school, such as Yale, and there is such ignorance.

Only occasionally do white, middle-class members of the Yale community perceive the racism and elitism on campus, as one such woman did.

I feel I've met a few people here that are . . . they are very elitist and very racist and it's really annoying, but I think that I've sort of, I mean, it's very easy when your family is not suffering or struggling to get by or whatever. It's very easy to be sheltered and think that somehow you deserve it and other people who have less deserve what they get or something.

The historical legacy and demographic characteristics of Yale present particular challenges for racial minority and first-generation college students and require them to contend with a range of race and class issues that are largely nonexistent for other students. Furthermore, in my sample, all four of the Hispanic students and three of the seven black students were first-generation students, facing barriers of both class and color.

Going to College for Southern Students: Earning a Degree

If the Yale students saw the value of education in the journey, the Southern students set their sights on the destination. The project for them was not one of how to best avail themselves of an enriching college experience, but rather one of acquiring a college degree. When the Southern students described why they decided to attend college in the first place (see chapter 3), they often justified their choice in terms of the necessity of a degree for getting the kind of job they wanted. Once at college, their emphasis largely remained the same. As one student succinctly explained, "that's basically why I'm here, to get my degree." For the Southern students, getting a degree had three distinct dimensions: first, securing the credential that that piece of paper signals to potential employers; second, obtaining the knowledge, skills, and information required for future lines of work; and third, acquiring the markers of an educated person, specifically, a broader set of verbal and self-presentation skills. Within each of these dimensions, the notion of *earning* one's degree holds relevance. The Southern students tended to conceive of college degrees as rewards for their hard work and dedication.

Living on campus, as most Yale students do, is not the norm for those attending Southern, who are also much more likely to work, and to work more hours, during college.* These factors mean that Southern students have less time and opportunity for involvement in extracurricular activities and social events. Seventy-six percent of the Yale students in my survey participated in volunteer services, athletics, or organized extracurricular activities, compared with only 24 percent of the Southern students. The Southern students were also only about half as likely as the Yale students to mention the importance of friendships.

With less investment in campus life and a stronger focus on earning their degrees, the Southern students' college experience occurred primarily in classrooms and libraries. Their replies to the interview questions about their college years centered much more on professors, courses, and bureaucratic requirements than on experiences, activities, and friends. While for the Yale students even negative experiences were considered a valuable part of their overall college experience, the Southern students did not evaluate their experiences in terms of their richness or their potential for contributing to their personal growth, but rather in the extent to which they expedited the goal of earning a degree. Indeed, in discussing their interactions with peers and professors and their overall experiences, the Southern students drew distinctions between those aspects that facilitated their goal of earning a degree and those that hindered that goal.

Practical Help from Peers and Professors

The Southern students were much less likely to discuss the importance of their close friends than the Yale students. When they did talk about their peers, they were much more likely to comment on the practical help provided by friends than on the friendships themselves. The students often spoke with appreciation of students they met who shared information, advice, or practical help on course assignments.

---

* I found little difference, in terms of experiencing college life, between the Southern students who lived on campus and those who lived with their families. Those students who lived on campus did spend more time "partying," and also remarked on how difficult it was to study at times, given the distractions of living in a dorm. A few students who had previously lived on campus commented that their marks had improved once they moved back home. Perhaps the relatively small proportion of students living on campus discourages a more active institutional culture.

People who have taken classes before me in my department kind of tell me what went on last semester, or I get to share my experiences this semester with them for the classes they're taking, and if you have a project to do, everybody's always willing to help out, and what not . . . They're very, very, they're really supportive. That's why I enjoy it so much, because you always know there's someone there to help you if you're wondering about a test.

I met a lot of nice people that I keep following in all my classes. They're in all the classes with me, so we get together in like study groups. They help you out, you know. Everybody's really friendly. We're like, "Oh, how did you do, how did you do?" and "I'll help you with this" and "Come see me."

While the Southern students commented on actively helping each other, they rarely discussed learning from their peers. Only about 20 percent of the Southern students mentioned this, compared with about 60 percent of the Yale students.

Though the Southern students were less likely to learn from, or form strong bonds with, their peers than the Yale students, the Southern students more often reported important interactions with their faculty members. One of the striking differences between the two groups was that while the Yalies often complimented their professors on their brilliance and renown, the Southern students were more likely to discuss whether their professors were helpful or not. The Southern students tended to describe their professors in terms of being caring, motivating, and encouraging, or in providing practical help in navigating departmental and university requirements.

I've had all the professors pretty much, and you see them in the hall and they say "Hi" and, you know, you feel like they're there for you. If you had a problem, you could go sit down with any one of them and say, "You know, this is what happened." So I think that my experience at Southern from that aspect has been great.

What's been most helpful to me would be just the teachers. My professors. They've helped me out a lot, you know, in every way that they could, you know. A lot of times you hear that professors in college they don't care about you, you know, they just go do their work and make sure that you hand in your work. If you don't, you fail. I've experienced that, but in the program that I'm in now the teachers are not like that, you know. They get to know you and they try to help you out, they honestly [do], and that's helped me out a lot, you know.

These accounts suggest that the helpfulness of these faculty members was not just confined to clarifying course materials, but extended to helping in other ways. If a student ran into an administrative problem or began falling behind in class, the professors often helped them resolve issues and get back on track. In addition, many of the students encountered difficulties with the demands of college-level coursework and found that they were unprepared. For some of them, their professors played a key role in helping them gain confidence in their academic abilities by encouraging and motivating them.

> She's, her lecture is very, very interesting. I have to say, she encourage [*sic*] us to learn and it's hard to find a professor like that. She help [*sic*] you any way she can, and English is not my field. I'm very bad at English, writing or anything like that. I'm very bad, but that class, after I took that class, my English improved a lot and also my writing.

> There's a math teacher that I have right now who is just absolutely wonderful. She's just very, very funny. She has a very, very relaxed approach to math. And I'm usually really horrible at math and I really don't grasp the concepts very well, but in that class I'm doing very well, and I'm enjoying it very much. And she's always there for support. She always has office hours and she's always there if you want to talk and she's very funny, and she's very friendly. And I respond to that.

> First of all, organic chemistry is very difficult, it's too abstract, so you either know it or you don't know it, and so it was hard to begin it. He helped me out. And when I knock on his [the professor's] door, and he was always there, he always helped me. He tried to push to see who I was, where I was coming from, why I was there, and he's the only one who basically say [*sic*] "How are you doing? Are you doing all right? Okay, where are you going to be? What do you want?" He's the one who just sit [*sic*] in there and say, "Yes. You can do it but take little steps at a time, like little by little. Don't push too far, too hard." So that's why he stands out . . . Not only me, he encouraged a lot of people. But he takes the time just to listen and he's always there. And he's always there, not only in the course but sometimes if you have a personal [concern] or a problem, he'd at least try to listen to you and try to say, "Okay, this is what you can do, this is what you should do."

Hindrances

On the other hand, the Southern students raised a number of complaints about professors who were not helpful. In some cases, the students felt their professors did not take into account or accommodate their life situations, since commuting and holding jobs sometimes made it difficult to manage their academic work. At other times, the students commented on how their professors criticized or shamed them because of their academic difficulties.

> Some professors, they were just like, "Oh, you know," basically telling you you're a dummy if you don't know how to do this work.

> One of my biology teachers, she just all of a sudden picks on you when you don't know why. She makes you stand out right in front of the class . . . Since I'm taking biochemistry, it's very hard, I got a tutor for it, and sometimes you're frustrated. It's a frustrating course, and sometimes you don't go smiling to her class, so she picks on you or makes you feel like you're the worst person, the stupid [*sic*] person in the world and you shouldn't be there and you shouldn't go to like your standards.

> I think that teachers don't take people into consideration who work and go to school full time. I feel like they give more . . . attention to people who work full-time and come to school part time, at night, you know.

> And, just some of the teachers they don't seem to care at all, you know. It's like their class is everything and it doesn't matter how much other work you have to do, they're still gonna give you an incredible amount.

The students gave these examples as instances in which they felt professors were working against them instead of helping to facilitate their mastery of the course materials. Their accounts also touch on these students' frustrations with difficult and time-consuming coursework and with being labeled as inadequate by their professors. The final quote again equated caring with the professors' ability to understand their students' situations. In this instance, a professor giving what was perceived as an unreasonable amount of work was thought to demonstrate a lack of concern for the students and with the demands they faced in other courses.

Wastes of Time

The most common complaint among the Southern students was about courses that were a waste of time. The students made such comments if they did not feel that they were learning anything or, more commonly, when they thought the material in the course would not be helpful to them in the future.

> I guess my only complaint would be like some classes that I've taken that seem pointless to me . . . that you're just like, "What does this have to do with anything?"

> Quite a few of the classes I've taken, don't seem to . . . I just feel it's been a complete, like, waste of time because they aren't . . . either I haven't learned anything, or when I get out, it's not gonna do anything for me.

> Social work program, I'm not gonna lie, I hated it last year. I hated it. Like the professor was always complaining about everything. I didn't feel that I was learning . . . I just thought the teacher would just get up there and talk all this nonsense, and I wasn't learning. I actually wasn't learning. I wasn't doing the readings, 'cause we didn't talk about 'em in class.

> They were just giving you so many papers. You had to write like twenty-five-page papers, on an agency, on community. I was doing so much work. I didn't know why, you know, like is this gonna help me for the future?

In these quotes, the students made plain their preference for the kinds of learning that would be useful to them in the future. The value of their courses came from providing them with relevant knowledge, and, in cases where this criterion was not met, the courses were perceived as a waste of time. Their preferred courses prepared students for future jobs, as one student explained in his description of what had been most important to him about his education.

> Well, I guess some of the classes I've had and how they've prepared me for what I'm gonna do, physical education. They're really good, some of them. They've really prepared me for going out to get a job, I guess.

In terms of the general education requirements of the university, the Southern students frequently spoke about "just getting them out of the way." Far from seeing these courses in the way the university envisioned—as an opportunity to broaden their knowledge—the students often regarded the required general education courses as necessary but burdensome steps toward their degree. This approach contrasts with one in which the emphasis is placed on how learning may contribute to the students' intellectual development.

Bureaucratic Frustrations

The Southern students directed their most vociferous criticisms toward the advising and bureaucratic processes. Registering for courses and completing the paperwork for financial aid were unnecessarily cumbersome and time consuming, with long lines, inadequate information, and frequent complaints of lost forms or files. The students recounted their frustrations in receiving inadequate advising about the requirements for their majors and for graduation, and often had difficulty determining whether in fact they had met the requirements for graduation. Several of the students, for example, stated that they would have graduated a semester or a year earlier if they had received advice about how to properly plan their course of study. Failing to take certain prerequisites in the correct sequence often meant a delay in finishing their degree. Those students who had begun their education at other institutions often found that not all of their courses transferred or that courses taken at other institutions did not count toward Southern's requirements, but instead could only be counted as elective courses. The extensiveness and vehemence of the students' criticisms suggested that the registration and advising systems at Southern could certainly stand improvement. On the other hand, the students' comments also revealed the extent to which they prioritized graduation over the college experience. For example, when I asked one student what had been most helpful about being at Southern, she replied, "I guess just like wanting to graduate and like looking forward to that. I guess it like motivates me to help things through, you know, that kind of thing."

Many of the other students noted how their motivation as students had shifted from high school, because of the incentive of earning a college degree.

> I think I take my work a lot more seriously now than I did in high school. I definitely do, because I'd say I'm working for something, my degree, which motivates me. That's what motivated me to get my bachelor's.

> I don't know, high school to me seemed like you would graduate if you just played your cards right, but like here, like if you don't do certain things or whatever, I mean, you build up credits, you have to do all this stuff, like that's it, you don't graduate. And I know lots of people who have like gotten like all these credits and just haven't graduated. So I don't want to be like that.

I'm 100 percent more focused [than in high school]. Things to me are more real, they're more relevant to the rest of my life, whereas in high school, it was just like I had to be there . . . and all I cared about was what I was doing after school. All day you sat around with your friends, joking around, clowning, daydreaming, and then, you know, that's it. But here it's like everything is tentative. If I get a bad grade in this class, it's gonna affect everything that I've done, everything. You know, if I fail a class, boom, my GPA goes down, I get kicked out of my program, and then for me to come back up, I'm looking at like two more years of like taking classes that make no sense to take, so I got to crawl back up the mountain.

All three of these quotes showed an emphasis on graduation over the college experience or simply over learning. While not receiving adequate advising would certainly frustrate any student, for those who prioritized the goal of graduation above all else, the possibility of delay became a much more serious aggravation. In addition, these students' accounts also suggested how college, for them, equated with work. In the first quote, the student described "working" toward her degree, a phrase commonly employed by the Southern students. Similarly, in the last of the three quotes above, the student likened earning a degree to crawling up a mountain.

Beyond these challenges, many of the students who did not particularly enjoy high school found college perhaps even more wearing, as evidenced by some of the replies when I asked the students what would stay with them about being at Southern.

Not a whole lot, I guess. I suppose I enjoyed my theater classes a lot, I enjoyed some of my lit[erature] classes, and a couple political science classes, but other than that . . . I didn't really, I didn't particularly enjoy doing it. I still don't really enjoy school.

I'm really looking forward to getting out of here . . . I'm just looking forward to leaving, because, see, I started out wanting to be a teacher . . . and I really realized that I was really getting sick of school and that if I wanted to be a teacher I was gonna have to go back to school. I mean, not as a student but as a teacher, but I would still have to go back and have to be working in a school and I don't really think that I want to be working in a school.

Academic Challenges

Perhaps an additional contributing factor toward equating education with work stemmed from the difficulties many of these students faced with meeting a new level of academic challenge. The students frequently commented on the change in expectations between high school and college and on how they did not feel sufficiently prepared in terms of their academic background or study skills. In high school, many of the students could get by rarely studying, but they quickly found that that was not the case in college. This led to initial difficulties for many of the students as they struggled to develop their study habits and adjust to more demanding coursework.

> In high school I never really learned how to study, and so like I have a hard time memorizing and stuff like that. So I guess now like professors have showed me different ways to study, like using note cards or that kind of thing.

> The coursework, at first, it was very challenging. I had a hard time, 'cause journalism is a whole different level of writing. It's a whole different style. I remember just the first little thing. We had to write like a three-paragraph news story about somebody who had gotten shot or something, and I was like, "How hard can this be? I read newspapers all the time." And I got like a C minus on this. I was like, "Are you kidding me?" you know? It was like, "Oh god!"

Thus, while the Yale students were moving toward becoming more autonomous learners and distancing themselves from their marks, the Southern students expended their efforts on becoming better students, learning how to manage and complete the requirements for their courses. The Southern students also differed from the Yalies in that they placed less emphasis on learning in and of itself, as part of their own self-development, and more emphasis on acquiring useful knowledge for their futures. The Southern students tended to disparage courses that would not be applicable to what they envisioned as their future careers.

This difference between the two groups of students stood out most strongly in their responses to questions about whether they had changed during college. While the Yale students generally had varied but detailed responses to these kinds of questions, the Southern students were more likely to simply reply that they had not changed in significant ways.

Has being here changed the way you see yourself?

Um . . . not really, it hasn't changed that much. I'm basically pretty much the same.

Have you come across any new ideas here that have changed your perspective or your view of the world?

I don't really, I don't think so . . . I don't think that being here changed my perspective on anything in a major way, no.

What became apparent from these responses was how little they saw college as an avenue toward personal growth or change. While some of the students did talk about gaining maturity and independence, they described these changes as ones taking place more from growing up than from attending college. For most of the students, college itself was not perceived as or expected to be a meaningful route toward personal growth. Education, for the Southern students, was not valued as a means of effecting internal change. Rather, for them education worked as an external attribute, a kind of resource that attached to, but did not essentially modify, who one is. One student, in describing how going to college had increased her confidence, explained this point of view.

College was not a path to learning about oneself or for Personal growth

> Well, it just added to [my confidence], I think . . . because I know I have these degrees now and I know that I worked hard, I graduated with honors.

She identified the value of college not from how she had changed or what she had learned, but from the confidence she had gained by obtaining a degree.

While these differences generally held true across the two groups of students, there were exceptions. Though the majority of the Southern students saw their college courses primarily as job preparation, some did find required courses unexpectedly interesting, and a minority began to find pleasure in learning for its own sake.

> I took a, what's it called, Females in Literature [course] . . . It was, I don't know, she made us read a lot of different books from like Europe, from Africa, from China, all about females and it has nothing to do with my major but I really liked it. It was just . . . she gave you a perspective of how women were treated in history or something. I thought it was really interesting.

> I like to learn more things now, 'cause back in high school, I didn't, I mean, I don't think I opened a history book. And I did well in history but I don't think I ever read anything. So now, it's strange to me, but I really like to read history.

I don't know, learning just kind of hooked me. Let's see . . . all during my life, I hated to read. Now I read all the time, and I love to read more and more. It just kind of finally just caught on, in a way like a light bulb went off and said, "Hey, you know what, there's a lot of opportunity out there if you just would take ahold of it." Maybe it's from watching *Dead Poets Society*, you know, *carpe diem*, seize the day kind of thing. It's like, "Now's the time to do it, let's go," you know [laughs].

Others took pleasure in becoming "smarter" or "more educated."

I think about myself when I first came here. As far as education-wise, I'm 100 percent smarter in the way I think, in the way I read, in the way I write, and even in the way I convey myself, the way I speak to people.

I feel, I guess I feel smarter now [laughs], 'cause of the classes and other things I've taken. 'Cause I enjoy a variety of different things, that's why I really, I wanted to get a basic overall knowledge about it, you know . . . I've taken acting classes, all kinds of theater classes, music classes, art history classes, foreign language classes. I'm not really into science and that kind of stuff but I took some science classes, history classes.

•   •   •

The ten-and-a-half million students currently enrolled in four-year college programs probably share the common goals of clarifying their career paths and graduating with a bachelor's degree. For those just coming out of high school or those in their early twenties, going to college also coincides with a time of maturing and gaining confidence and independence. However, beyond these similarities, college students vary tremendously in their approaches to college. For the Yale students, college was viewed as an experience directed toward their own self-development. These students valued friendships, extracurricular activities, and courses as important components, or resources, in their processes of self-discovery and change. For the Southern students, the primary project was not one of crafting an enhanced self, but of acquiring a bachelor's degree. One of the Southern students likened this degree to a prize.

I want to graduate. This is like this thing . . . almost like a prize, and it's like I can't quite grasp it yet, you know? I'll know I'm graduating once I start walking down the little aisle there, you know?

From their descriptions of college, the Yale and the Southern students by and large held different ideals of education. However, most of the Southern students also lacked an opportunity to have the college experience available to the Yale students, because the former lived off campus and spent their spare time working. Indeed, several of the Southern students commented on this aspect of their education.

> I don't know if I'd come back here [for graduate school], just because . . . this place is dreary, you know? They nicknamed it "Suitcase Southern" when I was a freshman, 'cause everybody goes home on the weekends, nobody stays here. There's no ambiance for people to stay. Sometimes it seems like there's no reason for anybody to stay here during the weekends.

> Southern is such a commuter environment, and that affects the basis of your schools. Like when you have a university that's completely noncommuter, everyone is on campus, or at an apartment . . . so there's much more student interaction. Here, everyone's sort of detached . . . You could be a student here and not know anyone, because if you live in Seymour and you come in for classes and you leave . . . you miss "college," "college life" . . . which is a shame.

> I don't think I got the whole, complete experience. I was talking to my girlfriend yesterday. I was like, "I don't think I got the whole college experience, I don't know why." Maybe because I don't socialize . . . They say college life is supposed to be the best years of your life. It was regular to me. I didn't have any high points.

These passages raise important questions. Did the Southern and the Yale students begin with different objectives for their college education? How much did the institutions they attended influence their outlooks? Did the difference lie in commuting to college versus residing on campus? Such questions are difficult to answer with the data collected for this study, because I spoke with students only near the end of their college years and thus have no way of knowing how their perspectives may have shifted during college. However, it is worth reviewing the three strands of sociological research that have tackled these questions. First, studies have shown that first-generation students are generally less academically and socially involved than students from more educated families (Nuñez and Cuccaro-Alamin 1998). Second, research comparing commuter students with those residing on campus generally finds that the latter group shows much greater change across a wide array of psychosocial, attitudinal, and value measures, net of background traits and confounding influences. Living on campus positively impacts "intellectual orientation, autonomy, and independence; tolerance, empathy, and ability to relate to others; and the use of principled reasoning to judge moral issues" (Pascarella and Terenzini 2008, p. 603), while commuting provides fewer opportunities for these kinds of cognitive and psychosocial changes. On the other hand, they note that studies have found little difference in learning outcomes between students living on and off campus. The third strand of research examines the effects of attending institutions with a liberal arts emphasis. Students who choose to enroll in such institutions come from families with higher levels of education and income; have higher levels of extracurricular and volunteer involvement as high school students; and start college with more strongly developed critical thinking skills, more openness to diversity, and a greater orientation toward learning for self-understanding. However, even after taking into account these precollege differences, students attending liberal arts institutions show greater increases in intellectual and personal growth during college (Pascarella et al. 2005; Seifert et al. 2008). This is probably because liberal arts colleges provide a distinct quality of education. Their faculty members are more interested in the students' academic and personal problems, interact more frequently with students, and involve them in their own research projects. These institutions also place more emphasis on writing and independent study and less on multiple-choice exams (Astin 1999a). Taken together, these findings suggest that the Yale students in my sample most likely differed from their counterparts at Southern before even beginning their college education, but that attending a liberal arts institution and living on campus further amplified those differences.

Residential liberal arts colleges certainly offer students far more opportunity for a greater level of interaction with their peers, more involvement in college life, and better opportunities for intellectual and personal growth than commuter colleges.* Unfortunately, the likelihood of attending a residential liberal arts college is one that depends greatly on a student's socioeconomic status. The vast majority of first-generation, working-class, and lower-middle-class students attend commuter colleges in part because they lack the financial means to live on campus. Thus, while variations in their goals and expectations help

---

* There is also a considerable body of research identifying specific institutional features and practices that increase student engagement and learning. Freshman interest groups, formal social activities, tutoring, orientation, active advising, and learning communities all help foster student integration (Bean and Eaton 2001/2002; Eaton and Bean 1995; Engle and Tinto 2008; Tinto and Goodsell 1994). Various organizational attributes and structures, such as institutional communication, fairness in policies, and investment in student affairs, exert an effect on student learning (Astin 1999b; J. Berger 2001/2002; J. Berger and Braxton 1998). This research shows that all institutions, regardless of their type, can take steps to increase student engagement and learning.

shape individual students' college years, disparities in their material resources also contribute to whether students will even have the opportunity to have a college experience. (as opposed to just going after a degree)

These differences carry implications that extend far beyond the memories students take away from their college years. The activities that make up college-as-an-experience provide their participants with a range of opportunities to hone their social skills, build networks, and develop cultural capital. Some of these activities also help pave the students' ways into graduate programs and prestigious scholarships. An article by a Yale student (Kotch 1997) notes how some students established new community-service groups for the express purpose of getting into law school and goes on to describe how leadership roles in some political groups are a "gateway to a Rhodes Scholarship, to Yale Law." The author also outlines the future usefulness of skills learned in Yale's extracurricular groups.

> Yale is no bastion of immaturity, but a breeding ground for real-life movie villains: sly politicos and businessmen who learned how to play the game, and play it very well. It hardly surprised me that Yale produces more managers, more Congressmen, and more governors than any other college. In spite of the fine liberal education it purports to provide, Yale's real school is its brutal culture of advancement, existing not in its classrooms, but in its viciously competitive extracurricular world . . . Yale's microcosm is not much different from the real world, where Yale alumni are playing the game and climbing the ladder, their eyes forever on the next rung. When politicians return to Yale . . . someone will ask them where they learned politics. "Here, of course," they invariably reply. (p. 6)

CHAPTER SIX

Majors and Knowledge

At some point during their college years, students declare a major field of study and then complete the required courses in that field on the way to earning a bachelor's degree. Majors represent a sort of envisioned future, connecting students to images of the kinds of work they might do and the kinds of people they might become. Choosing a major is also one of the most important decisions students make, influencing not only what they will learn in university but, to an extent, their possible graduate school opportunities, career trajectories, and potential earnings. Not inconsequentially, the choice of a major corresponds to a student's class and gender.

By class, privileged students gravitate toward liberal arts fields of study,* while their less privileged peers tend toward applied and preprofessional fields, a pattern identified not just in the United States, but in several other countries (Bourdieu and Passeron 1977; Goyette and Mullen 2006; Sanderson 1993; Thomas 1990; Van de Werfhorst 2002). By gender, major choices consistently and sharply diverge. These gender differences in fields of study hold across

* Liberal arts fields comprise disciplines in the arts, humanities, mathematics, and social and natural sciences. Liberal arts are also sometimes referred to as "liberal arts and sciences."

institutional types as well as across the students' social backgrounds. Highly selective institutions are just as segregated as less selective institutions (Mullen and Baker 2007, 2008). Moreover, high-SES men and women differ as much in their choices of fields of study as low-SES men and women. While high-SES men and women are both more likely to select liberal arts over preprofessional majors, they diverge in terms of which of the liberal arts fields they select. Among high-SES students, men more commonly choose science and math majors, while women choose arts and humanities. Among their lower-SES counterparts, men more commonly choose engineering, while women choose education (Goyette and Mullen 2006). In these ways, the choice of a major becomes a further point of stratification by class and gender. To the extent that a college major is linked to educational and employment outcomes, these patterns contribute to reproducing gender and class inequalities.

Even as little as a year after graduation, salaries vary tremendously according to one's field of study. As shown in table 6.1, graduates in the fields of engineering and computer science enjoyed hefty salary advantages over those who chose majors in education, the humanities, and the social and life sciences. For example, in 2001 a graduate in a life science field earned just 55 percent of the salary of a computer science major. Generally, graduates in preprofessional fields command higher starting salaries than those in arts and science fields. In addition, the fields in which women predominate (e.g., education and the life sciences) appear at the bottom of this table, while male-dominated fields such as engineering and computer science come out at the top.

Yet these figures do not tell the whole story. Students in some fields are more likely than others to continue their education with a graduate or other advanced degree. Indeed, 38 percent of life science majors entered a graduate or professional program within one year of receiving their bachelor's degree. Graduates in the highest-paying majors (engineering and computer science) are among the least likely to continue their education, with only 22 percent and 15 percent, respectively, entering a graduate program (Bradburn et al. 2003). This pattern also follows the liberal arts/preprofessional divide. Forty-one percent of students graduating with a bachelor's degree in the arts and sciences in 1993 had entered a graduate program within four years of graduation, compared with only 24 percent of preprofessional students. The differences are even more pronounced in relation to enrollment in PhD programs; nearly eight times as many liberal arts graduates enroll in PhD programs as do preprofessional graduates (Goyette and Mullen 2006).

Table 6.1   Median annual salaries of 1999–2000 bachelor's degree
recipients in 2001

Undergraduate major	Median annual salary (in dollars)
Computer/information science	47,885
Engineering	46,286
Business/management	34,933
Math	34,146
Health	34,061
Physical sciences	30,553
Other technical/professional	30,170
Vocational/technical	29,959
Humanities	27,396
Social/behavioral sciences	27,309
Education	26,983
Life sciences	26,336

Source: Compiled from Bradburn et al. 2003, p. 128, table III.3

These patterns suggest a set of tracks running through the higher educational system. In one track, students attend more prestigious institutions, major in liberal arts fields, and then continue their education with a graduate or professional degree, a package leading to lucrative and high-status jobs. In the other track, students study applied fields at less prestigious institutions and then take their acquired skills directly into the labor market, often earning a relatively decent starting salary. While their earnings in the early years after graduation will be higher than liberal arts majors who choose not to attend graduate school, in the long run there is little doubt that those on the first track do better. The kinds of jobs open to those with graduate and professional degrees generally far surpass the opportunities available to those with bachelor's degrees in preprofessional fields. The probability that a student takes one track or the other varies by social background; children from high-SES families are far more likely to follow the first track, while students from less advantaged backgrounds, if they make it to college, generally take the second track (Mullen, Goyette, and Soares 2003).

In addition to these class-based tracks, there is also a set of gendered tracks. While women now earn a slightly higher share of bachelor's degrees than men, gender differences in the choice of a college major contribute to the earnings disadvantages experienced by women. Graduates in female-dominated majors are more likely to enter female-dominated occupations and earn substantially lower salaries than graduates of male-dominated fields of study. In 2004, for example, the median annual earnings of all full-time working women between the ages of 25 and 34 with bachelor's degrees were $40,300 compared with $50,700 for men, or 79 percent. This percentage has barely changed since 1980, when women earned $34,100 to men's $46,300 (in constant 2004 dollars), or 74 percent (Snyder 2007).

On the surface, it might appear that students simply differ in their proclivities for fields of study. Indeed, the selection of majors is typically portrayed as an individual choice, where students decide based on their particular preferences and career goals (Cebula and Lopes 1982; Davies and Guppy 1997; Hearn and Olzak 1981; Wilson 1978). Certainly, a number of individual characteristics do influence or constrain the choice of a major. This choice will depend in part on one's plans for graduate school. Students planning to attend graduate school have more liberty to postpone their vocational training until after receiving an undergraduate degree. Students intending to complete their education with a bachelor's degree must make sure they have labor-market-ready skills by the time they finish. Because more privileged students have educational aspirations beyond a bachelor's degree (and the means to realize those aspirations), they have more freedom of choice at the undergraduate level. Students may also be limited by their own academic abilities. Those who struggle academically, have difficulty in quantitative-based disciplines, or lack a strong background in science are likely to avoid certain fields. Finally, cultural capital influences choice in at least two ways. First, students with greater levels of cultural capital will have a more extensive knowledge of the various offerings in the higher educational system and the range of possible occupational starting points. Second, because cultural capital facilitates a student's mastery of abstract and theoretical disciplines (Bourdieu and Passeron 1977, 1979; Bourdieu 1984), students with high levels of cultural capital may be more likely to choose fields in these areas.

Beyond these individual characteristics, the features of the institutions students attend also influence their choices. The range of choice is restricted to the majors offered by an institution and further weighted by that institution's focus. For instance, the higher proportion of liberal arts fields at more prestigious institutions increases the likelihood that a student will choose one of those fields. In addition, degrees from more prestigious institutions derive a larger part of their value from the name of the college or university than from the particular kind of degree. If students can count on getting jobs because of the name of the institution on their diplomas, they can afford to be less concerned with acquiring marketable skills during college. Finally, depending on their class backgrounds and the institutions they attend, students likely anticipate entering different segments of the labor market. The segments differ in terms of the types of employment available, the gendered divisions of the labor market, and the varying job requirements. Some labor market segments expect prospective employees to be pretrained with the required job skills, while others are more open and provide training for new hires. In the face of these differences, students may plan their credentials accordingly. Likewise, depending on the market segment, acquiring a job may hinge more on connections than on a particular credential. In these segments, students with a substantial array of social connections may worry less about their marketable skills.

Yale offers only one undergraduate degree in an applied field, engineering, which accounts for less than 2 percent of all degrees awarded. Yale is similar in this regard to most other Ivy League institutions. The more selective the college or university, the greater the proportion of degrees awarded in liberal arts fields (Brint et al. 2005); indeed, the prestigious private liberal arts colleges almost exclusively offer liberal arts degrees. At Southern, degrees in preprofessional fields constitute around half of all degrees awarded, but if we add in the students earning degrees in liberal arts fields while simultaneously earning their secondary education certificate through the School of Education, the balance shifts to 67 percent applied degrees versus 33 percent liberal arts degrees.* The figures for Southern are in line with the national average. Over the last several decades, the national trend has shifted in favor of applied fields of study. Currently, about 60 percent of all undergraduate students choose a preprofessional field, up from around 45 percent in the mid-1960s (Brint et al. 2005).

As expected, a higher proportion of the Yale students that I interviewed planned to continue their education beyond a bachelor's degree than the Southern students in my sample. Table 6.2 lists the graduate education plans discussed by the students in their interviews. Exactly half of the Southern students did not intend to pursue further education after their bachelor's degree, in comparison with just less than a quarter of the Yale students. In addition, of those Southern students intending to go on to graduate school, the majority (fifteen out of twenty-five) planned to enter a master's program. The women in my sample were somewhat more likely than the men to plan to pursue a master's degree. The Yale students, in contrast, were more likely to plan for law, medical, or doc-

---

* This is based on an estimate provided by Professor James Granfield, Interim Dean, School of Education, Southern Connecticut State University, in a telephone conversation on May 24, 2007.

Table 6.2 Graduate education plans of the Southern and the Yale students

	None	Master's	MBA	Law school	Medical school	PhD	Mix or unsure
Southern women	11	9	1	1	1	1	1
Southern men	14	6	0	0	0	1	4
Yale women	4	1	1	1	10	3	5
Yale men	7	0	0	4	2	2	10

Note: N = 100.

toral programs, with a large number either still deciding or considering multiple degrees. In my sample, a much higher proportion of the Yale women intended to pursue a medical degree, compared with the men.* The Yale students' greater propensity to attend graduate school presumably allows them more freedom of choice at the undergraduate level.

Next to the decision to go to college and the selection of an institution, a student's choice of a major has the greatest bearing on his or her future trajectory. Further, choosing among the 1056 fields of study currently available depends not only on individual preferences, but also on the particular kinds of constraints and opportunities a student faces. How did these influence how the students at Southern and Yale thought about college majors and went about the process of selecting them? Why were the Southern students more likely to choose applied fields of study, compared with their counterparts at Yale? How closely did the Yale students fit the liberal arts ideal of selecting fields based on intellectual interests? Why did the men and women on both campuses diverge in their choices? Exploring these questions brings to light not just differences in how students decide on majors, but also the students' perspective on what they were learning in their classes and their opinions about the value of different kinds of knowledge.

Not surprisingly, the Southern students regarded majors primarily as career choices, and they prioritized courses and knowledge that would facilitate their career goals. The ideal at Yale is to allow students to prioritize intellectual explo-

---

* The higher proportion of women planning to attend medical school, as compared with men, may be an anomaly of my sample. Yale reports that just 7 percent of the class of 2008 had entered medical school one year after graduation (Yale University 2007b). Nationwide, men and women are now nearly on a par in their likelihood of earning medical degrees (Snyder, Dillow, and Hoffman 2009).

ration and growth, ostensibly free from the immediate concerns of career planning. Indeed, given that Yale almost exclusively offers degrees in the arts and sciences, nearly all of its students select a field of study in these areas. In this way, one imagines that liberal arts students, as opposed to vocational students, accord greater value to the pursuit of knowledge and the development of their minds over more mundane, practical concerns. However, in taking a closer look at the logic the Yale students used in selecting majors, the distinction between liberal arts students and vocational students becomes blurred. While the Yale students did study liberal arts and science fields, they often did not fully match the spirit of the liberal arts ideal. However, students vary, and for reasons explored later in this chapter, of all the students in my sample at Yale, the privileged women came closest to the liberal arts ideal.

Choosing Majors at Southern

At Southern, majors were chosen not for what a student wanted to study, but for the kind of occupation a student planned to enter. While the Yale students tended to first select a major and only then began thinking about career options, the Southern students worked in reverse, choosing their future occupations and then selecting the most appropriate major. This logic makes sense for those students going into applied fields. After all, why study social work, education, nursing, or business other than to enter those occupations? However, this pattern also held true for those Southern students majoring in the liberal arts, as in the example of a biology student explaining why she chose her field.

> I knew that I wanted to work with people or animals, so I was either gonna be bio. or soc[iology], and I wound up choosing to major in biology and minor in soc.

Generally speaking, the students selected fields on the basis of the career options to which they were linked. The process described by the social work student below is typical of most of the Southern students. He initially chose sociology because he wanted to teach, but later switched to social work, not on the basis of what courses he wanted to take or the knowledge he would gain, but in terms of what kind of work he thought he would most enjoy.

> Initially, I wanted to be a sociology major. My senior year in high school, I wanted to be a sociology major and I wanted to teach. But I was confused, and one of my best friend's mom, stepmom, was a social worker, and she goes, "But what do you

want to do in sociology?" I said, "I don't know. I want to work with people." She goes, "Sociology's a lot of studying, it's a lot of research." She said, "Why don't you do social work? You'll definitely work with people," and I said, "All right."

For the Southern students, majors represented not bodies of knowledge or academic disciplines, but rather occupational fields. Indeed, the Southern students rarely drew distinctions between an academic field and the occupations associated with it. When comparing different majors, for example, the students did not refer to differences in the academic disciplines, but rather to differences in the career lines associated with those majors. This contrasts with most of the Yale students, for whom majors represented branches of knowledge.

For those Southern students who had difficulty choosing a future line of work, business and psychology remained their preferred choices, because these fields were considered to be more open-ended.

> I started out in business because when you don't know what you want, you go into business. I think that Dad helped me along with that one. "When you don't know what you want, Brian, you know, try business. You can always fall back on it." So, it seemed logical to me. So I did that.

> I'm not sure what kind of field I want to go into, where business management covers all of them.

In some cases, the students started by considering the available majors and then evaluating them according to their career options. In these instances, liberal arts majors were often the first to be discarded because of their perceived lack of career potential. One student explained why he briefly considered but then rejected the fields of history and sociology.

> I really didn't see a future in like sociology, especially . . . There's no jobs. I don't know, I guess what do you do in sociology? But it's just like, it's hard to get a job, I think. That's what I was told and I've read a little bit. And history . . . what do you do with a history major? Become a teacher with it? And I didn't want to do that.

Two students discarded English and math in part for the same reasons.

> I decided to do English because I was always told I was a really good writer, and a very good, you know, grammar, you know, all that kind of stuff. So I tried that and I couldn't stand reading all the books and books of literature. And then I thought about all I could do with it is either write or teach, and that wasn't gonna get me too far.

It was more thinking about the avenue, like, "All right, if I do this major . . . what are the options that this leads to?" If you're a math major, if you think about it, there's not much new research in the field of math. What's there is there, all the problems have been figured out for the most part, so . . . I would see only teaching math . . . and I don't want to be a math teacher.

Students also took into account whether, and how much, graduate education might be required for an occupation. For example, several of the students mentioned an interest in psychology, but once they discovered that they would not be able to practice without a doctorate, they opted for social work instead. An additional factor was the level of difficulty for a given major. Particularly for students already finding their college courses demanding, an easier major often held appeal.

I contemplated biology for some reason. Nah, it's not me. It's a lot of work, and, I don't know, if I was to be a bio. major, that's a lot of work, and if I was gonna be a biology teacher say at high school, that would still be a lot of work, because of the amount of knowledge you'd have to take in.

Coming here, taking a couple of psychology classes, I didn't do good, I got Ds in those, and I was, "This is harder than what I thought, you know, I thought it was just sit down and chat with people, know their business," but I found out it takes a lot more.

Finally, in some cases the students arrived at their choice of a major by pragmatically adding up their credits and grades and making a determination as to which major would be the quickest to complete. One student used this method in choosing psychology.

I had the most credits in it. And I had the best grades in it. So I decided on psychology because I thought I would get out faster.

Because the choice of a major was so tightly linked to occupational considerations, the extent of the Southern students' knowledge about possible jobs played a strong role in their decision making. To feel comfortable about their choices, the students wanted to have a clear idea of the exact occupations they would enter. This eliminated a large number of possible but less defined options, such as working in particular industries like publishing or banking. In contrast, the Yale students more commonly identified broad occupational areas without having a specific idea of their probable position within a given area.

Moreover, the range of occupations familiar to the Southern students was actually quite limited. Because the students' knowledge and sense of possibility was shaped in part by the occupations of their parents, their parents' friends, and their relatives, the Southern students, particularly those from working-class backgrounds, confined their choices to a relatively small set of occupations. Teaching was a common choice, in part because of its familiarity. Their limited knowledge also meant that the Southern students' choices sometimes depended on chance conversations with friends or relatives. Much more so than the Yale students, they spoke of choosing a major after learning about a possible occupational field from a friend or relative.

> People around me, like my family and friends and stuff, have always said that "you work well with people." And I had no idea, you know. Social work meant nothing to me, you know. I didn't know what it was, but I guess my parents have kind of, had an idea that that would be, you know, psychology, things like that, so, we just looked up in the curriculum and it just said, you know, "social work" and take these kinds of classes, and I was like, "All right, I'll try it, you know," and I just stuck with it.

> I was still thinking math, but my grandfather suggested to me if I had thought about computer science. I'd never heard of computer science. I didn't know what he was talking about, but he suggested to try it out and to see if I liked it. So when I became a freshman here I signed up for straight computer science major as a freshman, based on his advice, just to see what it is, and 'cause I figured if I didn't like it I could always change.

> My cousin's an architect, and he made a lot of money, so I was like, "Okay, let's try that."

In addition, when discussing various occupational options, the Southern students sometimes revealed a great deal of misinformation about what different careers entailed. For example, one student decided against pursuing law because he didn't want to defend criminals. I asked another student whether she had considered psychology.

> No, psychology scares me for some reason. Like I wouldn't want to be a psychologist and like administer drugs and tie people up or something, that whole thing scares me. And I didn't know that psychology, you know, if you were just a psychologist, and not a psychiatrist, it was different. I just assumed it was all different levels of the same thing.

Another student gave a related rational for choosing social work over psychology.

> I enjoy psychology, but even psychology's just like a narrow path, you know? They focus on mental illness, mental health, and that's it. Social work, you can help people find jobs, you know, you can help people find places to live, provide food for people.

Still another student originally declared a major in psychology, only to find out from her adviser that she would need a doctorate to do clinical work. Up until then, she had not considered social work, because she did not know much about it.

> I only knew psychology, I didn't know social work. I used to think about social work as welfare. "Oh, welfare people had to take kids out of the homes," that's how I knew social work. I didn't know much about it, so I always used to say, "I'm gonna be a psychologist, I'm gonna sit down and help people with their problems." And also they make good money, that's what I thought about . . . And I spoke to my advisor and she told me, "Oh, you know, and for psychology, you will need a PhD to really do clinical work. You can't just have a bachelor's and do clinical work. That's not how it works." So I was like, "Oh, then what can I do? I really want to counsel, I really do want to do clinical work." And she said, "Well, you know, you could do social work." And I said, "Oh, what can you do with social work?" And she told me what you could do . . . So, I said, "Well, I'm gonna give it a try." So I switched from psychology to social work.

In a final example, one student with an initial interest in law turned away from that goal after his teachers explained that he would mostly be doing research.

> One day, my teacher was talking to me and said, "Most of your time's gonna be spent in a library, researching the work." And I thought about that. I never thought about that before, and I was like, "That's not what I want to do. I don't want to be locked up in a room all the time." And so then my mother, at that point, I was confused, I wasn't really sure what exactly I wanted to do. So my mother knew and she one day came with a book full of jobs, different jobs and stuff, job descriptions. And so I was looking through it, and I happened to land on TV reporter, TV anchoring, television news. And I found the qualities, it had a list of qualities, like you can be investigative, you can have your face on TV, all that stuff, so that attracted me to it right away. I said, "This is something I would like to do," you know. I liked writing, I liked creative writing and stuff, I liked to write, and I thought that,

you know, I could make a difference in some kind of way, through the stories I do, to help somebody out, and to reveal a lot of the corruption in this world. I mean, that's the best way, TV, that's the biggest medium, and so hopefully that's what I'll be able to do in the future.

While most of the students fit the general pattern described above, there were some exceptions. Of the fifty Southern students I interviewed, thirty-six (72%) chose applied fields, while fourteen chose fields in the liberal arts. As at Yale, these students' choices related to their social backgrounds. While just over half of all the students in the sample were first-generation college-goers, only 29 percent of the liberal arts majors were first generation. However, of the fourteen liberal arts students, eight of them had chosen their major primarily for occupational reasons (such the biology student above). Only six of the students (three men and three women) selected their fields primarily because of their interest in the actual area, with future job considerations playing only a small role. One of these students explained choosing chemistry simply because he really liked it and it was "very interesting," rather than for its career possibilities. He did very well in this major and, at the time of our interview, had been accepted into the PhD program at the University of Arizona. Another student had always loved writing, but initially felt that "it wouldn't be worthwhile to pursue as a major because I wouldn't be able to get a job out of it." She eventually changed her mind after realizing "I was happy doing it and I liked it." Like many of the women I interviewed at Yale, her career interests centered on an ideal, as-yet-undefined job that would allow her to do meaningful work and continue her writing. "I'd like to have a job where I could express, where I could do something that I really cared about, where I could enjoy what I was doing enough, and have enough money and then still have time to write."

Gender Divisions at Southern

Because majors were so tied to future occupations for the Southern students, gendered patterns of choice reflected gender-typed notions of appropriate work for men and women. Women at Southern were more likely to choose majors in education, public health (including nursing), social work, and psychology, while the men more commonly chose computer science and business. These preferences reflected both a gendered occupational structure and the asymmetrical character of gender change (England and Li 2006). Women have made considerable inroads into some previously male-dominated occupations, such as law, medicine, and university professorships. Women made up only 7 percent of all lawyers in 1975, but by 2006 they constituted 26 percent. In medicine, the comparable figures were 13 percent and 32 percent. However, the integration of occupations has mostly been a one-sided process; while women have moved into many previously male-dominated occupations, men have not moved into female-dominated ones. Consequently, the proportion of women in occupations such as nursing, social work, and elementary school teaching has barely changed over the past thirty or so years. Women made up 97 percent of all nurses in 1975; by 2006 this had dropped only slightly, to 92 percent. Women constituted 85 percent of all elementary school teachers in 1975, and 81 percent in 2006. Social work has become even more female-dominated than before; women made up 61 percent of the social workers in 1975, and 83 percent in 2006 (U.S. Bureau of Labor Statistics 2007; Wootton 1997). These patterns reflect the way status in occupations relates to gender. Because our culture devalues women, the kinds of work typically done by women are also devalued. Thus men face a more pronounced stigma for entering nontraditional fields, because they enter the devalued realm of things associated with femininity (England and Li 2006; Williams 1995). However, when women make the nontraditional choice of a typically male occupation, they generally benefit from the higher social value of the occupation (in addition to better pay and elevated status).

Because the Southern students chose majors based on perceptions of their links to occupations, the gender-typing of a particular occupation influenced whether students considered the occupation, and thus the major, to be gender appropriate. These distinctions were perhaps most strongly reinforced in the major and occupation of education. Because women make up 98 percent of all preschool and kindergarten teachers, and 82 percent of all elementary and middle school teachers (U.S. Bureau of Labor Statistics 2007), the vast majority of the Southern students went through their early years of schooling with all-female teachers. It is noteworthy that many of the women in my study discussed forming their aspirations to be teachers at a very young age. In addition, some came to the realization that they wanted to be teachers by "playing school," a distinctly gendered children's game. Two of the Southern students discussed how the early development of their aspirations to be teachers came partly from this practice of playing school.

I always wanted to teach. When I was little, I used to play school. I had a nice little chalk board.

My mother thought that I should be a teacher because she always thought that I would. She'd always observe me with kids, and she always thought that I was good with them and thought that I should be a teacher. And I was always playing school when I was little, so she thought that I would like to be a teacher and she encouraged that.

The influence of the family also comes across in the last quote, with the student's mother encouraging her to take up the teaching profession because she thought her daughter was good with kids. Other students also noted the influence of their families, either through encouragement or by example, such as having female family members in the teaching profession. One student tied her interest in teaching to the fact that she came from a family of teachers, including her mother.

So I always knew that I wanted to do something around the area of teaching, even if it wasn't 'specially becoming a teacher. So I explored that and then that lead me to college because that was my final goal was to . . .

And so you'd always wanted to do something in teaching?

Um-hmm. I come from a family of teachers. My mom, I think every single school in the system in the town I live in has a teacher with my last name, and they're all relatives.

Early work experiences, which tended to be gender typed, also influenced the students' choices. Some women linked their decision to go into teaching to their teenage experiences with babysitting.

How did you know you wanted to be a teacher?

I don't know, I just always, I always loved kids. Every job I've ever had involved kids, so, I don't know, it just sort of happened. Ever since I was, you know, started babysitting I knew that I wanted to be a teacher.

Because babysitting is done almost exclusively by girls, it contributes toward setting more women than men on the track to teaching.

When men do enter education majors, they tend toward higher levels (secondary instead of primary education) and typically male-curricular tracks (technology and agriculture). Men also earn the majority of degrees in physical education teaching and coaching (Snyder 2007). For the Southern men, these aspirations, too, were influenced by family and by the students' childhood experiences with gender-typed activities, as shown in the statements by two male students, both studying education in order to be coaches.

> Freshman or sophomore year [of high school], I decided that I probably wanted to go into phys[ical] ed[ucation] and be a gym teacher or coach.
>
> *How did you make that decision?*
>
> Well, I played sports all my life since I was five, and it's a major interest is [*sic*] sports, and athletics, and . . . baseball since I was five, hockey since I was nine. So I've been around, my father's coached me since I was five, so he's been involved in sports his whole life, too. So sports is a big background.

> *Tell me the whole story of how you chose your major.*
>
> I've always played hockey all my life, so I was always involved with the high school teams, and I went back and I'd just skate around with them and stuff even after I graduated . . . I'd skate with them all, through all the practices, and I'd show up at games and stuff. And it happened to be that one of the assistant coaches was quitting, and the guy that I played for said, "Do you want to come aboard and be the assistant coach?" and I said "Yeah, sure." So I started doing that, and I really enjoyed being around the kids and being able to show them "All right, this is the play we want to do and this is how we want to execute it," and then have them go do it in a game, really like gave me, I was satisfied. So I was like, this is something I think I might look into, so that's what I started looking into . . . I thought about it, and I said, "Yeah, that's something I would like to do."

Because sports activities, and in particular hockey, tended to be a larger part of the boys' childhoods than those of the girls, these earlier experiences laid the groundwork for making coaching a more "natural" choice for men than for women. This also extended to the men who majored in other fields, such as one student who majored in journalism in order to pursue a career in sports information.

> 'Cause I think the whole sports thing is . . . I mean, I just love being around sports, and it's just, it's something I've grown up with, you know, my dad's very sports

oriented, my brother was beyond sports oriented, that was his life, and it still is, and it's something that I can have fun with that.

Likewise, another student explained how his interest in business came from watching his father run a store and then helping him.

Tell me the whole story of how you chose to major in management.

'Cause, uh, since my father was running a business trade, I was always into business, even in high school . . . And then I said, "Well, since I'm good in business and since I watch my father every day running a store, managing a store," that's what I wanted to do, pursue.

The accounts related above suggest how childhood experiences and observations shaped these Southern students' occupational aspirations. The students' experiences with gender-typed activities and professions influenced their own career inclinations. In addition, gender-essentialist beliefs also contributed to the students' choices. This became most apparent in the comments made by a few of the men who had chosen stereotypically female fields. When asked to describe the kinds of students in their majors, two social work students, both men, immediately focused on the gender composition of their major.

Do you see any similarities among the social work majors?

The only thing I notice is that there's very little males, very small percentage of, I mean, there's some classes where I'm the only male. I think we have like eight in our whole program.

Why do you think that is?

It's a female-dominated field.

Why is that?

Because women are more nurturing by nature, sometimes more sensitive.

Do you see any similarities among the social work majors?

Yeah, they're mostly women. I mean, um, similarities, yeah, I think a lot of them are open, are very open minded, just have a very caring side to them, and yeah, I think that's . . . but also a lot of women.

Why do you think that's so?

Because, because, ah, maybe it's society the way it is, you know, men are supposed to be, you know, hard core, I don't know, you know, tough, and being a social worker you're kind of, it's kind of the opposite of all that. So maybe that's why, I don't know.

In the first account, the student explained the scarcity of men in social work by attributing what he saw as the necessary characteristics of social workers, nurturing and sensitivity, to women. "By nature," women have more of those characteristics than men. In the second account, the student offered more of a gender-socialization explanation, suggesting that men are supposed to be tough and hard core, rather than open-minded and caring. Both of these descriptions reveal the men's awareness of crossing gender lines when they entered the field of social work. The lines are not so rigid that it becomes impossible for men to enter social work, but strong enough so that only one in ten social work majors is a man (Snyder 2007).

Interestingly, in the interviews none of the women entering traditionally male fields of study made mention of the gender composition of their field. This again suggests that women, while certainly facing other barriers, do not risk the same kinds of stigmatization that men do when entering typically female fields of study.

The Value of Knowledge at Southern

One of the central ways in which the Southern students evaluated the content of their courses was in the extent to which the materials would be useful in their future lines of work. Most of the time, this meant that they were looking for knowledge that could be directly applied. This point was expressed most clearly in the students' negative evaluations of certain courses.

I had a couple of classes that were a waste of time, I think. Like zoology, it was kind of like memorizing. It was really like, you don't really need it after college.

All we learn is classification, which I'll never use. I'll never say, "All right, what's the Latin name of that animal." No one will ever ask me that.

I had to take physics, and I know that I'll never use physics again.

In each of these cases, students regarded learning they would not later use as a waste of time. On the other hand, the students reserved their praise for knowledge and courses that were directly applicable to their future occupations.

I guess learning what classes I have taken that I have liked and felt that I have learned material that, you know, that does apply, you know, as far as my major goes, I guess. You know, it's not all the classes I've taken I've been fed up with, but, you know, there are quite a few that I have taken that I can really look at the material and say, "Wow, you know, this is like really what goes on in real life," that kind of stuff, where I can really see that it does apply to what I'm gonna need to have to do . . . Yeah, the teachers, they'll come right out and say, you know, "You're gonna have to know, you need to know this, you have to do this, blah, blah, blah, blah." And I'll say, "Oh, you know, that's great, I'm glad I'm learning that now and not later."

In some fields, this meant that the students critiqued knowledge for being out of date.

Quite a few of the classes I've taken don't seem to, I just feel it's been a complete like waste of time, because they aren't either, I haven't learned anything, or when I get out, it's not gonna do anything for me . . . I feel it's scary sometimes, 'cause I feel, especially in this field, almost unprepared, like I'm going to be unprepared because there's so much to learn. I mean, I go to, you know, like Walden Books, or, you know, Barnes and Noble, and there's just racks and racks of books in the computer thing and I just look at 'em all, going "I got to know that, I got to know that, I got to know that," and I haven't learned any of it yet. And I just go out and buy the books and just read 'em. You have to, because the things that they teach you, some of it's out of date, or a lot of it's out of date . . . I just don't feel like I'm learning everything that I need to be.

I'm a computer science major . . . A couple of [my classes], I was like, "Hmm, I don't see why I have to take this class." Like my assembly language classes. They don't use assembly language anymore in the computer field. It's like "Why do I have to take this?"

Even some of the students who enjoyed liberal arts courses expressed the view that what they learned in their classes should be contemporary or have relevance to their current lives.

Yeah, I don't particularly enjoy writing an eleven-page paper on the *Canterbury Tales*, because, I mean, there's nothing you can really add to it. It's been analyzed for the last 600 years, so I hated doing something like that, because it just seems pointless. And, you know, I mean, I like the *Canterbury Tales*, but I didn't particularly see how the, you know, Wife of Bath or whatever related to anything that was going on today. Not that it has to, but it just seemed a little odd to write about the Black Plague of the thirteenth century.

Because of the emphasis the Southern students placed on courses and learning that would be applicable to their future lines of work, these students showed little patience for general education courses that they did not see as relevant to their careers. While the university itself maintains a system of general education requirements with a stated goal of providing students with a well-rounded education, the students often did not share this goal.

> I feel like more of a focus should be on your major, you know. We had to take all these other classes that I don't really feel, and I'm sure a lot of other students feel that way, apply to your major. I mean, I understand having to take a few general courses, but . . . it's like "What am I ever gonna do with this stuff [general requirements]?" you know?

> I would never have come to a four-year college if I would have known [about all the requirements]. Like I said, I don't have a problem with the major classes, that's fine, but all these requirements? I didn't think they'd take up at least two years, and then the other two we're doing, that you have to do as far as your major. I'm telling you, if they would have told me, if someone would have told me that I would take all these requirements, I would have never come to a four-year school.

> Some of the core requirement stuff, some of 'em I found to be very good, that I'm glad that I was required to take them. Others, they were pointless to my major. I mean, they're something that I might come across but most likely not, and so it was sort of wasted time. Others, like I mean, it just basically took up time away from my other classes, or away from working.

These cases evince the most explicit line of difference between the priorities of many of the Southern students and those of the institution. While the university is invested in providing students with a well-rounded education, this view of education was not always embraced by the students (though to be sure, there were some students who did value the required-curriculum courses).

Along with their appreciation of applied knowledge, the Southern students highly valued hands-on learning (over book learning) and learning that related to real-life experiences.

> Some of the professors are too wrapped up in being professors and reading the book, and then other professors are the complete opposite, are very real, they

describe what it's like to be providing therapy, to going out into the field. And those are the professors who make it worth while, 'cause they make more sense than the ones that sound like a book.

I had a radio-broadcast news class . . . which I really enjoyed, because it was a very hands-on class. You got to do all your editing. You were out there in the field getting sound bites and interviewing people.

I think that more of the education should be hands on. You should be out in the field, because you learn twice as quick . . . 'cause you have to. Under a controlled environment where you're expected to make mistakes, it's a lot easier than just jumping into it when you graduate.

The class that I most enjoy is the class that I'm taking now on studio production. And it's hands on, that's how I know that that is my calling, to do something else where I'm actually physically doing something [other] than taking classes and all that, 'cause I really enjoy it and I'm doing well in the class.

These accounts reflect another way in which the Southern students appreciated a certain efficiency about their education. They wanted to have their education focused as much as possible on their future jobs. For them, what was valuable about learning was what could be readily applied in their future job contexts. Underlying these immediate preferences, the Southern students also expressed a more general appreciation for applied knowledge in and of itself, along with skepticism toward theoretical knowledge.

I mean, you could read all the theory you wanted about interventions in the book, but until you get to apply it, it doesn't make sense . . . You use what you have to use and you don't, everything's not a textbook. That's the biggest thing I've learned.

I was also considering psychology, but I kind of gave up on that because . . . to go back and study Freud and Jung and Erikson, it seemed to be so old that, it seemed so vague, I guess, in a sense. And it seemed like what, bottom line, what you wind up doing is just talking to people about, you know, trying to, you know . . . let them vent on you, and kind of guide them. That's all you really can do.

Their comments made clear that theoretical approaches held little interest for these students, in contrast to their appreciation of the usefulness of knowledge, applicable more for doing than for thinking.

While the above perspectives on the value of knowledge captured the general pattern found at Southern, there were also many students who did take an interest in their general education requirements and spoke with enthusiasm about their courses in liberal arts fields. Most commonly, the students described these courses as "interesting," often unexpectedly so. Frequently, though, these courses, too, were valued for the skills they imparted.

> [My favorite courses] academic-requirement-wise, I would say either any of my English composition courses, 100, 101, or Major American Authors. I, from what I understand, I guess I lucked out with the professors I had, and they were great in helping my writing style, which has been applied in all my other classes.

Like the student above, a number of the other Southern students commented on how their literature courses had been beneficial in improving their writing skills.

In sum, in both their choices of majors and their views toward knowledge, the Southern students approached their education from an applied perspective. This corresponds to the rationale employed by most Southern students of going to college for the explicit purpose of getting a job. Given Yale's long liberal arts history, we might imagine that the Yale students chose majors for intellectual rather than career reasons. However, many of the Yale students had more in common with the Southern students in the ways that they chose majors than one would expect. The greater divergence between the two groups of students lay in the ways they thought about knowledge.

Choosing Majors at Yale

Yale proclaims that its undergraduate program is not about "training students in the particulars of a given career," but rather in providing students with a "broadly based, highly disciplined intellect." The rhetoric suggests that intellectual quests precede career decisions, and that students develop their minds "without specifying in advance" how their capabilities will be used in "whatever work they eventually choose" (Yale University 2005b). Regardless of the extent to which they might embrace this educational philosophy, the Yale students had three reasons not to be as concerned as the Southern students with having concrete skills to take into the job market. First, most of them were going on to graduate school. Only about a fifth of the Yale students, compared with half of the Southern students, planned to complete their studies with a bachelor's degree. The 80 percent of the Yale students who would be pursuing graduate and professional degrees knew that they would receive their applied training after their bachelor's degree, so they did not need to be as concerned with what kind of a job they could get with an English or a sociology degree.

Second, the Yale graduates, irrespective of their majors, had a clear advantage in the job market because of Yale's name on their diplomas. The Yale students were quite cognizant of the value their degrees would derive from the name of the institution, as opposed to their field of study. In terms of job interviews, one student commented that "it's amazing what just the name of the university can do sometimes." As another student succinctly explained, his diploma would have four important letters on it, which he clearly expected would facilitate his future objectives.

> I'm getting a diploma with four letters, Y-A-L-E, on it. I should be able to have the sky be my limit. I mean, actually, I should be able to do anything I want to.

This statement illustrates the student's awareness of the significance of holding a degree from an elite institution, as expressed by the unlimited possibilities he perceived in his future. His estimation of the value of a Yale degree is not unfounded (see, for example, Bowen and Bok 1998). In the next excerpt, one of the student-athletes made a similar argument. He explained why he did not worry too much about studying, but was content with getting by. While he hoped to play sports professionally, he was also banking on his Yale degree. In contrast to the logic applied by the Southern students, it was not the specific training he had received, his major, or his grades which he connected to his likelihood of getting a good job, but rather the Yale name.

> I skate by a lot . . . I always think, you know, I'm gonna graduate from here anyway, and once I get out there I'm not gonna look back at GPA or major or anything. I mean, it's, Yale is Yale . . . [Ten years from now] I would like to be thinking I'll be playing baseball. I mean, that's my ultimate goal . . . And then the thing I'll have that a lot of those guys won't, is that if it doesn't work out for me, then I graduated from Yale, and hopefully I'll have a good job somewhere.

Later in the interview he returned to the same points and contended that a Yale degree carried even more weight in other parts of the country than it did in the Northeast. He posed the comparison of earning a 4.0 grade point average at a state school with getting a 3.0 at Yale and concluded that there was no question that the Yale credential would still be far more valuable. These kinds of calculations were neither rare nor unconscious. For example, in an opinion piece in the Yale undergraduate newspaper, the author made explicit this same kind of reasoning.

> We like to pretend that the purpose of our Yale education is to prepare us better to confront the world, to make us well-rounded, deep, morally enriched persons. But what is on our résumés, top line, in italics? *Education: Yale University*. Graduating from Yale will put us in a certain class, a process entirely separate from the stated goals of education. When we graduate, grades—arguably the real measure of what we have learned—will be irrelevant for most of us. It will be enough to have the degree, the name, the label. (Sigel 1997)

There was an important difference between the Yale and the Southern students in terms of what their degrees would signal. The Yale students were freer from the necessity of graduating with practical skills, because they knew that the university's name on their diplomas would carry them far. They expected to obtain good jobs on the basis of their Yale degrees.

Finally, the Yale students benefited from wider access to an impressive array of social connections. The students made references to their peers moving into "cushy jobs their daddies got for them" after graduation and joked about being asked to find jobs for their friends' children in the future (Benton 1997). While this resource was not equally accessible to all, many of the students could, in fact, count on family connections or their Yale network for assistance in getting good jobs, rather than needing to rely on marketable career skills. Even some of the first-generation students took advantage of this.

> I also feel that I have just tangible contacts with people and some things about Yale. You know, if I read something interesting or I want a job lead or something, like I won't hesitate to call up a professor who did this or that, and . . . on my internships, I've always contacted whoever was the Yale person who was there and they've always been willing and able to help me.

The comments of one student summarized these themes, providing a depiction of the high occupational expectations held by many of the Yale students, based on their calculations of the value of their elite degree, rather than of their field of study, and the kinds of connections linked to their privileged social backgrounds.

> So many people are going into the sort of mentality, "Well, I want a high-paying job, I want the job that Yale can get me after I graduate, you know, I want a

$90,000-a-year salary as soon as I leave the university, and a setup in New York or San Francisco," and I think too many people at Yale are sure that they're gonna get something like that, whether it be from family connections or from their expectations of going to such a nice school.

For these reasons, the Yale students enjoyed the luxury of not having to concern themselves as much as the Southern students had with acquiring preprofessional training during college. However, this did not mean that all of the Yale students chose majors solely out of intellectual interest. Indeed, only about a quarter of the Yale students, mostly the privileged women, chose majors in this manner. For most of the Yalies, career considerations, to varying degrees, did weight their choices.

About a third of the Yale students—a group disproportionately comprised of student-athletes, first-generation students, and less affluent students—described choosing a major primarily for its connection to a particular career. Some of these students, in fact, felt uncomfortable being at Yale, given the paucity of applied fields from which to choose. One student, who came to Yale as an athletic recruit, talked about this dilemma.

> That's another thing I stressed about [choosing a major], because, you know, Yale's a liberal arts school and there isn't like a business major, or a marketing major, or a communications major, which is definitely, you know, one of those things I would have done like at Michigan State or Michigan or wherever . . . and econ. is the only thing that's business related, but it's not really. It's pretty much all theory, and it doesn't interest me, 'cause there's so much math and it's really dry.

He also mentioned the influence of his father, who raised a concern about selecting a major that would lead to a definite job.

> I liked psych[ology] and soc., but my dad, for some reason, his big worry, concern, was that I was going to be a psych. or soc. major . . . but, to get a practical degree or whatever . . . He had a big influence on what I decided to major in.

His uncertainties led him to seek advice from career services, where he was told that "the best thing you can do is major in something that emphasizes communication, orally and written . . . something like English or history would be great."

In the end he chose history, finding both that he liked it and that his "communication skills improved a lot." Still, he continued to be anxious about his employability, explaining that "it ma[kes] me nervous, because I don't have any practical skills to speak of, to offer any company. But I guess everyone's in the same boat coming out of here." Two other less advantaged students expressed similar concerns in terms of the choice of a major.

> I kind of feel that I have to do something that has, for me, I have to do something that's either kind of a set, not necessarily a profession, but something that's kind of set, you know? Coming into college, I was saying, "Well, what do I want to be? Do I want to be a doctor or a lawyer?"

> My dad had suggested engineering, because basically because you can do anything with an engineering degree. If you want to go into business, it's fine to have an engineering degree. If you want to go into teaching, it's fine to have an engineering degree. If you want to go into law, fine to have an engineering degree. If you want to be an engineer, engineering degree. But like if you're a history major, you can't be an engineer. So his reasoning was that if you're an engineering major you can do anything you want. If you do basically anything else, you're limiting yourself . . . And it made sense to me . . . [but] I decided at the end of my freshman year . . . I just didn't want to be an engineer . . . And I talked to my dad about it and he said, "Fine. Major in whatever you want, but the only thing I ask of you is that you make yourself, you know, when you graduate, you're marketable, you're somebody that people want."

Nearly all of the first-generation students (nine out of ten) chose majors on the basis of practical rather than intellectual concerns. While most of these students enjoyed their courses and were often quite engaged in their learning experiences, their focus was directed toward their career goals. One first-generation student had herself observed class differences in the process of choosing majors and offered her own analysis during our interview.

> I find that people from lower socioeconomic levels do not choose majors the same way that people from higher socioeconomic levels [do]. Like, I'm a double major in economics and international studies. I'm lucky that I genuinely have a passion for economics, and that's how I chose it. But I don't think, like, it being something where I could have a secure job and I knew I was gonna make, you know, a certain level of money, like it has, like, a floor to what my earnings are going to be, really affected it . . . I'm lucky that this is what I wanted to do, but I think that if this wasn't what I wanted to do, I would have still been thinking about something that was gonna be concrete. Like I would never have done, like, art history, or like French, or just something like that that you never know, or, either that you know

you're not gonna make a lot of money in it no matter what, or it's very unclear what
job you can get after it . . . I also think that, this is just a generalization, that people
who come from wealthier families feel less great pressure, because they know . . .
it's like social contacts will be able to get them jobs . . . And I think that for them,
the emphasis is on learning for learning's sake.

In these comments, she admitted that she would choose a major that was not her
real preference, but had secure job and earnings prospects, over majors without
specific job possibilities. She also pointed out that her wealthier peers might rely
on social contacts to get them jobs. That, along with their greater familiarity
with the market value of an elite degree, probably contributed to their likelihood of pursuing learning for its own sake, as she suggested.

Finally, six of the seven student-athletes chose majors not out of interest,
but either as a preparation for a future occupation or for even more practical
reasons. For example, one athlete chose his field of study primarily for its ease
and low reading demands.

[I chose American Studies] 'cause after my third semester here, I looked at my
transcript and I was like 60 percent done if I chose that major. So I just, it fell into
my lap, too, kind of, 'cause I was almost done with it, I guess, 'cause I don't like
taking classes that I know nothing about . . . And then I wasn't gonna be an English
major or a Spanish major . . . 'cause I don't like, pretty much in those majors you
have to read a lot, I mean, so, like, I started taking a lot of history classes, 'cause
you can get by in history without [reading], you really can, but most people say
you can't . . . I'm taking American Studies. I mean, if I take American Studies
classes I'm gonna know something about the material going into it, as opposed to
taking something that . . . So it was easier. I started choosing classes that I knew I
was gonna be all right at, and then it just kind of snowballed . . . And I mean, it's
generally considered a pretty easy major, too, as opposed to calculus or math or
whatever. I didn't want to do that.

In addition to the student-athletes and those from less privileged family
backgrounds, many of the students planning on pursuing graduate degrees also
chose their majors for career-related reasons. While postponing career-relevant
training until their graduate education allowed some students more freedom of
choice with their undergraduate fields, for other students the requirements of
their graduate programs dictated the selection of their college majors. Many
of the Yale students majoring in biology or chemistry chose those majors not

out of a love of science or an intellectual curiosity, but as preparation for medical school. As one student explained, even though she eventually intended to become a doctor, she would much rather have studied English in college, but, because of trying to get into medical school, chemistry became a more practical choice for her.

> Well, I was considering being an English teacher for a while, but that was in high school. But then it occurred to me that I'd really like to be a doctor, and I thought, "Well, I could just be an English major and then become a doctor," and then I thought, "Well, that's gonna be very difficult, finding summer internships, and that's gonna put me in a really bad position" . . . so I think I should pick a chemistry major just to be practical.

This pattern also held true for many of the students intending to go into law and business. As with the Southern students, these Yalies' choices were made instrumentally, to fulfill a particular career goal, in these cases one that would begin with admission to a professional graduate program.

> *How did you come to pick poli. sci.?*
> Well, I basically wanted to be a lawyer and that's what I want to do . . . I guess since I decided that I really would like to go to law school . . . I think the obvious choice, well, for me the obvious choice would be poli. sci., just 'cause there's not much else. I guess you could do history or something like that, but other than that, there aren't really too many majors that lead into that.

> Yeah, [the choice of] political science was, you know, 'cause I sort of knew that I wanted to be a lawyer, and, to be honest, there are like standard majors for lawyers, political science and history, particularly.

> *Why were you considering econ.?*
> Because I want to go to business school.

Each of these accounts showed how career goals involving a graduate degree motivated the choice of a major. Rather than the desire to study the fields of political science, history, or economics, the students' awareness of admissions requirements at law and business schools influenced their decisions. While planning for graduate school does allow students to put off their professional training, it can also constrict their choice of a major.

In contrast to the students described above, who chose their majors primarily for career-related reasons, a larger group of the Yale students, about 40 percent, chose their fields for a mixture of both intellectual and career considerations. All of these students embraced the liberal arts approach, yet at the same time wanted some assurance of future career prospects. They spoke in detail about their appreciation of their chosen academic discipline and, unlike most of the Southern students, clearly regarded majors as bodies of knowledge. At the same time, they also had an eye on the career opportunities associated with their fields. For example, a geology major explained that he chose that field because "I like studying things that happened and why things happen and how things happen." Later in the interview, he shifted to discussing the job prospects associated with geology, noting that he was attracted to the field because of the opportunities to work outside, instead of in an office environment.

In some cases, students balanced intellectual and practical concerns by choosing fields at least in part for the kinds of skills they would acquire. One student spoke about his interest in the field of political science, but also noted that he chose it because he "wanted to focus a lot more on analytic skills." Other students chose to double major, selecting one major to satisfy their practical proclivities and a second major strictly because of their intellectual interest in the field. While these students were similar to the Southern students in their concern for how their education would prepare them for a career, they differed in that the Southern students preferred explicit career links, whereas the Yale students were satisfied with an idea of the general area or broad direction of their future work.

Whether students tried to accommodate both intellectual and career interests or chose majors primarily for career reasons, all told, most of the Yale students (about 75%) took career considerations into account to some degree. Only about 25 percent chose majors based solely on their intellectual interests, with seemingly little or no regard for their connections to future careers. These students tended to come from the most affluent backgrounds, and more women than men fit this profile (eight women versus four men). The following section explores the gender divisions in the choice of a major at Yale, and explains why women were more likely than men to embody the liberal arts ideal of spending their undergraduate years in the pursuit of knowledge for its own sake, rather than in career preparation.

Gender Divisions at Yale

Gender divisions run just as strongly across liberal arts fields as they do across vocational fields. In the humanities at Yale, men tend to study philosophy and history, while women enter English, religion, area studies, and the visual and performing arts. In the social sciences, women opt for sociology, anthropology, and psychology, while men select economics and political science. In the sciences, women prefer biology, while men gravitate toward the physical sciences, math, computer science, and engineering.* These gender divides are quite sharp. For example, men earn almost 80 percent of the degrees in economics at Yale and over 70 percent of the philosophy, math, and computer science degrees. Conversely, women earn over 70 percent of the sociology, psychology, and anthropology degrees. Gendered choices at Southern were driven to some extent by a gendered occupational structure and the asymmetric nature of gender change. These influences were less predominant at Yale, in part because the Yale students were less likely to as directly link their majors to their future occupations, and in part because most of the occupations under consideration by these students were more gender-integrated than those contemplated by the Southern students. Women have successfully entered many previously male-dominated professions, such as law and medicine. Indeed, women have now nearly reached parity in graduate degrees earned in the fields of law, medicine, and business, as well as doctoral degrees in a wide range of fields (Snyder 2007). What, then, explains the difference in choice? The men and women I interviewed at Yale differed in the ways that they imagined their future family roles. The men also carried more concern for status than the women. Further, bodies of knowledge themselves have become gendered, and their associations with masculinity and femininity helped shape the students' choices.

While the men and the women overlapped significantly in their substantive interests, the women were much more likely than the men to choose majors on the basis of these interests, with little regard for the future career opportunities associated with their fields. In response to being asked to tell the whole story of how they chose their majors, the narratives of the women, in particular the most privileged women, focused almost exclusively on their likes and interests. Com-

---

* These statements are based on bachelor's degrees in all fields conferred by Yale University, from data available through the Integrated Postsecondary Education Data System (IPEDS), http://nces.ed.gov/ipeds/datacenter/.

ments taken from four women's explanations of their choice of a field illustrate this approach.

I was fascinated by the subject.

I really enjoyed the courses in that field.

I loved the reading.

I decided that I really liked interdisciplinary things.

The language used by these women conveyed a keen interest, or even a passion, for their fields of study and an enjoyment of the courses, readings or labs, and assignments. One woman recounted how her biology adviser "swept her off her feet" and described how "the information is just fascinating to me." Another woman spoke about how "literature was the first thing I was really drawn to . . . just because I had sort of an immediate response to it." One noted that "I always really loved science," and another described finding her "niche."

When asked about their futures, many of these women either had no concrete career plans or only vague and indefinite ideas about their future work (with the exception of most of the first-generation women and those who intended to be doctors or who had been pursuing a particular avenue for some time, such as filmmaking). For example, a philosophy major described her future work in these terms:

All I kind of think of is that it would be some combination of being with kids somehow, and probably painting. So maybe painting kids . . . No, I would rather *do* something with kids than paint them, but it would involve painting somehow, and kids, and philosophy somehow, if that were possible.

Another woman, a biology major, said:

I'd like to be either traveling somewhere and studying things with some population of animals somewhere or somehow being connected, affiliated, with a zoo.

A third woman was even more general:

What I hope is that whatever I'm doing is sort of something where I get to learn a lot of new things, where there's a high rate of turnover in what my tasks or my projects are. I hope to meet a lot of people. I just like to engage people somehow, and I like to read a lot of stuff, and I like to write a lot, so I hope to do those things in terms of like a career.

What is notable in these mostly hazy descriptions of future work is that these women's ideas about their careers were built on a natural continuation of their likes and intellectual interests, rather than on any practical or financial concerns. Concerns about salaries were rarely a factor, much less a priority, in their decisions. When asked, about two-thirds of them responded that considerations of salary were not important at all.

> If I was worried about salary, I wouldn't be going into this field. I mean, it is important, I would like to survive, but to me it's just a more fundamental desire to do it [biology].

> Not important at all, really. As long as I have enough money to pay my rent and keep my car running and be able to buy food and, hopefully, eventually, I'll have enough money so that I won't have to be worried about which kind of bread I'm buying, and then I'll be pretty happy.

Nearly all of the women emphasized that what was important was the kind of work they would be doing, not the salary. Of the women who did express concerns about their salaries, these were voiced in terms of wanting to "live comfortably" or "not having to worry about money."

When asked about family plans, almost all of the women wanted to have a family at some point, and most planned on taking a few years off to raise their children. Remarkably, very few of the women conveyed any concern about having the financial stability to do this or indicated that the decision to take time off would depend on their family's resources at that time. Rather, the majority of the women visualized working for self-fulfillment, not economic necessity, with the option of stopping work for a period of years to raise children. These imagined plans suggested the assumption of a financially successful partner, prepared to support the woman and her future children. Only a few of the women spoke about not wanting to rely on a partner or about the importance of having enough money to financially take care of future children.

In sum, many of the Yale women, particularly those from higher-SES backgrounds, came to college to pursue their intellectual interests and passions and, for the most part, chose majors on that basis. When they envisioned future careers, they imagined doing what they most enjoyed. Even the women going into science entered it out of a real love for the field and a deep attraction to scientific knowledge. By and large, these women showed little concern for either future salaries or their specific occupations, assuming that they would follow their passions into the labor market. In terms of family, while most of the women intended to have children and take time off to raise them, they expressed few worries about the economic feasibility of this arrangement, seemingly taking for granted a future in which there would be enough money to support them during this time.

These women's male counterparts matched them in regard to their intellectual engagement and the enthusiasm and detail with which they described their favorite courses and important learning experiences. However, a different picture emerged when the Yale men recounted how they made decisions regarding their majors. While they overlapped with the women in their intellectual interests in their fields of study, the men tended to be pulled away from these interests by two concerns that were not shared by the women. The first involved considerations of status, and the second, concerns about making enough money to reproduce the affluent lifestyle they experienced in their childhoods.

The men's interest in status had two dimensions: status within the university in terms of professors and departments, and the status of their future line of work.* The interviews with the men were sprinkled with references to issues of status and prestige, relating to several different aspects of their education. When giving reasons for selecting the university, for example, they would often mention its reputation, far more so than the women. They were also quite cognizant of the fame of their professors, frequently remarking on their public achievements and renown. For example, one student gave this description of his history professor: "He's famous. He just wrote this essay for *Time* this week . . . he just teaches very well and he's famous." Beyond specific professors, the men tended to show an awareness of which academic departments had good reputations and which did not.

The status of academic departments was often cited as a factor influencing the men's choice of a major, but not the women's. In some cases, it made the students more likely to consider a particular major. One student entertained the idea of majoring in English because of the reputation of the department. "English I also considered, I think in part because of the department. It's just so well renowned [and] that definitely attracted me." More often, however, the standing of a department discouraged male students. Two different students decided against a major in philosophy because of the low stature of the department.

---

* Status concerns surfaced only once in my interviews with women, when a Japanese-American woman explained to me that even though she wanted to be a psychologist, she would have to become a psychiatrist, because psychologists were still not respected in Japan, where she wanted to work.

It seemed silly to go through the effort of doing it [majoring in philosophy] if people would always look down on the degree afterwards.

I love philosophy, and I [thought] philosophy would be a great major, but it's such a bad department, [and] I need a major that's impressive. I've still got to keep up with the expectation. And so poli. sci. seemed like a very nice go-between, because there's a lot of respect for being a politician. Like, if you have aspirations for being like a president or an ambassador, then that's the right thing to be in.

For the latter student, the status of the academic department clearly influenced his choice, but it was also linked to a larger set of status issues related to his future work. While many of the men, like the women, were unsure of the specifics of their careers, the men's descriptions were marked by wanting to be in positions of power and wanting to make an impact, such as the above student's aspiration to be either president or an ambassador. As one student remarked to me, "I now study Chinese because I know it will help me in the business world and in the political world, and because it's going to be such an influential, great power, eventually."

Thus the men in this study, in contrast to the women, were mindful of status issues, and their perceptions of the status of an academic department could positively or negatively influence their choice to enter that field. This concern for status was sometimes enough to pull the Yale men away from the fields in which they were most interested. In the case of the student above, his need for an impressive major trumped his love for philosophy in his final decision. As another, and more extreme example, one student described at length his deep interest and love for architecture ever since he was a small child. However, after a summer internship at an architectural firm, he realized he would not be able to make the kind of money he had anticipated in that field, so he switched to economics.

I'm a student that's not actually very interested in my subject matter, which is economics . . . Economics was chosen because it was the safest major, in that it gives me a sense of the business world, it teaches me how things work.

Later in the interview, when I asked him about his future work, he replied that he wasn't sure what he'd be doing, but knew he would be quite successful.

As far as ten years, well, I'd like to see myself financially sound, and able to take exotic trips. I see myself [as] very successful, regardless of where I am, and I see myself in a position of leadership . . . I really, I always see myself as making a huge impact somehow on this planet.

While there was continuity for most of the women between their interests, their choice of a field, and their plans for their future work, for the men the quest for status and power often created breaks, or disjunctures, between their intellectual interests, their decisions about a major, and their plans for the future. These breaks occurred in two different ways. First, there were the men who simply did not consider the possibility of majoring in their favorite areas. These men would describe in great detail their intellectual interests, but they still selected a major in an unrelated field, such as the two students who "loved" philosophy and architecture but settled on political science and economics, respectively.

Second, some of the men did select majors based solely on their interests, but they then turned away from those interests when considering future careers. For example, one student considered several majors—English, art history, and biology—before settling on history. He spoke extensively of his love for history, the wonderful seminars he had, and the interesting reading he'd done. His major complaint about his university education was that he hadn't gotten to read enough Shakespeare, Faulkner, and Tolstoy. Yet after describing these interests with great enthusiasm, he then explained his plan to enter law school following graduation. A few of the men divulged the conflicts brought about by these decisions. One economics major had always loved music and had performed extensively with singing groups, even touring with them, yet he never considered majoring in music. During the interview, he reflected on this decision.

> Who's to say that my life wouldn't have changed a lot had I just recognized the fact that music was something I was good at, I enjoy doing? Why not take classes in music? It never occurred to me.

In addition to weighing the prospects of power and status, the men were constrained in their choices by potential future incomes. Whereas most of the women gave little thought to income, the men nearly always answered the interview question about the importance of income in two parts: income level was not important at that point, while they were single, but it would be important in the future, after they got married and had a family, when they would want to live in the suburbs, take their families on ski vacations, and send their children to private schools. A full two-thirds of the men gave this response, showing the expectation that they would be supporting a family in the future and the desire to support their family in the manner to which they'd become accustomed.

> I don't think about money now, to be honest with you. But I think if I have a family, and I want to take them skiing, and I want them to have a nice life . . . I want them to be able to do some of the things that I did. You need money to be able to do that. If you want to show them some sort of cultural experience, you need money. That's important. So, while I'm single and independent, I don't think it's much of an issue, but when you have a relationship and a family, it's a much different incentive.

Several of the men commented specifically on the costs of education for their future children. Many intended to send their children to private high schools and colleges without loans, a remarkable expectation given the heavy tuition costs of such institutions. The men consistently noted that money was not important in their own lives, but would become important once they had a family.

> And if I have to think about kids way down the line, then it will be even more difficult, because then I'm providing not just for myself, but for them, and I'm gonna want to make sure that they can get as much as I did out of their education, out of their life. So then the standards would increase. But that's not gonna happen for a while, so I don't have to think about money immediately.

> I mean, I figure that when I'm young, it's less important that I make money and it's more important that I have fun and enjoy myself . . . But on the other hand, once I get older, I'll want to have enough money to send my kids to private school and to put them through college without any debts or anything.

The desire to support a future family at such a high level clearly influenced their evaluation of career prospects. The following student described discarding his preference for a government job and searching for alternatives that would allow him to take care of his future children's education without making major sacrifices. His narrative illustrated how his own childhood experiences set the expectations for his role as a father, attaining an income level sufficient to provide for private schooling for his own children.

> I've grown up with a pretty decent life. Like, my dad is a very successful corporate lawyer. He doesn't pull in bazillions, but he pulls in enough that all of our needs are taken care of and that we don't have to make major sacrifices for me to go to school . . . I went to public school through sixth grade, but after that I went to a private

school. And my parents are able to handle that and law school and it's pretty much all okay. That's something that I'd like to be able to provide for a kid. And that's my most major consideration in terms of salary. And I'm pretty aware that most positions in government would not really afford that sort of thing, and because of that I'm now looking at two major alternatives . . . And, in terms of my own lifestyle, I really don't care that much as long I could live in a decently safe part of the world and have enough money to make myself pasta or something. It's pretty much my child or children's education that would concern me the most.

The onus the Yale men felt to support their families at such a high level complicated their career considerations. Whereas the women could follow their passions, the men faced the difficulty of finding meaningful *and* highly profitable work. One man described this as the "trick" of finding "something you love where you make a lot of money." Many clearly found this quandary frustrating.

I'm sure there are things that I could do that would be both financially and intellectually rewarding, but I don't know what they are. If I knew that, I'd have a much easier time of it.

Part of my problem is that, the family that I grew up in, I've been kind of a little bit spoiled. I went to boarding school, and my life has never been that hard, but I kind of have been used to living at a certain standard and you don't want to, or at least I don't really want to abandon that. Which definitely pushes me towards something that I can make money doing. But at the same time, I don't really find a lot of that work kind of gratifying or satisfying. So, I'm really thinking a lot about what it is that I, you know . . . Everyone's thinking about making that decision, you know.

Only two of the men said that money was not a priority, and another three said that it wasn't a concern, but they then said that that was because the kinds of jobs they were applying for were high-paying jobs anyway. Only one of the men mentioned the possibility that his wife might earn as much or more than he did and that, if she did, it would free him to pursue other career options.

In the end, it was the elite Yale women who most lived up to the liberal arts ideal. While the women chose fields and then imagined future careers based on their intellectual interests, many of the men were pulled away from pursuing their interests because their criteria for selecting a major included concerns about status. In addition, they expected to eventually assume economic responsibility for their future families, meaning that they were not at liberty to pursue careers in painting and philosophy, but instead had to begin to move toward more assuredly lucrative endeavors. These dynamics were most pronounced among the most privileged students. Among the first-generation students at Yale, both the men and the women had a more applied focus. At Southern, the women also intended to take time off to raise their children, yet their male counterparts did not describe the kinds of pressures experienced by the Yale men. This is probably because their expectations for taking care of their families differed. The Southern men most often mentioned owning a home and a car as their measures of success, while the Yale men required a great deal more.

The Value of Knowledge at Yale

In comparison with the Southern students, the Yale students evaluated knowledge less on the basis of its usefulness and more for its intrinsic qualities. Instead of ranking courses by how readily the content could be applied, they ranked the caliber of the knowledge. The Yale students also differed from the Southern students in that they classified not just courses and departments, but entire academic disciplines. The Yalies deemed some forms of knowledge as more valuable than others, though they varied both in the standards they employed to appraise the quality of knowledge and their preferences for certain forms of knowledge. Further, their evaluations of knowledge carried an important gendered component. An additional reason for the gender disparity in majors at Yale came from the association of bodies of knowledge with masculinity and femininity. Just as at Southern, where the students chose majors within a gendered occupational structure, at Yale the students made choices within a gendered knowledge structure.

Academic fields embody qualities closely linked to ideas of masculinity and femininity (Harding 1986; Keller 1995; Noble 1992; Thomas 1990). In general, there is a strong association between masculinity and objectivity, and femininity and subjectivity. For example, Keller (1995) describes the mythology "that casts objectivity, reason, and mind as male, and subjectivity, feeling, and nature as female" (p. 7). Scholars in this area maintain that science has evolved around a particular ideal of masculinity and that it continues to be associated with the concepts of masculinity, objectivity, hardness, difficulty, and values (Keller 1995; Noble 1992; Thomas 1990). This view has also been articulated by Harding (1986), who writes about the scientific norms of detachment, distance, and rationality corresponding to those of a masculine culture. Thomas (1990) suggests that the high status accorded to science is dependent on its association with masculinity and with the related values of objectivity and impersonality. The arts, on the other hand, are linked to effeminacy, softness, easiness, and lack of worth. English, for example, is associated with qualities generally regarded as feminine, such as emotional response and subjectivity. The traditional women's fields have the lowest status. Similarly, Bourdieu (2001) states that disciplines can be arrayed between "soft" and "hard," representing gendered divisions. Even within fields, gender distinctions are still manifest; women often enter the soft as opposed to the hard sciences. Likewise, in literary criticism, epics are regarded as masculine, in contrast to the lyric, which is seen as ornamental and feminine. Thus branches of knowledge themselves become associated with heterosexual ideals of masculinity and femininity.

Thomas (1990) finds that students choose which subjects to study on the basis of the perceived qualities of the fields, and that views on the arts and sciences become shaped by notions of masculinity and femininity. Students think of disciplines in a hierarchy, which weighs the difficulty and usefulness of a field in determining its importance. While many men do go into English, she finds that students perceive those who major in English as "feminized men." Students make an identification with their field of study. Men gravitate toward physics in part for its elevated status as a body of knowledge and as a career track, which affirms one's own sense of masculinity. Physics students, she found, looked down on students in English because the latter field is associated with pleasure, laziness, and subjectivity. For women, entering physics was problematic, partly because physics is bound up with notions of masculine success; success in physics depended on a negation of femininity (see also Ong 2005).

These theories help explain why even in the realm of academic disciplines, we see the same asymmetrical change found in occupations. The gender divisions of fields of study shift over time largely because women enter previously male-dominated fields, rather than because men enter previously female-dominated ones (England and Li 2006). Further, when enough women enter a male-dominated field, it becomes devalued by the high proportion of women in it, causing men to leave. While not minimizing the obstacles facing women who enter male-dominated fields of study, these findings suggest that the psychic costs to one's sense of gender-appropriate identity are higher for men entering female-dominated fields than the converse. Men may find it stigmatizing to enter fields associated with women.

Both the men and the women at Yale drew distinctions between different kinds of knowledge. The women, however, more frequently explained why a certain field appealed to them on the basis of its qualities of knowledge. The men, on the other hand, were more likely both to make distinctions and to draw on evaluations of knowledge as reasons why they rejected certain fields of study. In several cases, the men dismissed female-dominated fields such as English and anthropology on this basis. Their accounts are reminiscent of the students in Thomas's (1990) study. In each case, the men discarded these fields because of a perceived subjectivity and lack of rigor.

For both the men and the women, one of the characteristics commonly taken as an indicator of the value of a particular kind of knowledge was rigor. The students judged courses and fields alike on their degree of rigor or softness.

> I guess the reason ultimately that I decided to major in [philosophy] was because I felt like that's where I really was working at Yale, and it was a whole different level of reading and thinking and writing for me than other classes I was in. And I felt like it was really rigorous. I still feel that way, so that's probably both why I chose it and the thing I like best about it.

> I would shop classes in anthropology, and they just struck me as being so boring, and just not as, I guess, intellectually rigorous, I would say. See, what always appealed to me about those, well, especially about something like anthropology, would be the active fieldwork aspect. But I always, whenever I would go to classes and see the mental side of it, I felt it was somewhat lacking.

In these two passages, the students showed how their evaluations of the demands of knowledge in a field of study influenced their choice to major in that field. In the first quote, a woman chose philosophy for this reason, and in the second, a male student decided against anthropology, in spite of his interest in fieldwork, because he found the intellectual side of the field to be wanting.

One component of rigor was objectivity. Some of the students disparaged fields they thought were too subjective, and these distinctions often served to separate scientific fields from the humanities. Facts, or the concrete aspects of a field, indicated that discipline's degree of objectivity. One male student explained why he rejected English, a predominantly female field, and instead chose political science, in part because of its more scientific nature.

> I was really interested in English, but I don't like the subjectiveness of it . . . I walked into my first English class freshman year, and we were analyzing a poem, and some kid in the room just decided to go off on maybe two or three words in the poem,

and he just talked about it for ten minutes. Everybody was kind of nodding their heads, saying "Yes, yes," and I was just thinking "No" . . . So it was on the basis of that that I wanted something more concrete, as close to a science as possible.

A second criterion the students employed in ranking knowledge was the fundamental nature of a discipline. The Yalies valued fields that they perceived to be closer to essential truths. This criterion was most often applied to scientific disciplines, where the students made claims about which was the most constitutional of all the science fields. A woman going into biology explained her decision on the basis of the fundamental quality of the knowledge in her field.

Biology just seemed to me like the fundamental, even though all science, different sciences, will argue, "Well, everything comes down to physics" and "Everything comes down to chemistry" or whatever, and they're probably right. But to me, like, biology was just the most interesting, the most fundamental thing, like, to me.

The students used this criterion to rank both scientific and nonscientific fields. The following student saw knowledge existing in tiers, with the most essential knowledge, scientific, on the first tier. He placed disciplines such as sociology and literature on the second tier, and philosophy on the third tier. He claimed that one tier was not better than another, yet he deemed the first tier to hold more essential knowledge.

I see society and, like, intellectual culture kind of on tiers. And I'm not saying that one's better than the other, but I see that there's like basic, like what we are . . . So you can study what we are, or you can study who we are, or we can study the people who study who we are . . . I mean, basically I think . . . like intellectual spheres are built around studying, like, humans, either what we've done or what we are. And I always just thought it was more interesting to study what we are, because on a level, to me that's where you're getting, science to me is kind of my truth, in a way. It's sort of like a religion to me. And so I feel like you're studying fact, and then you're studying what makes us up, and then once you get to that level, then the people who do things, they write, they interact with each other, that's sociology, that's literature, that's studying them, and that's like the second tier. Then there's like, kind of, philosophy, that studies those people. So I always felt, not that there's anything better at any level, but I always wanted to get to just what was the essence of it.

A broader, but perhaps more commonly used gauge to evaluate academic disciplines was that of the field's explanatory value, or ability to arrive at the truth.

The students sometimes criticized fields for their inability to explain behavior, for example. One student chose to major in economics but regretted the decision, in part because of his disappointment about the quality of knowledge in that field.

> One of the biggest things in econ. is to derive an indifference curve . . . That's the curve of happiness, basically. That's what it turns out to be. And you actually plot this out. And it's just the fact that you can actually derive something like that, showing somebody's happiness between two different things, you know, whether they would like to have X or Y, showing what their preferences would be if they could have different levels of X and Y. It was something that was just way too . . . made up, contrived to fit a theory that didn't even really exist, or a theory that could never really happen. On the basis of those little kinds of idiosyncrasies, that really just kind of set me off from it.

Another student weighed in on what he perceived as the weakness in the field of psychology: its application of a scientific approach without gaining much payoff.

> I think that psychology as a discipline, or at least how it's taught here, is kind of bogus, just because it shrouds itself in these scientific elements, like, you know, its obsession with statistics. And obviously statistics is how things are measured in almost all the social sciences. But psychology, especially because it overlaps into prescribing medicine when it's psychiatry, had some sort of questionable blurring, to me, of the lines. So I was definitely turned off by psychology as a field. Also . . . maybe one or two things I probably read influenced, or some book in freshman year, but mainly stating very, very, very obvious things with its own particular terminology.

While in some cases this kind of evaluation appeared to follow the divide between the scientific and the humanities fields, other students were more concerned about whether the aims of a particular field were achievable. One student saw political science as a weaker field than history, because the latter, though less ambitious, was more likely to realize its ambitions.

> It always seemed to me a little bit that poli. sci. was the evil twin of history, in the sense that, and this is kind of a real biased generalization that I'm not gonna support very well, but it's just that poli. sci. is . . . the idea that you can make a science out of complex human interactions and make models is very ambitious. And that's why it's very attractive, but I would use the word seductive as opposed to attractive

because, if you compare it to history, history is much less ambitious and I think it's far more realizable. Like, you can actually achieve what you're trying to, what you set out to achieve, as opposed to poli. sci., where that whole idea of politics as a science is, in itself, very suspect in my mind.

Alternatively, critiques were leveled at the theoretical development of a field.

I think some of the international relations theories are wrong. I mean . . . I just think that a lot of the major theories that exist in poli. sci., in international relations, are just really, really inadequate, and they're just really not, for a major that is supposed to be analytical, at least, I mean, maybe not like math, but close to that, at least, it really, some of those theories really lack in any common sense or in true analytical qualities. So, I mean, that's just one thing that, it's a little pet peeve that I have.

Of course, not all of the Yale students concerned themselves with evaluating the quality of knowledge across academic disciplines. Nonetheless, it is true that the Yale students studied in an environment where assessments of knowledge by their peers were commonplace. They also felt comfortable evaluating and weighing different academic programs. Whereas the criticisms of the Southern students were limited to how up-to-date the curriculum was, the Yale students posed a broader critique of the very construction of the curriculum itself, including the analytical and substantive biases of various departments.

The whole school of deconstruction is still like lingering over the lit. department and parts of the English department, and their approach to reading literature here is very, very cultural context. So my big thing, Shakespeare, if I read Shakespeare and I talk about it, I want to say, "Why is this so great?" . . . Their perspective is almost to the extreme of "How can we show that he can't escape being an Elizabethan man of this educational background, of this regional geography of England?," which you can show if you dig around, but I don't know why you want to show it.

[The] music [department] is very stuffy and old fashioned . . . The music department only studies Western music. They have like *a* jazz class. That's pretty ridiculous, because jazz is pretty much across the country an established, okay thing to study in academics. It has its own rules, well, a little fuzzier than, like, nineteenth-century German music, but definitely has its own rules. It definitely is a fairly critically acclaimed style of music. There's one jazz class, and god forbid there be like a world music class or a non-Western music class or a popular music class of the twentieth century or any century. There's none of that. I took one class on Gershwin and

Porter, which is the music department letting down their hair. I think, compared to most schools, that's not terribly far to let your hair down. So that's dumb, and it's very snobby, and it's kind of like if you don't write pretty good imitations of Bach inventions, you get low grades, and they're like "You're not gonna make it."

I wanted an education in aesthetics that was geared towards the creating of things as opposed to the deconstructing of things, which I did not find present here . . . I mean, the undergraduate art department is extremely backwards in a certain way . . . It seems to me that having a course in Master Drawing that is constructed the way courses are constructed here is the equivalent of having a course in macramé.

These examples show the extent to which the Yale students felt comfortable, or entitled, to critique the programs of study put together by Yale's faculty.

Overall, then, while the Southern students primarily rated knowledge for its usefulness, the Yale students evaluated knowledge for its intrinsic qualities. These differences, far from being arbitrary, reflected the purposes for which the students acquired knowledge. For the Southern students, the information they learned was important for the ways in which they would be able to apply it in their work. It was valued for its role in increasing their chances of success in obtaining a job and performing well in it. For the Yale students, the quality of knowledge was important not because of how it fit into their careers, but in terms of what it contributed to themselves, in how it became an attribute of the self. This logic was apparent in the description one Yale student gave for moving from an engineering major to religious studies.

I didn't feel that I got as much out of it [engineering], out of the study in itself. I felt that I would be a wonderfully practical, competent person after it, but I just didn't feel that the curriculum would make me into the type of person that I wanted to be eventually.

She explicitly rejected engineering because it would make her practical and competent, but it would not make her into the type of person she wanted to be. Given the critiques of engineering education, it may be that choosing engineering also involved a choice concerning her femininity (Ong 2005). Two additional examples revealed the same logic at work.

Art history I loved. It was just too flaky, though. It was so much fun, but I couldn't face myself in the mirror. I had friends who were art history majors, and I was just like "No, I need something more challenging than that."

I had a friend Catherine . . . And she said to me one day . . . you know, we were
sitting talking about some Hegel or something like that, she said, "You don't seem
like an anthro. major, you seem like a lit. major or a philosophy major." And I
thought about it and I thought maybe she was right. But it was also partially a
social choice, but, um, in that what intellectual identity I wanted at the time.

In the first quote, the student described not being able to face himself in the
mirror, an image suggesting that studying art history would change the way he
saw himself. Somehow, by becoming a person who studied art history, the very
nature of the discipline would become intrinsically associated with him. Art
history, at Yale and across the country, is a heavily female-dominated field. Men
make up only 14 percent of all art history majors (Snyder 2007). This student
described it as "flakey" and not challenging enough, similar to characterizations
the students in Thomas's (1990) study made of English. In the second quote,
the student referred to choosing his intellectual identity in declaring a major.
His friend, in her comment that he did not seem like an anthropology major,
pointed to an incongruity between that discipline and his intellectual identity.
For these students, their chosen field of study formed part of their intellectual
identity—a part of who they were, not just what they could do.

•   •   •

The differences between the Southern and the Yale students in choosing majors
and evaluating knowledge demonstrated different kinds of logic at work. The
Southern students viewed college primarily as career preparation: the project of
going to college involved selecting a career and acquiring the necessary training in that area. Far from the lofty liberal arts ideal of learning for the sake of
learning, most of the Yale students also had their eye on how their education
would prepare them for a chosen career. Altogether, about 75 percent of the
Yale students chose majors for a blend of career and intellectual considerations.
For about a third of the Yale students, career considerations dominated their
choices, much as they did for most of the Southern students. Ironically, majoring in the liberal arts was part of a calculated strategy of getting ahead for some
of these students. In addition, while both the Yale and the Southern students
shared a concern for what kinds of work their education would lead to, they
differed in that the Southern students preferred training that was linked to a
well-defined job, while the Yale students were comfortable having only a general
idea of their future work. The Yale students also took a longer view regarding the establishment of their careers, because most of these students expected

to obtain a graduate degree. Of all the students in my study, the Yale women most closely fit the liberal arts archetype. They were guided primarily by their intellectual interests and allowed these evolving interests to predict their future occupations. In the end, the Southern and the Yale students were more similar than different in choosing majors in anticipation of their future careers. The greater division between the two sets of students lay in their appreciation of learning and their use of knowledge. Even when choosing majors for career-related reasons, the Yale students generally enjoyed learning and appreciated their courses, rather than recounting the drudgery of taking classes, as so many of the Southern students did.

Tying in with the logic of choosing majors, because the Southern students went to college primarily to obtain jobs, their priorities rested on acquiring knowledge that would be useful for those jobs. The Yale students had a more complex relationship with knowledge; it became incorporated into their own identities. For that reason, the qualities of particular kinds of knowledge held much more salience for the Yale students. In fact, both groups of students appreciated *useful* knowledge, but they intended to employ it in disparate ways. The Yale students used learning as a means to build their own identities, whereas the Southern students used it for its exchange value in the labor market. These differences in the acquisition of knowledge may be linked to how graduates are assessed on the labor market. The Southern students would perhaps get jobs based on what they know and what they can do, whereas the Yalies would be awarded jobs for who they are, in other words, for being a certain kind of person, rather than for having a certain set of skills. In these ways, the dichotomy between the preprofessional and the liberal arts fields is more complicated than it first appears. In some senses, the liberal arts curriculum can be regarded as a vocational course of study for the middle and upper classes (Rose 2008).

There is evidence that class-based patterns of choosing majors hold true even within institutions. The first-generation students and those from less affluent backgrounds attending Yale more closely resembled the Southern students in employing a practical approach to college and worrying about having marketable skills. The first-generation students at Southern were more likely to choose an applied over an arts and sciences field than their peers at either institution who came from better-educated families. There are also numerous ways in which the likelihood of adopting a practical versus a liberal arts approach to college can be traced to the privileges or disadvantages of social background.

For starters, the academic preparation of many of the Southern students played a role in the kinds of fields they were willing to consider. Not having the benefit of the superior secondary schooling of most of the Yale students, many of the Southern students did not have the appropriate academic preparation to take on some of the more demanding fields of study. Second, the Southern students did not have the luxury that the Yalies did of assuming that they could follow up their undergraduate degrees with several more years of graduate training. When the Southern students did consider graduate programs, they mostly imagined two-year master's programs. Third, the institutions themselves played a role. As some of the Yale students pointed out, the prestige of a Yale degree meant that their chosen field of study would be of less importance in obtaining a good job. The Yale students knew that their prospects were largely assured by that university's name on their diplomas. The Southern students realized that their future employers would be evaluating their educational credentials less on the name of their university and more on the nature of their studies. In addition, many of the Yale students knew they could rely on an extensive and powerful family network in their job searches. For these reasons, the Yale students were more insulated than the Southern ones from having to acquire vocational training during their college years. The Southern students operated under a much more limiting set of constraints. Their choices were confined by the extent of their academic preparation, their lower aspirations for graduate education, their restricted knowledge of possible occupations, and the prestige of the institution from which they would graduate. These realities meant that only a particularly courageous or inspired student would pursue a liberal arts path through college.

In addition to the economic and social resources noted above, the cultural capital the Yale students inherited through their families facilitated their academic mastery of liberal arts fields, in particular those requiring abstract and theoretical thinking (Bourdieu and Passeron 1977, 1979). Their taste for this kind of knowledge was reinforced through the curriculum at their private, college-prep high schools, which corresponded to that of elite universities. Studying liberal arts fields at the university level then built up these students' cultural capital, both in the form of greater intellectual knowledge and in the degree itself. Just as liberal arts fields lend status to an institution, they also "ennoble" those who study them, by their strong association with higher levels of intelligence (Lewis 1993; Rose 2008).

In Bourdieu's (1984) view, the "distance from necessity" also helps explain class-based patterns in the choice of a major. Those with few economic or cultural resources must direct a large part of their energies toward the practicalities of making a living. The dominant class's freedom from material constraints allows it to develop tastes for the impractical, such as gourmet food and abstract art. This distance from necessity aligns with fields of study, providing privileged groups with the freedom to pursue abstractions having little practical application, such as theoretical knowledge. Put another way, the most privileged have the luxury of choosing liberal arts fields, whereas the least privileged face the necessity of studying something more practical. These varying tastes in knowledge become imbued with cultural distinctions, as such tastes appear to originate from different degrees of natural intellectual aptitude. The choice of a liberal arts field comes to signify the chooser's greater inherent intelligence or broadmindedness, effectively disguising the accumulation of advantages that made this choice possible.

The extent to which this translates into greater success in the labor market has not yet been adequately investigated. A liberal arts degree is certainly no guarantee of an immediate and high-paying job, as satirized by the old joke about what the liberal arts graduate says to the business major ("Do you want fries with that, sir?"). Even Yale graduates can attest to the difficulties of finding a good job after graduation (Olson 2003). Yet research also shows that many firms welcome those with liberal arts degrees and that these individuals are just as likely to advance up the corporate ladder as those with degrees in engineering and business (Useem 1989). There is also considerable evidence that degrees from elite institutions result in higher long-term earnings and entry into positions of power, as opposed to degrees earned from less selective institutions (Bowen and Bok 1998; Kingston and Smart 1990; Useem and Karabel 1990).*

---

* Estimating the returns associated with degrees from elite institutions is complex, in that students attending elite institutions are generally more talented and more academically qualified than their peers in less selective institutions. Studies can control for academic variables, such as high school grade point averages and SAT scores. However, there are other variables that are more difficult to measure, but that may make a student more likely either to apply to an elite institution or to be accepted at one; such qualities may lead to higher rewards in the labor market, independent of the selectivity of the institution the student attends. In this way, studies may confound the qualities of a graduate with the benefits bestowed by an elite degree. The matter is further complicated because the rates of entry into graduate programs and the types of graduate programs vary, both by the students' characteristics and by the characteristics of the undergraduate institutions they attend. Further, most studies have done a poor job of adequately controlling for major fields of study, often aggregating fields into just a few broad categories. Because less selective institutions will be more likely to offer fields with relatively high, early labor market returns, such as computer science and engineering, it is possible that studies overstate the long-term

Because elite institutions offer majors primarily in the liberal arts, this suggests that some of the effects discussed above may be due to these fields of study. On the other hand, it is possible that the value of a liberal arts degree works best when coupled with a prestigious institution; liberal arts degrees awarded by less selective institutions may not confer the same ennobling status. Answering the question about the precise payoff of a liberal arts degree is quite difficult, because of the problem of disentangling the effect of the institution from that of a particular field of study. Further, liberal arts majors are more likely than students from preprofessional fields to continue their education with one or more graduate degrees (Goyette and Mullen 2006), complicating comparisons between the two groups. It may also be the case that the signaling effect of a liberal arts degree works best for those individuals who already have high levels of inherited cultural capital.

In addition, the concept of distance from necessity did not entirely fit the privileged men at Yale, who bore the considerable pressure of achieving the same earning power as their fathers. While they might share a taste for abstract and theoretical knowledge, their choice of a liberal arts field did not stem from the freedom from material constraints posited by Bourdieu (1984), but rather was based on the necessity of tracking toward a lucrative career. Indeed, while the Southern men and women may have felt with more immediacy the need to prepare for a job, the Yale men surely felt with more intensity the weight of preparing for financial success.

Turning to gender, in some respects the findings presented here confirm earlier studies showing that men gravitate toward fields with higher prestige and better economic payoffs (M. Berger 1988; Davies and Guppy 1997; Hearn and Olzak 1981). However, my findings also provide a corrective to the simple socialization explanations that predominate in this area of research. Typically, the research on gender and majors either implicitly or explicitly attributes differences in the choice of a field to early childhood socialization. Socialization models conceive of gender primarily as an individual attribute, rather than as an institutionalized system of social practices (Ferree, Lorber, and Hess 1999). These models see men's and women's preferences essentially as the result of socialization without taking structural influences into account. Moving be-

---

earnings of graduates from less selective institutions by not including more detailed controls for majors. Because of these factors, scholars come to conflicting conclusions and continue to debate the true payoff to earning a degree from an elite institution. See Gerber and Cheung (2008) for a critical review.

yond this limited framework in order to demonstrate the powerful effects of institutionalized gender norms on students' preferences for different occupations, Correll (2001, 2004) shows how cultural conceptions of gender work to constrain the early career-relevant choices of men and women. Cultural beliefs about gender and task competence bias individuals' perceptions of their own competence in different areas and consequently influence their preferences for entering fields requiring those skills. Correll's important work points to the inadequacy of early childhood socialization models for explaining gendered preferences; rather, in what is an ongoing process, cultural conceptions of gender bias a person's perceived competence, which then influences that individual's preferences. The results presented here show additional ways in which choice is much more than the result of socialization. Gendered associations with bodies of knowledge, as well as gendered occupational structures, both influence choice. Choice may also be seen as a product of the structure of the curriculum (Charles and Bradley 2009; Gaskell 1992). The organization of the family is important, too, in that it relates to how students anticipate their future roles. Thus, while the socialization that men and woman receive before they arrive at college decidedly explains some of the differences in their preferences, gender biases in institutions, opportunity structures, cultural beliefs, and social practices also exert a continual and powerful effect on their choices.

Although women have entered higher educational institutions and now attend them in greater numbers than men, this has not resulted in the same kind of success in the labor market. Women and men are still largely segregated into different types of occupations, and women still earn far less than men do. Even more troubling, the narrowing of the gender wage gap has slowed considerably since 1990. These labor market trends are directly linked to the gendered segregation of major fields of study (Bielby 1978; Bradley 2000; C. Brown and Corcoran 1997; Snyder 2002). In these ways, women's inclusion in higher education has not resulted in commensurate advances in gender equality. In sum, not only does the choice of a major field reflect gender and class divisions among students, it also perpetuates those same divisions, serving as another point of stratification within higher education.

Conclusion

The last half of the twentieth century saw the sweeping expansion of the U.S. higher educational system. Once a relatively rare choice for young people, going to college has now become commonplace. Most students from all social backgrounds now expect to attain a college degree, and scholars predict that by 2125 postsecondary attendance will be almost universal (Gamoran 2001; Goyette 2008). However, while educational expansion is promoted under the rubric of equal opportunity, what is often lost in this college crusade is recognition of the increasing stratification of higher education. The American system is now more socioeconomically stratified than at any other time during the past three decades (Astin and Oseguera 2004), and social origins continue to shape nearly every facet of going to college. In addition, the high levels of gender segregation in fields of study have barely changed over the past twenty years. The educational journeys of the Yale and the Southern students in my study illustrate these inequalities in the higher educational system, along with the intricate social processes animating them.

Well before students begin to apply to college, differences in the advantages provided by their families and schooling converge to engender profound disparities in students' levels of academic achievement, motivation, educational expectations, and even in their sense of what it means to be a student. Privileged parents invest heavily in actively producing exceptional levels of accomplishment in their children (Stevens 2007). Their efforts are reinforced by the kinds of schools to which they can afford to send their children, and by the kinds of children attending those schools. This fortuitous accumulation of advantages often results in the distinguished academic performance and ambitious expectations requisite for applying to an elite university. An important component of this eventual success derives from the way privileged students' environments activate their academic motivation.

These early advantages influence both the students' decisions to attend college and their choice of where to attend. For most of the Yale students, college was simply the next step in the natural progression of their education; these students did not decide *whether* to go to college, but only *where*. Conversely, the Southern students did not take this step for granted. Instead, they consciously chose to attend college, often in spite of an aversion to schooling, in order to improve their career prospects. Social privilege thus influences not just whether a student goes to college, but whether going reflects a strategic choice or a nondecision. When it comes to choosing colleges, the direct benefits of family background become amply evident. Understanding the higher educational game and how to play it is a vital form of cultural capital. With few exceptions, the Yale students drew on a remarkable set of resources, including the collective knowledge of an educated and informed group of family, friends, and school personnel to navigate the college application process, as well as their families' economic resources to cover multiple campus visits, exam-preparation courses, and application fees. The Southern students typically decided on their own, or with the advice of one or two friends or family members, making do with more limited information and fewer financial resources. These differences in resources affected the degree of constraint the students faced in the range of options available for their consideration.

Once at college, the students' divergent goals for their education and understandings of the purpose of education become markedly apparent. The Yale students expected college to encompass a full life experience, involving not only academics, but living on one's own for the first time; gaining independence and confidence; engaging in extracurricular activities, sports, and volunteer work; and making friends. The Yalies pursued these endeavors for personal enrichment, centering their college years on the aim of crafting an enhanced self.

The Southern students' approach may be best characterized as *earning* a degree. Far fewer students lived on campus or participated in campus activities. Instead, setting their sights on the credential, most of the Southern students viewed college as a burdensome, often tedious process of deciphering and meeting organizational regulations, fulfilling program requirements for their majors, and doing enough work to pass their courses. For them, college became more a matter of manipulating bureaucracy than of cultivating the self.

When it came to choosing majors, the Southern students selected fields not for what they wanted to study, but for the kinds of occupations they hoped to enter. In fact, the Southern students rarely drew a distinction between academic and occupational fields. Because semiprofessional majors closely align with highly sex-typed, semiprofessional occupations, gender lines for these students were reinforced by notions of the gender-appropriateness of different kinds of work. The Southern students also approached academic knowledge from an applied perspective, evaluating course content in terms of its usefulness to their future lines of work. General knowledge and theoretical approaches held less relevance than applied, hands-on, or real-life approaches. In contrast, the Yale students prized theoretical or abstract knowledge and evaluated knowledge less for its applied purposes and more for its intrinsic qualities, such as rigor and objectivity. Further, these students associated bodies of knowledge with characteristics of masculinity and femininity, which contributed to the gendered division of fields of study. In spite of Yale's long liberal arts history, surprisingly few students chose their majors for primarily intellectual reasons (and most of those who did were privileged women). Most of the students chose fields, at least to some degree, for pragmatic reasons related to their long-term career interests. The onus on the Yale men to secure status for themselves and reproduce their class position by providing privileged lifestyles for their future families contributed to their choice of moving away from their intellectual interests in order to select disciplines with more assured and lucrative returns in the labor market.

These broad patterns captured the experiences of the majority of students in my sample. At both institutions, however, some of the students did not fit into these categories. One of the challenges in writing this book has been in portraying the wide range of differences between the Yale and the Southern students while not losing track of the diversity present within each institution. The reports from some of the student-athletes at Yale helped confirm the suggestions of earlier researchers, who noted the existence of a culture of athletics on college campuses. While certainly not true for all student-athletes, a majority of these students from my sample at Yale identified much more strongly with athletics than with academics. I also found occasional points of overlap between the two institutions, where some of the Yale students more closely resembled typical Southern students, and, more rarely, vice versa. In many cases, class conditioned the students' educational approaches, independent of the institution. Less privileged students at Yale, including many of the athletes, held views more typical of the Southern students, such as preferring preprofessional fields over liberal arts disciplines. Finally, as with any research project, there were students at both institutions whose answers to my questions did not fit into any category.

Comparing the educational trajectories of these two sets of students makes the influence of social background on educational attainment stand out in stark relief. The quality and quantity of one's family resources (economic, social, and cultural) contribute to almost all aspects of a student's educational progression. The students who matriculated at Yale generally arrived on the back of tremendous childhood advantages. Just as important as these resources themselves, each student's habitus shaped the kinds of choices he or she made. Habitus reflects the students' sense of what is reasonable to expect, from themselves and from their education; what makes some choices thinkable and others unthinkable; and what lies in the realm of the possible and the impossible. It explains why none of the Southern students I interviewed even considered applying to Yale. A deeply ingrained sense of one's place served to guide these students toward the destinations they regarded as appropriate for persons with their background. In this way, habitus becomes a powerful mechanism for self-selection. The Southern students did not end up at Southern because their applications to Yale were rejected, but because they never applied to Yale in the first place. Even more to the point, the Southern students often did not fully dedicate themselves to their high school studies, because institutions such as Yale were outside of the realm of reasonable possibility. By the time they finished high school, these students' lack of academic preparation became a concrete manifestation of their ineligibility.

On a collective level, habitus helps explain the smooth connection between social origins and academic destinations. Aspirations and expectations for any particular social class adjust to the objective probabilities of success or failure for those belonging to that class (Bourdieu and Passeron 1977, 1979). Individuals internalize these probabilities, thereby generating self-fulfilling prophecies in accordance with their class positions. Even with equivalent academic credentials, lower-SES students are less likely to apply to more selective institutions than are their higher-SES peers (Mullen and Goyette 2009). In the end, without overt coercion, most individuals gravitate toward their prescribed location within the social hierarchy, a process Bourdieu (1977) likens to a conductorless orchestra. The sum of these individual tendencies contributes powerfully to the reproduction of social stratification.

Habitus also maps onto competing narratives about the meaning of education. As Swidler (1986, 2001) points out, there are many more cultural meanings or notions available than the ones that people actually use. Individuals selectively adopt or reject those pieces of culture that help them make sense of their own experiences. In the case of education, the dominant narratives center on either education as a means of gaining the requisite skills and credentials for occupational advancement or education as a means of cultivating one's intellectual and personal qualities for the intrinsic satisfaction of doing so. A student's habitus finds expression in the ideal of education he or she adopts, in whether that individual finds it reasonable to think of education as a means of self-cultivation or whether education makes more sense as job preparation. Notably, it was rare to see the students I interviewed consciously struggle to define their sense of education; for most of the students, one particular educational narrative had become so ingrained that it was taken for granted. A Southern student might have wrestled with which preprofessional major to choose, but majors that did not appear to lead to concrete chances of employment were quickly eliminated from the range of possibilities. The few of the students in the sample who did consciously engage with these narratives were those whose sense of education conflicted with the possibilities available at their institution. This was the case for some of the first-generation students at Yale, who would have preferred more applied majors offering safer routes to specific occupations. Because Yale does not offer applied fields, these students had to select among the liberal arts majors, and, in the process, rethink their ideals of education. This was also the case for the privileged Yale men, who, while embracing liberal arts notions of education, also had to contend with the competing objectives of securing both their own status and their ability to support their future families.

As different class positions relate to different habitus, gender also finds expression in habitus. The gendered dimension of habitus is present in the kinds of future roles men and women imagine for themselves and, consequently, in the kinds of educational expectations they hold. It can be seen in the Yale men's general acceptance of taking on the role of primary breadwinner, as well as in the privileged Yale women's sanguine plans to pursue intellectual passions. At Southern, it can be seen in the taken-for-granted notion of teaching as an appropriate occupation for women. At both Southern and Yale, the students formulated plans based, in part, on what they envisioned their future family roles might entail and on the kinds of occupational lines that appeared more open or closed to those of their gender. In most cases, the students took up these roles without much conscious consideration.

The disparities in resources between the Southern and the Yale students and the ways that these translated into different degrees of educational advantage and achievement meant that by the time they graduated, the Southern and the Yale students would be heading off toward very different futures. In terms of continuing their education, nearly 80 percent of the Yale students intended to pursue a graduate degree, mostly in doctoral or professional programs. Only half of the Southern students planned to go on, mostly into master's programs. The divergence in their directions also became evident in the students' discussions of their general plans for the future. While most of the Southern students held the relatively modest ambitions of having a decent, stable, white-collar job and owning their own home, the Yale students entertained much more expansive notions. Like the student who said that he saw himself "as making a huge impact somehow on this planet," many of the others held similarly far-reaching ambitions. The Yale students who considered careers in journalism saw themselves working at the *New York Times* or the *Wall Street Journal*. Those who thought about law anticipated making so much money that they could rely on their investments and pursue humanitarian causes. Those who planned to go into writing intended to publish their novels with the top presses. The Yale students anticipated earning significantly more money than the Southern students. When asked to estimate their salaries at the age of forty, the Yale men expected to earn *nearly double* the amount of the Southern men and the Yale women expected to earn one-and-a-half times as much as the Southern women. (The women at Yale, however, anticipated earning only 83% of the salaries of their male peers, probably an accurate guess, given the continuing gender wage gap.) Moreover, the Yale students, especially the men, recognized that they were being trained as a class of leaders.

> Looking at what people are interested in and what they're doing, just my fellow classmates, I think, basically, I'm looking at the future generation of leaders in America right now. And not just in a homogenized sense, not like strictly politics, not strictly this or that, but very like [a] motley crew of leaders, in many different fields, in art, and literature, and in drama, as well as in politics.

The expectation of assuming positions of leadership also corresponded to a sense of entitlement. The Yale students banked on the value of their degree to carry them in the job market.

> I know, based on my Yale degree, my intelligence quotient, as well as, you know, where I'm headed, that I'll be comfortable.

The Yale students did not just come to expect top jobs with high incomes; they also took away ideas about how they should be treated by the rest of the world, as conveyed in the remark by one student concerning what he had least liked about being at Yale.

> I needed to take a makeup final and [the professor] refused to give it to me. And there was this whole headache with dealing with the dean, and this guy was just being an absolute jerk. And I couldn't believe it. It's just ridiculous. For $30,000 a year, I think he should shine my shoes if I ask him.

Though the student admittedly made this comment in jest, the anecdote revealed his sense that the professors should accommodate the needs of the Yale students because of the high tuition the students pay. What was not stated directly was his sense of worthiness, because of both getting into Yale in the first place and having parents wealthy enough to pay full tuition. It is interesting that he compared his professor with a shoeshine boy, one of the lowest possible service-type jobs.

The benefits of graduating from a place like Yale extend beyond the concrete aspects of jobs and money. An elite degree also serves as a kind of consecration, permanently marking its holders as worthy and entitled. Bourdieu (1984) describes the symbolic consecration conferred by diplomas from elite institutions as assuring, "without any other guarantee, a competence extending far beyond what they are supposed to guarantee" (p. 25). To quote an old Spanish saying, "No one explores a good man's pedigree" (D. Brown 2001, p. 27). To quote a Yale student, "[the Yale name] gives us the magic password we will use for the rest of our lives to signal membership in that elite" (Sigel 1997, p. 6).

It is no coincidence that elite degrees provide this consecrating function for their graduates. One of the roles of colleges and universities is to symbolically redefine people to make them eligible for membership in various social categories (Kamens 1977). To do this, institutions create and then dramatize legitimating myths about the quality of their students' education. Institutions differ in regards to the symbolic conceptions of graduates that they attempt to create, based on the level of intellectual training and the degree of socialization their students receive. Elite institutions convey the idea that they rigorously select their students and then provide them with intensive intellectual and leadership training. Lower-status institutions promote the idea that their graduates possess technical skills, a kind of training that sets them apart from those who do not attend college. Elite colleges and universities work to sustain their legitimating myths by publicizing their selectivity (via admission rates and the average SAT scores of their accepted students) and requiring students to live in campus residence halls (thus proving the in-depth socialization their students receive). These elite institutions also emphasize the intellectual training they give their students by offering a liberal arts education, small classes, and high teacher-student ratios. Some institutions even unjustifiably make claims to a liberal arts curriculum as a strategy to bolster their prestige and legitimacy (Delucchi 1997), attempting to capitalize on the association of the liberal arts with intelligence and high-mindedness. Elite institutions also intentionally remain small in size, as another means of proclaiming their selectivity.

In this fashion, credentials work on a symbolic level, communicating a particular image of the degree holders. This perspective challenges the standard human-capital theory, which maintains that the value of educational credentials rests primarily on the skills they certify in the degree holders. Indeed, scholars find that the actual skills required by most jobs are modest and can be learned relatively quickly once a person is employed (Collins 1979). So, rather than acting as markers of skills or competencies, credentials may serve a signaling function, indicating that their holders have certain characteristics, such as intelligence, trustworthiness, or acceptance of the norms of the business world. These signals will vary, depending on the type of institution from which one graduated. Degrees from elite institutions signal their holders' social superiority and qualifications for leadership, while diplomas from less selective institutions may primarily indicate their holders' compliance with bureaucratic work values (D. Brown 1995).

In these ways, the elite tier of higher education is a powerful engine of social reproduction, whereby accidents of birth are transformed into legitimate achievements. Social privilege is first converted into educational advantages, which then result in admission to elite institutions. Elite colleges and universities consecrate their graduates as superior individuals, enhancing the students' sense of entitlement. When they graduate, Yale students meet the world assured of their own talents, intelligence, and worthiness. From their perspective, they arrived at Yale through their abilities and hard work during high school. Admission to Yale was an appropriate reward for their intelligence and preparation. Making it through four years at Yale further confirms their innate capabilities and their deservedness of their future successes. Twenty years from now, Yale graduates will not only be enjoying comfortable lifestyles, they will also be ready to pass on their privileges to their own children in the form of good neighborhoods, excellent high schools, and the strong likelihood that they, too, can enter the elite educational realm. Thus social privilege will once again become transformed into receipt of an elite diploma, and thus disguised.

While the elite tier largely serves to reproduce social privilege, for those disadvantaged students who did attend Yale, their education could provide them with a powerful source of mobility. One first-generation student spoke at some length about how attending Yale had changed her sense of expectation and even placed her in a new socioeconomic level.

What will stay with you the most about your experiences at Yale?

I think that Yale has opened up a lot of doors for me that I didn't know existed . . . I've become, I feel like even in a whole other socioeconomic level, once you come to Yale. Like I was able to . . . meet people, that I could get involved in different channels that I didn't even know existed or that I could access before. And I don't think that I would have even thought about those things before . . . I wouldn't say I didn't think big, but, you know, you may think you're thinking big now, but you don't know that there's bigger things . . . I think [Yale's] just given me a whole new outlook about myself and the things that I can accomplish, and I think that I'm leaving from here with a lot more social capital than when I came here . . . And I just think also to be able to formulate, or just to be empowered enough to think about things in a certain manner, or to place yourself in a certain manner, or just to think that you can accomplish certain things . . . And then, I just think that it's thinking that you belong to a certain social class, and I didn't belong to this social class, or think about it at all before I came here. And I think that once I've come to Yale, I'm moving in completely different circles, and yeah, I just think that I have a whole bunch more resources that I didn't have before I came here.

What stood out in this student's reflections were her comments on how being at Yale had changed both her level of aspirations for herself and her confidence in placing herself. It was as if her very sense of self had been transformed. She found that Yale had empowered her to think big and act in new ways. Attending Yale boosted her social-class standing, and she discovered a new vision of herself, in the world and in the possibilities ahead of her. As one of the few first-generation students attending Yale, this student was an exception to the high level of class homogenization within elite higher education.

The Southern students, too, experienced social mobility through education, albeit on a more modest scale. The half of the students in my sample whose parents had not graduated from college would probably attain a higher socioeconomic status than their families, one that they, in turn, would pass down to their own children. Consciously striving for mobility, these students sought a college degree as an escape from the blue-collar work of many of their parents. In this way, higher education serves as a key factor in both social reproduction *and* upward mobility. However, while higher education can play an important role in individual mobility, it is far less successful in redressing social inequality. The broader issues of access and equity as they pertain to social policy will be discussed later in this chapter, but let us initially consider possible directions for future research in the sociology of higher education.

Directions for Future Research

First, in order to better understand the consequences of stratification in higher education, the body of research on educational outcomes needs to be strengthened by more updated and detailed analyses of the occupational destinations of graduates of different types of postsecondary institutions. Rather than simply looking at the effects of institutional selectivity, as most of the studies have done, researchers should begin to explore other characteristics of institutions. Further, analyses need to focus on the outcomes for different groups of students, by race, ethnicity, gender, and social background. Much of the present research on outcomes, moreover, fails to take into account students' likelihood of attending graduate institutions. Estimates of the salaries associated with different fields of study are often biased because of this omission. Earnings for undergraduate liberal arts majors, for example, appear low when compared with the salaries for preprofessional majors, but this is mostly because liberal arts majors are more likely to enter graduate programs (Goyette and Mullen 2006). Finally, the majority of studies confine research on outcomes to only a limited number of years after college graduation. For a more comprehensive understanding of the benefits of attending different types of institutions, such studies should follow graduates over much longer time periods.

With regard to the outcomes associated with degrees from elite institutions, little research has been done on how those outcomes are achieved. There is much speculation about the role of the social networks students build during their college years, but little in the way of empirical studies. How big of a role do social networks formed during college play in students' future occupational outcomes? Do men and women have the same access to those networks, and do they gain the same rewards? What about students from different socioeconomic backgrounds and from different races and ethnicities? How important are networks at non-elite institutions? Further, research should be designed to investigate the consequences of the process of consecration. An experimental study of hiring practices, comparing employers' evaluations of résumés that are equivalent *except* for the status of the undergraduate degree, would help shed light on the payoff of an elite degree.

In general, research on postsecondary students and their choices and experiences should better situate these students in their particular institutional and cultural contexts. Researchers too often either lump all students together or look at a subset of students without specifying how they differ from the norm. Studies need to take into account what kinds of institutions the students attend, what educational ideals these institutions promote, and to what extent their students identify with liberal arts and vocational notions of education. While the research in this book has compared an elite university to a mass university, there is much variation within and between both of these institutional types that could fruitfully be explored. Studies also need to look more carefully at the implicit assumptions made with regard to how students make decisions. Too often researchers apply a rational-choice perspective, presupposing that students carefully weigh the costs and benefits of each choice before making a decision. The data in this book show that many decisions are in fact *not* made in a rational, calculating manner. Further, for certain students, some steps never even require a conscious decision.

Researchers could fruitfully pay more attention to educational trajectories. Too often studies focus on students at a single point in their educational histories, without taking into account either their previous educational experiences or their future expectations. Putting their current experiences and choices into the broader context of a longer educational trajectory can provide an important perspective to help us understand their current position. Researchers should pay particular attention to the cumulative advantages students gain as they move through various stages in their educational progression. All too often, the educational advantages associated with social background in the early years of schooling appear in later years as simply higher levels of achievement.

There is also a need for more finely tuned research on race, ethnicity, and immigration in higher education. Race and ethnicity influence educational choices and experiences much more than the data used for this book were able to capture. Studies such as Vivian Louie's (2004) wonderful book on Chinese-American students at two institutions have much to offer. In particular, more research should focus on the experiences of racial and ethnic minority students in elite institutions, building on existing studies such as that of Bowen and Bok (1998). Since these bastions of white privilege have only recently begun to move toward racial integration, minority students there face qualitatively different experiences and challenges. Finally, as more and more foreign and immigrant students undertake their studies in the United States, research should devote more attention to their experiences.

Higher education research also needs to move beyond looking at specific groups and pay more attention to intersections. For example, studies on gender and the choice of a major have almost entirely failed to take into account differences in social backgrounds. By looking at these intersections, we begin to see very different processes at work in gender differentiation. Similarly, many theoretical concepts in the sociology of education have been inadequately specified in relation to gender and other dimensions of identity. The concept of habitus, for example, was developed around the idea of social class and has yet to be fully adapted to an understanding of gender (for efforts in this direction, see Bourdieu 2001; McNay 1999).

Policy Recommendations

Sociology books generally close with a discussion of the policy implications of their research and the provision of specific policy recommendations. Indeed, there is no shortage of higher educational policy recommendations coming from sociologists. Curiously, we persist in the belief that policy innovations will be up to the task of evening out deeply entrenched social inequalities. Worse, too often policy recommendations focus on limited, short-term goals without taking long-term implications or consequences into account. The implicit aims of proposed educational reforms are often not fully considered. Both scholars and policymakers seem to operate under the maxim that any step to increase access to higher education for anyone will be unambiguously positive. The comforting rhetoric of educational reform fails to reason through long-term consequences or to address the underlying issues of class inequality in society. It is puzzling how, as a society, we persist in the belief that education is the solution to all manner of social ills and, in particular, that it can serve as the "great equalizer," balancing all other forms and structures of inequality. Both the political left and right enthusiastically embrace educational reform, taking for granted the unexamined equation that simply making the proper adjustments to the U.S. educational system will result in greater social equality. My own conclusion regarding policy initiatives is considerably more pessimistic. The vast majority of higher educational policies, even if carried out, will be equivalent to only minor tinkering on the margins of educational inequality, while the larger forces driving inequality will remain obscured and deeply entrenched.

Let us consider the aims of the majority of reforms proposed for higher education. The most common suggestion is to increase access to higher education, the idea being that the more people who go to college, the better. Recommendations in this area favor different tactics. Educational expansion was founded on the idea that building more colleges means more people can go to college. More recent proposals include the perennial call for increases in financial aid and decreases in tuition; more academic and social support for students within colleges, particularly for students from disadvantaged backgrounds; and better student services in order to increase student retention.

Two assumptions guide proposals of this sort. The first is that increasing access to higher education (and ensuring students' ability to complete their degrees) is a good thing in and of itself, because it promotes equality of opportunity. If we can make college accessible to anyone who wants to go (whether that means providing sufficient space in college, enough financial aid, or adequate support structures to ensure success), we can uphold our commitment to equality of opportunity. If we are successful in these endeavors, then anyone, from any background, should be able to attend college and complete a degree. The second assumption is much broader and more ambitious: if we can provide enough equality of opportunity in education, we can work toward leveling social inequality. In other words, if there is enough educational opportunity so that both the rich and the poor have equivalent chances to attend college, then gradually the gap between the rich and the poor will close and there will be less overall social inequality. The logic here seems to be based on the observation that those in the middle class get good jobs because they have college degrees. Therefore, if we can increase college-going rates among the more disadvantaged groups, they, too, will receive the same benefits from their degrees and move into the middle class. If enough of them do so, there will be a larger middle class. Thus, if we are successful in our educational reforms, we will reduce the barriers for even the most socially disadvantaged individuals, increase college access, and, in the end, reduce the gaps between the social classes and decrease the size of the disadvantaged classes.

As promising as this picture seems, it is not supported by the evidence. Contrary to the widespread belief that educational expansion results in more equality of access, cross-national research conclusively shows that the expansion of higher educational systems does not necessarily lead to more equality of access, particularly in cases where this expansion is accompanied by increasing differentiation within the higher educational system (Shavit, Arum, and Gamoran 2007; Shavit and Blossfeld 1993). There are two issues here. First, when higher educational systems expand, members of previously disadvantaged groups do begin to enroll in greater numbers; however, at the same time, advantaged groups also increase their enrollment rates, so that as enrollment rates grow for both groups, the gap between the two groups remains constant (Raftery and Hout 1993). This process may continue until all members of the most advantaged groups enroll at any given level of education. At that point, disadvantaged groups may continue to increase their enrollment at that educational level, thereby closing the enrollment gap with the more advantaged groups (as has occurred in the case of high school enrollments). However, the most advantaged groups will then typically begin to increase their enrollment at a higher level of education. Once nearly everyone began to attend high school, members of the upper classes entered college in higher numbers. In more recent years, now that undergraduate degrees have become much more common, and consequently devalued, more advantaged groups have begun to consolidate their hold on higher levels of education, such as graduate programs (Mullen, Goyette, and Soares 2003).

A second issue is that in most cases the expansion of higher education is accompanied by increased differentiation of institutions and of fields of study. Rarely does the elite sector of higher education expand; expansion tends to happen at the bottom, at less selective colleges and universities and in more applied fields of study. As members of previously disadvantaged groups begin to participate in higher education, they tend to concentrate within the lower tiers of the educational hierarchy. These new opportunities have diminished value, because they are at lower levels (Lucas 2001). Instead of getting the same payoff for their credentials that middle-class students attending more selective institutions get, disadvantaged students find that their access to good jobs and incomes is more limited. The diversification that accompanies expansion may also serve to further entrench gendered tracks. For example, in an effort to "accommodate" women, institutions may develop more feminine-typed programs, such as teacher education (Charles and Bradley 2009). As a consequence, women's success in educational achievement often does not result in commensurate equality in the labor market.

Because of these two processes, a cross-national comparative study looking at several decades' worth of data found that in most countries, educational expansion did not reduce educational inequality (Shavit, Arum, and Gamoran 2007; Shavit and Blossfeld 1993). Though higher educational expansion means more people can go to college, the privileged classes retain their advantages over time. In line with these general patterns, a detailed analysis of educational expansion in the United States shows that as the system grew, it also became more differentiated (Roksa et al. 2007). Most of the growth came in lower-status institutions (both nonselective four-year institutions and two-year and community colleges), and the lower tier became increasingly vocationalized. This expansion solidified the existing educational hierarchy, since the split between the elite and the mass forms of education grew. As the bottom of the hierarchy enlarged, and it became easier to enter at this level, those places at the top became even more valuable. In line with predictions, as the system expanded, students from all SES backgrounds increased their entry into higher education. However, students from less advantaged backgrounds concentrated in two-year and less selective institutions. Meanwhile, the advantages associated with social background that lead to entry into four-year and elite four-year programs actually *increased* from the 1980s to the 1990s. Even after controlling for academic achievement, students with college-educated parents were far more likely to enter the upper tiers of the higher educational system. Overall, though access did improve considerably for women and African-Americans, inequality remained stable in terms of social-class background. Expansion did not result in greater equality of opportunity.

In the words of James Hearn (1984), the expansion of postsecondary educational opportunity can be a false promise. His description of the process by which the academically and socioeconomically rich become richer and the poor become poorer in the transition from high school to college succinctly summarizes the reasons why expanding postsecondary educational opportunity does not necessarily bring the hoped-for results.

Expansions means less in equity terms if it is accompanied *within* the educational
system by (a) the growth of hierarchical differentiation along status or quality lines
among institutions or curricula, (b) the use of that hierarchical differentiation in
status or quality to determine attainment opportunities for graduates of the various
institutions and curricula, and (c) the disproportionate channeling of the disadvantaged into the lower-status or lower-quality institutions and curricula. (p. 28)

If expanding higher education has not increased equality of access, has it
helped to level social inequalities at large? Again, the evidence is bleak. The
United States currently has the highest levels of income inequality of any rich
Organisation for Economic Co-Operation and Development (OECD) country.
The top 10 percent of Americans now collect nearly 50 percent of all reported
income, while the top 1 percent collects 22 percent of all reported income
(Johnston 2007). For both groups, these figures are higher than at any time
since 1928. In an international comparison of the income ratio between those at
the top and the bottom of the income distribution scale, the United States ranks
among the worst countries, placing at number twenty-eight out of thirty OECD
countries, just ahead of Russia and Mexico (Smeeding 2005). These increases in
inequality began in the 1980s, and grew more dramatically than for any other
of the seven OECD countries with comparable time-series data in Smeeding's
study. At the same time, the gender gap in earnings among college-educated,
full-time workers has barely improved over the past twenty years (U.S. Bureau
of Labor Statistics 2009). All of these trends have taken place at the very time
that postsecondary participation has been growing; indeed, up until recently,
the United States could boast the highest level of postsecondary educational
participation in the world. These patterns lend support to the conclusion Christopher Jencks (1972) made nearly forty years ago, when he found that the prior
twenty-five years of research suggested that equalizing educational opportunity
did very little to reduce economic inequality among adults.

For these reasons, I am cautious about policy recommendations advocating
increased access to higher education. There is certainly much to be done to
improve higher education as it now stands, and we can and should continue to
push for policies and programs that support students' success in higher education. We also should continue to advocate for institutions, especially in the elite
sector, to work toward diversifying their student bodies. However, we need to
be realistic about policies that simply endeavor to increase access. If previous
trends give us any guidance for the future, expansion will only further entrench

educational differentiation, whereby new distinctions (of either institutions or fields of study) will become even more prominent. We can expect to see the continuation of the pattern in which the benefits of higher education are disproportionately reaped by those already most socially advantaged. Further, the bachelor's degree will continue to depreciate, educational stakes will rise, students will increasingly seek to distinguish themselves through graduate degrees, and the graduate sector, in turn, will become more differentiated.

Some suggest that progress could be made by expanding or further diversifying the elite tier of higher education, making access to the most valuable kinds of degrees more equitable. Certainly, much could be done in terms of recruitment and admissions policies to attract, admit, and support a more diverse group of students. Some elite institutions have recently taken additional steps in this direction by providing free tuition to any student who is admitted and has a family income below a certain amount. There is also discussion of moving away from standard SAT scores and toward other, potentially less biased, indicators of academic ability or promise. However, while initiatives such as these can make a difference, the improvement will be negligible. To begin with, as much as we might tinker with the criteria for admissions, we will never match the determination and capacity of privileged families to ensure that their own children meet and exceed the new criteria. Moreover, elite private institutions, such as those in the Ivy League, rely on a certain percentage of their incoming class members paying full tuition and continuing to contribute to the institution as alumni (Soares 2007). For economic reasons, it is unlikely that elite institutions, in any significant way, will increase the proportion of their student bodies coming from lower-SES families. Further, it is also unlikely that the elite tier of colleges and universities will expand to any significant degree. In order to preserve their elite status, these institutions need to remain small and continue to be rigorously selective. The best colleges are the best "precisely because they are competitive and exclusive" (Jencks and Riesman 1968, p. 148). Indeed, elite institutions have become increasingly selective over the past several decades. As demand increases, these institutions respond not by accommodating more applicants, but by raising their admissions standards (Bound, Hershbein, and Long 2009).

Finally, much of the stratification within higher education stems from class-related differences in educational attainment before students even begin college. A more effective way of diversifying the upper sector of the higher educational system lies in working to equalize educational achievement at the primary and

[handwritten margin notes: "making elite institutions more accessible" with arrow down; "move away from SAT scores"; "free tuition if you're accepted and make below certain amount"; "BUT economic reasons hinder desire for elite institutions to implement these initiatives"]

To equalize field in the playing field in post-secondary education, we must change primary and secondary institutions.

secondary school levels. This undertaking would involve making changes in the ways public schools are financed (moving away from a reliance on local property taxes), as well as improving the health and out-of-school environments of disadvantaged students (Bowen, Kurzweil, and Tobin 2005). Integrating public schools by students' social backgrounds would also be a successful means of narrowing the achievement gap between the rich and the poor (Kahlenberg 2001). According to Kahlenberg, economic integration would be more effective than vouchers, standards, or reductions in class size.

Returning to the goals that motivate educational expansion, if the United States is serious about reducing social inequality, then it should abandon its attempts to achieve social equality by increasing access to education. Instead, it should address social inequality directly. The growing gap between the rich and the poor in the United States has been linked to wage inequality, government policies, and social spending (Smeeding 2005). Compared with other countries, the United States has fewer antipoverty measures, and its tax and benefit systems are ineffective in reducing social inequality. The United States might also turn to the recommendations made by Jencks in 1972. Arguing that economic reforms will be more consequential than increasing educational opportunities, he suggests measures such as progressive taxation, direct governmental regulation of wages, or tax incentives for employers to equalize wages. He also calls into question a system that finances higher education in part out of general tax revenues but then allows individuals to use their education for private gain. In this system, everyone shares the costs of higher education (through taxes), but the benefits accrue primarily to those who are already most advantaged. As a remedy for this inequity, Jenks proposes equalizing adult incomes; if the better educated and the less educated have equal incomes, then we can be assured that the economic benefits of higher education are being equally distributed, making it a reasonable supposition that the costs are also equally distributed. Alternatively, those individuals who reap the greatest rewards from higher education could pay most of its costs. In this scenario, college would be free for anyone who wanted it, along with a stipend to support general living costs. College graduates would then pay an income tax surcharge, which would vary according to the amount of their earnings. In this way, those who use and benefit from higher education would be the ones to pay for it. If the United States wants to tackle gender inequality, rather than simply encouraging more women either to earn degrees or to earn more degrees in male-dominated fields, it could reevaluate the ways work is valued and rewarded. Rather than asking women to go into typically male fields, Americans could start asking why typically female fields pay so much less.

To my knowledge, none of Jencks's policy recommendations were ever implemented, and it is highly unlikely that any of them will be taken up now. Nor is it foreseeable that Kahlenberg's proposal to economically integrate schools will gain traction. The United States seems to be comfortable with maintaining the illusion of equality of opportunity while turning a blind eye to increasing inequality. As Collins (2002) puts it, expanding higher education palliates the problem of class conflict in the United States. By increasing access, America promotes the idea that it has enough equality of opportunity while continuing to deny the reality of acute and increasing social inequality. By celebrating women's entry into higher education, it ignores the reality that in the first year after college graduation, women earn only 80 percent of what men do, a figure that drops to 69 percent ten years after graduation (Dey and Hill 2007). Without fundamental changes to U.S. economic and social policies, Americans can hardly hope for higher education alone to produce a moderating effect on social inequality.

Note on Methodology

The data for this study come from in-depth interviews conducted with a stratified random sample of one hundred junior and senior students, fifty from Yale
University and fifty from Southern Connecticut State University. Yale randomly
assigns each new undergraduate student to one of twelve residential colleges,
and students remain affiliated with this college throughout their time at Yale,
whether or not they choose to later live off campus. The names of twenty-five
junior students and twenty-five senior students were randomly selected (using a
random number table) from a list of all students at one college, excluding foreign
students. I chose to exclude the foreign students from the sample because of the
need to ensure comparability among social-class backgrounds in the analyses.
Students were first contacted by telephone to arrange for an in-person interview. I was unable to obtain interviews with twelve of the initial fifty students, so
I continued to randomly select additional students until I had completed a total
of fifty interviews. In the end, a total of sixty-two students were contacted, for a
response rate of 81 percent. Of the twelve students who were initially selected
but did not complete an interview, six had either taken a leave of absence, were
studying abroad for the semester, or had graduated early. I was unable to reach
four other students after repeated phone calls. One student declined to be interviewed, and another twice failed to attend a scheduled interview.

At Southern, the Director of Management Information and Research provided me with a list of students. The list included all full-time, nonforeign junior
and senior students under the age of 25. I limited the sample to full-time students in this age range in order to make the two groups of students comparable
on these characteristics. Names were selected from this list using systematic
random sampling. I first contacted students by telephone to arrange for the
interviews. In total, I telephoned 74 students, for a response rate of 68 percent.
Of the 24 students initially contacted whom I did not interview, half declined
the request for an interview, explaining that they were too busy. The other half
scheduled one or more interviews but then failed to attend. In cases where stu-

dents did not come to scheduled interviews, I made several attempts to reach them again to reschedule.

Comparisons of the samples of students to the entire student bodies at the two institutions show a close match (see tables A.1 and A.2). At Yale, in both my sample and the entire student population 92 percent of the students come from out of state, and the proportions of students of different races and ethnicities are comparable. There is some divergence in terms of the types of high schools attended by the two Yale groups. In the sample, 57 percent attended a private high school, compared with only 47 percent of the entire student body. However, the figures for the total student body include international students, who were excluded from my sample. It is possible that international students are more likely than domestic students to attend public high schools, which could account for the disparity. At Southern, the proportions of students by race, ethnicity, and state of residence also generally match. It is important to note that the gender proportions of the samples from both universities intentionally vary from the proportions in their student bodies. Because one of the goals of this research was to compare men and women, I sampled an equal number of men and women at each institution. However, at Yale, women make up slightly less than half of all students (47%), while at Southern women make up a full 60 percent. Also, because there is such a high dropout rate at Southern, the Southern sample more accurately represents students who have persisted into their final years of college, rather than the university population as a whole.

The interviews lasted an average of forty-five minutes each and followed a semistructured interview schedule. Students were also asked to complete a one-page form with demographic information. All of the interviews were taped and later transcribed verbatim. In addition to reading the transcribed interviews several times, the data were also analyzed by myself and two research assistants with the software program NVivo (QSR International, Doncaster, Victoria, Australia). The interviews were coded by section, according to a coding scheme, with new codes being allowed to emerge during the coding process. Throughout the process, we met frequently to discuss the coding of each section and the development of new codes. We verified the accuracy of the coding by independently coding several of the same interviews and then comparing the results.

Table A.1   Comparison of the Yale sample to all Yale students (in percentages)

	Yale sample	All Yale students
Out of state	92	92
Men	50	53
Women	50	47
Asian	10	16
Black	14	8
Hispanic	8	6
White	68	69
Other	0	1
Private high school	57	47
Public high school	43	53

Source: Beverly Waters (ed.), *A Yale Book of Numbers, 1976–2000*, Office of Institutional Research, October 2001. www.yale.edu/oir/pierson_update.htm.

Table A.2   Comparison of the Southern sample to all Southern students (in percentages)

	Southern sample	All Southern students
Out of state	6	7
Men	50	40
Women	50	60
Asian	4	2
Black	10	12
Hispanic	12	6
White	74	70
Other	0	9

Source: *Southern Connecticut State University Factbook*, Office of Institutional Research. www.southernct.edu/departments/research/.

Bibliography

Aschaffenburg, Karen, and Ineke Maas. 1997. "Cultural and Educational Careers: The Dynamics of Social Reproduction." *American Sociological Review* 62(4): 573–587.

Astin, Alexander W. 1998. "The Changing American College Student: Thirty-Year Trends, 1966–1996." *Review of Higher Education* 21(2): 115–135.

———. 1999a. "How the Liberal Arts College Affects Students." *Daedalus* 128(1): 77–100.

———. 1999b. "Involvement in Learning Revisited: Lessons We Have Learned." *Journal of College Student Development* 40(5): 587–598.

Astin, Alexander W., Kenneth C. Green, and William S. Korn. 1987. *The American Freshman: Twenty Year Trends, 1966–1985*. Los Angles: Higher Education Research Institute and Graduate School of Education, University of California, Los Angeles.

Astin, Alexander W., and Leticia Oseguera. 2004. "The Declining 'Equity' of American Higher Education." *Review of Higher Education* 27(3): 321–341.

Avery, Christopher, and Caroline M. Hoxby. 2004. "Do and Should Financial Aid Packages Affect Students' College Choices?" In *College Choices: The Economics of Where to Go, When to Go, and How to Pay for It*, ed. Caroline M. Hoxby, pp. 239–301. Chicago: University of Chicago Press.

Avery, Christopher, and Thomas J. Kane. 2004. "Student Perceptions of College Opportunities: The Boston COACH Program." In *College Choices: The Economics of Where to Go, When to Go, and How to Pay for It*, ed. Caroline M. Hoxby, pp. 355–394. Chicago: University of Chicago Press.

Ball, Stephen J., Jackie Davies, Miriam David, and Diane Reay. 2002. "'Classification' and 'Judgement': Social Class and the 'Cognitive Structures' of Choice of Higher Education." *British Journal of Sociology of Education* 23: 51–72.

Bean, John, and Shevawn Bogdan Eaton. 2001/2002. "The Psychology Underlying Successful Retention Practices." *Journal of College Student Retention* 3(1): 73–89.

Beller, Emily, and Michael Hout. 2006. "Intergenerational Social Mobility: The United States in Comparative Perspective." *Future of Children* 16(2): 19–36.

Benton, Joshua. 1997. "Yale College Is a Legend in Its Own Mind." *Yale Herald*, Vol. 23, No. 14, May 26, 10.

Berger, Joseph B. 2001/2002. "Understanding the Organizational Nature of Student Persistence: Empirically Based Recommendations for Practice." *Journal of College Student Retention* 3(1): 3–21.

Berger, Joseph B., and John M. Braxton. 1998. "Revising Tinto's Interactionalist Theory of Student Departure through Theory Elaboration: Examining the Role of Organizational Attributes in the Persistence Process." *Research in Higher Education* 39(2): 103–119.

Berger, Mark C. 1988. "Predicted Future Earnings and Choice of College Major." *Industrial and Labor Relations Review* 41(3): 418–429.

Berkner, Lutz, and Lisa Chavez. 1997. *Access to Postsecondary Education for the 1992 High School Graduate*. NCES 98-105. Washington, DC: U.S. Department of Education, National Center for Education Statistics, Institute of Education Sciences.

Berkner, Lutz, Shirley He, and Emily Forrest Cataldi. 2002. *Descriptive Summary of 1995–96 Beginning Postsecondary Students: Six Years Later*. NCES 2003-151. Washington, DC: U.S. Department of Education, National Center for Education Statistics, Institute of Education Sciences.

Berkner, Lutz, and Christina C. Wei. 2006. *Student Financing of Undergraduate Education, 2003–04: With a Special Analysis of the Net Price of Attendance and Federal Education Tax Benefits*. NCES 2006-186. Washington, DC: U.S. Department of Education, National Center for Education Statistics, Institute of Education Sciences.

Bernstein, Basil. 1975. *Towards a Theory of Educational Transmission*. Vol. 3 of *Class, Codes and Control*. London: Routledge and Kegan Paul.

Bielby, Denise Del Vento. 1978. "Career Sex-Atypicality and Career Involvement of College Educated Women: Baseline Evidence from the 1960's." *Sociology of Education* 51: 7–28.

Bound, John, Brad Hershbein, and Bridget Terry Long. 2009. "Playing the Admissions Game: Student Reactions to Increasing College Competition." Working Paper 15272, National Bureau of Economic Research, Cambridge, Massachusetts.

Bourdieu, Pierre. 1977. *Outline of a Theory of Practice*. Trans. Richard Nice. Cambridge: Cambridge University Press.

———. 1984. *Distinction: A Social Critique of the Judgement of Taste*. Trans. Richard Nice. Cambridge, MA: Harvard University Press.

———. 1986. "The Forms of Capital." In *Handbook of Theory and Research for the Sociology of Education*, ed. John G. Richardson, pp. 241–258. New York: Greenwood Press.

———. 2001. *Masculine Domination*. Trans. Richard Nice. Stanford, CA: Stanford University Press.

Bourdieu, Pierre, and Jean-Claude Passeron. 1977. *Reproduction in Education, Society, and Culture*. Trans. Richard Nice. London: Sage Publications.

———. 1979. *The Inheritors: French Students and Their Relation to Culture*. Trans. Richard Nice. Chicago: University of Chicago Press.

Bowen, William G., and Derek Bok. 1998. *The Shape of the River: Long-Term Consequences of Considering Race in College and University Admissions*. Princeton, NJ: Princeton University Press.

Bowen, William G., Martin A. Kurzweil, and Eugene M. Tobin. 2005. *Equity and Excellence in American Higher Education*. Charlottesville: University of Virginia Press.

Bowen, William G., and Sarah A. Levin. 2003. *Reclaiming the Game: College Sports and Educational Values*. Princeton, NJ: Princeton University Press.

Bradburn, Ellen M., Rachael Berger, Xiaojie Li, Katharine Peter, and Kathryn Rooney. 2003. *A Descriptive Summary of 1999–2000 Bachelor's Degree Recipients 1 Year Later, with an Analysis of Time to Degree*. NCES 2003-165. Washington, DC: U.S. Department of Education, National Center for Education Statistics, Institute of Education Sciences.

Bradley, Karen. 2000. "The Incorporation of Women into Higher Education: Paradoxical Outcomes." *Sociology of Education* 73: 1–18.

Brewer, Dominic J., and Ronald G. Ehrenberg. 1996. "Does It Pay to Attend an Elite College?" *Research in Labor Economics* 15: 239–271.

Brint, Steven. 1998. *Schools and Society*. Thousand Oaks, CA: Pine Forge Press.

Brint, Steven, Mark Riddle, Lori Turk-Bicakci, and Charles S. Levy. 2005. "From the Liberal to the Practical Arts in American Colleges and Universities: Organizational Analysis and Curricular Change." *Journal of Higher Education* 76: 151–180.

Brooks, David. 2005. "Pillars of Cultural Capital." *New York Times*, October 6, A37.

Brooks, Rachel. 2003. "Young People's Higher Education Choices: The Role of Family and Friends." *British Journal of Sociology of Education* 24: 283–297.

Broughman, Stephen P., and Kathleen W. Pugh. 2004. *Characteristics of Private Schools in the United States: Results from the 2001–2002 Private School Universe Survey*. NCES 2005-305. Washington, DC: U.S. Department of Education, National Center for Education Statistics, Institute of Education Sciences.

Brown, Charles, and Mary Corcoran. 1997. "Sex-Based Differences in School Content and the Male-Female Wage Gap." *Journal of Labor Economics* 15: 431–465.

Brown, David K. 1995. *Degrees of Control: A Sociology of Educational Expansion and Occupational Credentialism*. New York: Teachers College Press.

———. 2001. "The Social Sources of Educational Credentialism: Status Cultures, Labor Markets, and Organizations." *Sociology of Education* 74: 19–34.

Carnevale, Anthony P., and Stephen J. Rose. 2004. "Socioeconomic Status, Race/Ethnicity, and Selective College Admissions." In *America's Untapped Resource: Low-Income Students in Higher Education*, ed. Richard D. Kahlenberg, pp. 101–156. New York: Century Foundation Press.

Cebula, Richard J., and Jerry Lopes. 1982. "Determinants of Student Choice of Undergraduate Major Field." *American Educational Research Journal* 19(2): 303–312.

Central Advisory Council for Education. 1967. *Children and Their Primary Schools: A Report* [aka the Plowden Report]. London: Her Majesty's Stationery Office.

Chapman, Randall G. 1984. *Toward a Theory of College Choice: A Model of College Search and Choice Behavior*. Alberta, Canada: University of Alberta Press.

Charles, Maria, and Karen Bradley. 2009. "Indulging Our Gendered Selves? Sex Segregation by Field of Study in 44 Countries." *American Journal of Sociology* 114: 924–976.

Choy, Susan P., and Ali M. Berker. 2003. *How Families of Low- and Middle-Income Undergraduates Pay for College: Full-Time Dependent Students in 1999–2000*. NCES 2003-162. Washington, DC: U.S. Department of Education, National Center for Education Statistics, Institute of Education Sciences.

Coleman, James S. 1967. "Toward Open Schools." *Public Interest* 9: 20–27.

———. 1988. "Social Capital in the Creation of Human Capital." *American Journal of Sociology* 94 (Suppl.): S95–S120.

Coleman, James S., Ernest Q. Campbell, Carol J. Hobson, James McPartland, Alexander M. Mood, Frederic D. Weinfeld, and Robert L. York. 1966. *Equality of Educational Opportunity* [aka the Coleman Report]. OE–38001. Washington, DC: U.S. Department of Health, Education, and Welfare, Office of Education, National Center for Education Statistics.

Collins, Randall. 1979. *The Credential Society: An Historical Sociology of Education and Stratification*. New York: Academic Press.

———. 2002. "Credential Inflation and the Future of Universities." In *The Future of the*

City of Intellect: The Changing American University, pp. 23–46. Stanford, CA: Stanford University Press.

Connecticut Department of Higher Education. 2007. *Higher Education Counts: Achieving Results, 2007 Report*. Hartford: State of Connecticut, Board of Governors for Higher Education, Department of Higher Education.

———. 2009. *Higher Education Counts: Achieving Results, 2009 Report*. Hartford: State of Connecticut, Board of Governors for Higher Education, Department of Higher Education.

Cookson, Peter W., Jr. 1981. "Private Secondary Boarding School and Public Suburban High School Graduation: An Analysis of College Attendance Plans." PhD diss., New York University.

Cookson, Peter W., Jr., and Caroline Hodges Persell. 1985a. "Chartering and Bartering: Elite Education and Social Reproduction." *Social Problems* 33(2): 114–129.

———. 1985b. *Preparing for Power: America's Elite Boarding Schools*. New York: Basic Books.

Correll, Shelley J. 2001. "Gender and the Career Choice Process: The Role of Biased Self-Assessments." *American Journal of Sociology* 106(6): 1691–1730.

———. 2004. "Constraints into Preferences: Gender, Status, and Emerging Career Aspirations." *American Sociological Review* 69: 93–113.

Davies, Scott, and Neil Guppy. 1997. "Fields of Study, College Selectivity, and Student Inequalities in Higher Education." *Social Forces* 75(4): 1415–1436.

Davies, Scott, and Floyd M. Hammack. 2005. "The Channeling of Student Competition in Higher Education: Comparing Canada and the U.S." *Journal of Higher Education* 76(1): 89–106.

Delucchi, Michael. 1997. "'Liberal Arts Colleges' and the Myth of Uniqueness." *Journal of Higher Education* 4: 414–426.

Devine, Fiona. 2004. *Class Practices: How Parents Help Their Children Get Good Jobs*. London: Cambridge University Press.

Dey, Judy Goldberg, and Catherine Hill. 2007. *Behind the Pay Gap*. Washington, DC: American Association of University Women Educational Foundation.

DiMaggio, Paul. 1979. "Review: On Pierre Bourdieu." *American Journal of Sociology* 84(6): 1460–1474.

———. 1982. "Cultural Capital and School Success: The Impact of Status Culture Participation on the Grades of U.S. High School Students." *American Sociological Review* 47(2): 189–201.

Dougherty, Kevin J. 1996. "Opportunity-to-Learn Standards: A Sociological Critique." *Sociology of Education* 69: 40–65.

Dynarski, Susan. 2004. "The New Merit Aid." In *College Choices: The Economics of Where to Go, When to Go, and How to Pay for It*, ed. Caroline M. Hoxby, pp. 63–100. Chicago: University of Chicago Press.

Eaton, Shevawn Bogdan, and John P. Bean. 1995. "An Approach/Avoidance Behavioral Model of College Student Attrition." *Research in Higher Education* 36(6): 617–645.

Eckert, Penelope. 1989. *Jocks and Burnouts: Social Categories and Identity in High School*. New York: Teachers College Press.

Ehrenberg, Ronald. 2002. *Tuition Rising: Why College Costs So Much*. Cambridge, MA: Harvard University Press.

England, Paula, and Su Li. 2006. "Desegregation Stalled: The Changing Gender Composition of College Majors, 1971–2002." *Gender & Society* 20: 657–677.

Engle, Jennifer, and Vincent Tinto. 2008. *Moving beyond Access: College Success for Low-Income, First-Generation Students*. Washington, DC: Pell Institute for the Study of Opportunity in Higher Education.

Erdman, David G. 1983. "An Examination of Factors Influencing Student Choice in the College Selection Process." *Journal of College Admissions* (Summer): 3–6.

Feagin, Joe R., Hernán Vera, and Nikitah Imani. 1996. *The Agony of Education: Black Students at White Colleges and Universities*. New York: Routledge.

Ferree, Myra Marx, Judith Lorber, and Beth B. Hess, eds. 1999. *Revisioning Gender*. Thousand Oaks, CA: Sage Publications.

Gamoran, Adam. 1987. "The Stratification of High School Learning Opportunities." *Sociology of Education* 60 (July): 135–155.

———. 2001. "American Schooling and Educational Inequality: A Forecast for the 21st Century." *Sociology of Education* (Extra Issue): 135–153.

Gamoran, Adam, and Daniel A. Long. 2006. "*Equality of Educational Opportunity*: A 40-Year Retrospective." WCER Working Paper 2006-9, Wisconsin Center for Educational Research, School of Education, University of Wisconsin–Madison.

Gaskell, Jane. 1992. *Gender Matters from School to Work*. Milton Keynes, UK: Open University Press.

Geiger, Roger L. 2008. "The Ivy League." In *Structuring Mass Higher Education: The Role of Elite Institutions*, ed. David Palfreyman and Ted Tapper, pp. 281–302. London: Routledge.

Gerber, Theodore P., and Sin Yi Cheung. 2008. "Horizontal Stratification in Postsecondary Education: Forms, Explanations, and Implications." *Annual Review of Sociology* 34: 299–318.

Giroux, Henry A. 1983. *Theory and Resistance in Education*. London: Heinemann Educational Books.

Glennon, Lynda M. 1978. "Yale: Reflections on Class in New Haven." *Yale Review* 67(4): 627–640.

Goyette, Kimberly A. 2008. "College for Some to College for All: Social Background, Occupational Expectations, and Educational Expectations over Time." *Social Science Research* 37: 461–484.

Goyette, Kimberly A., and Ann L. Mullen. 2006. "Who Studies the Arts and Sciences? Social Background and the Choice and Consequences of Undergraduate Field of Study." *Journal of Higher Education* 77(3): 497–538.

Green, Patricia J., Bernard L. Dugoni, Steven J. Ingels, and Eric Camburn. 1995. *A Profile of the American High School Senior in 1992 (National Education Longitudinal Study of 1988)*. NCES 95-384. Washington, DC: U.S. Department of Education, National Center for Education Statistics, Institute of Education Sciences.

Grodsky, Eric, and Melanie T. Jones. 2006. "Real and Imagined Barriers to College Entry: Perceptions of Cost." *Social Science Research* 36: 745–766.

Hanushek, Eric A. 1997. "Assessing the Effects of School Resources on Student Performance: An Update." *Educational Evaluation and Policy Analysis* 19(2): 414–464.

———. 1998. "Conclusions and Controversies about the Effectiveness of School Resources." *Economic Policy Review* (Federal Reserve Bank of New York) 4(1): 11–27.

Harding, Sandra. 1986. *The Science Question in Feminism*. Ithaca, NY: Cornell University Press.

Harvard University. 2007. *The Harvard University Fact Book*. Cambridge, MA: Harvard University, Office of Budgets.

Hearn, James C. 1984. "The Relative Roles of Academic, Ascribed, and Socioeconomic Characteristics in College Destinations." *Sociology of Education* 57(1): 22–30.

———. 1990. "Pathways to Attendance at the Elite Colleges." In *The High-Status Track: Studies of Elite Schools and Stratification*, ed. Paul W. Kingston and Lionel S. Lewis, pp. 121–145. Albany: New York University Press.

Hearn, James C., and Susan Olzak. 1981. "The Role of College Major Departments in the Reproduction of Sexual Inequality." *Sociology of Education* 54(3): 195–205.

Heath, Shirley Brice. 1983. *Ways with Words: Language, Life, and Work in Community and Classrooms*. New York: Cambridge University Press.

Hoachlander, Gary, Anna C. Sikora, and Laura Horn. 2003. *Community College Students: Goals, Academic Preparation, and Outcomes*. NCES 2003-164. Washington, DC: U.S. Department of Education, National Center for Education Statistics, Institute of Education Sciences.

Horn, Laura J., Xianglei Chen, and Chris Chapman. 2003. *Getting Ready to Pay for College: What Students and Their Parents Know about the Cost of College Tuition and What They Are Doing to Find Out*. NCES 2003-030. Washington, DC: U.S. Department of Education, National Center for Education Statistics, Institute of Education Sciences.

Horowitz, Helen Lefkowitz. 1987. *Campus Life: Undergraduate Cultures from the End of the Eighteenth Century to the Present*. New York: Alfred A. Knopf.

Hossler, Don, and Karen S. Gallagher. 1987. "Studying Student College Choice: A Three-Phase Model and the Implications for Policymakers." *College and University* (Spring): 207–221.

Hossler, Don, Jack Schmit, and Nick Vesper. 1999. *Going to College: How Social, Economic, and Educational Factors Influence the Decisions Students Make*. Baltimore: Johns Hopkins University Press.

Hout, Michael. 1988. "More Universalism, Less Structural Mobility: The American Occupational Structure in the 1980s." *American Journal of Sociology* 93(6): 1358–1400.

Hurtado, Sylvia, Karen Kurotsuchi Inkelas, Charlotte Briggs, and Byung-Shik Rhee. 1997. "Differences in College Access and Choice among Racial/Ethnic Groups: Identifying Continuing Barriers." *Research in Higher Education* 38: 43–75.

Ikenberry, Stanley O., and Terry W. Hartle. 1998. *Too Little Knowledge Is a Dangerous Thing: What the Public Knows and Thinks about Paying for College*. Washington, DC: American Council on Education.

Ingels, Steven J., Michael Planty, and Robert Bozick. 2005. *A Profile of the American High School Senior in 2004: A First Look—Initial Results from the First Follow-Up of the Education Longitudinal Study of 2002*. NCES 2006-348. Washington, DC: U.S. Department of Education, National Center for Education Statistics, Institute of Education Sciences.

Jacobs, Jerry A. 1995. "Gender and Academic Specialties: Trends among Recipients of College Degrees in the 1980s." *Sociology of Education* 68: 81–98.

———. 1999. "Gender and the Stratification of Colleges." *Journal of Higher Education* 70(2): 161–187.

Jencks, Christopher. 1972. *Inequality: A Reassessment of the Effect of Family and Schooling in America.* New York: Basic Books.

Jencks, Christopher, and David Riesman. 1968. *The Academic Revolution.* Garden City, NY: Doubleday.

Johnston, David Cay. 2007. "Income Gap Is Widening, Data Shows." *New York Times,* March 29, C1.

Kahlenberg, Richard D. 2001. *All Together Now: Creating Middle-Class Schools through Public School Choice.* Washington, DC: Brookings Institution Press.

Kamens, David H. 1977. "Legitimizing Myths and Educational Organizations: The Relationship between Organizational Ideology and Formal Structure." *American Sociological Review* 42: 208–219.

Karabel, Jerome. 2005. *The Chosen: The Hidden History of Admission and Exclusion at Harvard, Yale, and Princeton.* Boston: Houghton Mifflin.

Karen, David. 1991. "The Politics of Class, Race, and Gender: Access to Higher Education in the United States, 1960–1986." *American Journal of Education* 99(2): 208–237.

———. 2002. "Changes in Access to Higher Education in the United States: 1980–1992." *Sociology of Education* 75: 191–210.

Katchadourian, Herant A., and John Boli. 1985. *Careerism and Intellectualism among College Students: Patterns of Academic and Career Choice in the Undergraduate Years.* San Francisco: Jossey-Bass.

Kaufman, Jason, and Jay Gabler. 2004. "Cultural Capital and the Extracurricular Activities of Girls and Boys in the College Attainment Process." *Poetics: Journal of Empirical Research on Culture, the Media, and the Arts* 32: 145–168.

Keller, Evelyn Fox. 1995. *Reflections on Gender and Science.* New Haven, CT: Yale University Press.

Kerr, Clark. 1991. *The Great Transformation in Higher Education, 1960–1980.* Albany: State University of New York Press.

Kingston, Paul William. 2001. "The Unfulfilled Promise of Cultural Capital Theory." *Sociology of Education* (Extra Issue): 88–99.

Kingston, Paul William, and Lionel S. Lewis, eds. 1990. *The High-Status Track: Studies of Elite Schools and Stratification.* Albany: State University of New York Press.

Kingston, Paul William, and Johns C. Smart. 1990. "The Economic Pay-Off of Prestigious Colleges." In *The High-Status Track: Studies of Elite Schools and Stratification,* ed. Paul W. Kingston and Lionel S. Lewis, pp. 147–174. Albany: New York University Press.

Knapp, Laura, Janice E. Kelly, Roy W. Whitmore, Shiying Wu, and Lorraine M. Gallego. 2002. *Enrollment in Postsecondary Institutions, Fall 2000, and Financial Statistics, Fiscal Year 2000.* NCES 2002-212. Washington, DC: U.S. Department of Education, National Center for Education Statistics, Institute of Education Sciences.

Kotch, Noah. 1997. "My Graduation from the School of Scandals." *Yale Daily News,* Vol. 119, No. 125, April 23, 1997.

Lamont, Michele, and Annette Lareau. 1988. "Cultural Capital: Allusions, Gaps, and Glissandos in Recent Theoretical Developments." *Sociological Theory* 6(2): 153–168.

Lareau, Annette. 1987. "Social Class Differences in Family-School Relationships: The Importance of Cultural Capital." *Sociology of Education* 60: 73–85.

———. 2003. *Unequal Childhoods: Class, Race, and Family Life.* Berkeley: University of California Press.

Lareau, Annette, and Elliot Weininger. 2003. "Cultural Capital in Educational Research: A Critical Assessment." *Theory and Society* 32(5/6): 567–606.

Levine, David O. 1986. *The American College and the Culture of Aspiration: 1915–1940.* Ithaca, NY: Cornell University Press.

Lewis, Theodore. 1993. "Valid Knowledge and the Problem of Practical Arts Curricula." *Curriculum Inquiry* 23(2): 175–202.

Lippman, Laura, Lina Guzman, Julie Dombrowski Keith, Akemi Kinukawa, Rebecca Schwalb, and Peter Tice. 2008. *Parent Expectations and Planning for College: Statistical Analysis Report.* NCES 2008-079. Washington, DC: U.S. Department of Education, National Center for Education Statistics, Institute of Education Sciences.

Long, Bridget Terry. 2004. "The Impact of Federal Tax Credits for Higher Education Expenses." In *College Choices: The Economics of Where to Go, When to Go, and How to Pay for It,* ed. Caroline M. Hoxby, pp. 101–168. Chicago: University of Chicago Press.

Looker, Dianne E., and Peter C. Pineo. 1983. "Social-Psychological Variables and Their Relevance to the Status Attainment of Teenagers." *American Journal of Sociology* 88(6): 1195–1219.

Louie, Vivian S. 2004. *Compelled to Excel: Immigration, Education, and Opportunity among Chinese Americans.* Stanford, CA: Stanford University Press.

Lubrano, Alfred. 2004. *Limbo: Blue-Collar Roots, White-Collar Dreams.* Hoboken, NJ: John Wiley and Sons.

Lucas, Samuel Roundfield. 1999. *Tracking Inequality: Stratification and Mobility in American High Schools.* New York: Teachers College Press.

———. 2001. "Effectively Maintained Inequality: Education Transitions, Track Mobility, and Social Background Effects." *American Journal of Sociology* 106: 1642–1690.

MacLeod, Jay. 1987. *Ain't No Makin' It: Aspirations and Attainment in a Low-Income Neighborhood.* Boulder, CO: Westview Press.

Maynigo, Traci. 2003. *A Girl's Guide to College: Making the Most of the Best Four Years of Your Life.* Boulder, CO: Blue Mountain Arts.

McDonough, Patricia M. 1997. *Choosing Colleges: How Social Class and Schools Structure Opportunity.* Albany: State University of New York Press.

McDonough, Patricia M., Anthony Lising Antonio, and Erin McNamara Horvat. 1996. "College Choice as Capital Conversion and Investment: A New Model." Paper presented at the 21st Annual Meeting of the Association for the Study of Higher Education, October 31–November 3, Memphis, Tennessee.

McNay, Lois. 1999. "Gender, Habitus and the Field: Pierre Bourdieu and the Limits of Reflexivity." *Theory, Culture & Society* 16(1): 95–117.

McPherson, Michael S., and Morton Owen Schapiro. 1991. *Keeping College Affordable: Government and Educational Opportunity.* Washington, DC: Brookings Institution Press.

Mullen, Ann L., and Jayne Baker. 2008. "Gender, Race, and Ethnic Segregation of Science Fields in U.S. Universities." *Journal of Women and Minorities in Science and Engineering* 14(2): 159–176.

———. 2009. "Uncovering Multiple Dimensions of Gender Segregation in U.S. Universities." Paper presented at the Gender and Education Association Meeting, Institute of Education, March 25–27, London, England.

Mullen, Ann L., and Kimberly A. Goyette. 2009. "Stratification in Higher Education:

Examining Social Background and Application Patterns." Paper presented at the ISA RC28 [International Sociological Association, Research Committee on Social Stratification and Mobility] 2009 Spring Meeting, Renmin University of China, May 14–16, Beijing, People's Republic of China.

Mullen, Ann L., Kimberly A. Goyette, and Joseph A. Soares. 2003. "Who Goes to Graduate School? Social and Academic Correlates of Educational Continuation after College." *Sociology of Education* 76: 143–169.

National Association of Independent Schools. 2010. *NAIS Facts at a Glance.* www.nais .org/files/PDFs/NAISMemFacts_Salaries_200910.pdf.

National Center for Education Statistics. *College Navigator*, National Center for Education Statistics, Institute of Education Sciences, U.S. Department of Education. http:// nces.ed.gov/collegenavigator/.

Noble, David F. 1992. *A World without Women: The Christian Clerical Culture of Western Science*. New York: Oxford University Press.

Nuñez, Anne-Marie, and Stephanie Cuccaro-Alamin. 1998. *First-Generation Students: Undergraduates Whose Parents Never Enrolled in Postsecondary Education.* NCES 98-082. Washington DC: U.S. Department of Education, National Center for Education Statistics, Institute of Education Sciences.

Olson, Beth, ed. 2003. *Life after Yale: A Survival Guide for the Class of 2003*. New Haven, CT: Yale College, Undergraduate Career Services.

Ong, Maria. 2005. "Body Projects of Young Women of Color in Physics: Intersections of Gender, Race, and Science." *Social Problems* 52(4): 593–617.

Padavic, Irene, and Barbara Reskin. 2002. *Women and Men at Work*, 2nd ed. Thousand Oaks, CA: Pine Forge Press.

Pascarella, Ernest T., and Patrick T. Terenzini. 2008. *How College Affects Students: A Third Decade of Research*, 2nd ed. San Francisco: Jossey-Bass.

Pascarella, Ernest T., Gregory C. Wolniak, Tricia A. Seifert, and Ty M. Cruce. 2005. *Liberal Arts Colleges and Liberal Arts Education: New Evidence on Impacts.* ASHE [Association for the Study of Higher Education] Higher Education Report, Vol. 31, No. 3.

Paulsen, Kenneth J. 2005. *Living the College Life: Real Students. Real Experiences. Real Advice.* Hoboken, NJ: John Wiley and Sons.

Persell, Caroline Hodges, Sophia Catsambis, and Peter W. Cookson, Jr. 1992. "Differential Asset Conversion: Class and Gendered Pathways to Selective Colleges." *Sociology of Education* 65: 208–225.

Planty, Michael, Robert Bozick, and Steven J. Ingels. 2006. *Academic Pathways, Preparation, and Performance—a Descriptive Overview of the Transcripts from the High School Graduating Class of 2003–04.* NCES 2007-316. Washington, DC: U.S. Department of Education, National Center for Education Statistics, Institute of Education Sciences.

Power, Sally, Tony Edwards, Geoff Whitty, and Valerie Wigfall. 2003. *Education and the Middle Class.* Philadelphia: Open University Press.

Raftery, Adrian E., and Michael Hout. 1993. "Maximally Maintained Inequality: Expansion, Reform and Opportunity in Irish Education, 1921–1975." *Sociology of Education* 66: 41–62.

Reay, Diane, Miriam E. David, and Stephan Ball. 2001. "Making a Difference? Institutional Habituses and Higher Education Choices." *Sociological Research* Online 5 (4). www.socresonline.org.uk/5/4/reay.html.

———. 2005. *Degrees of Choice: Social Class, Race, and Gender in Higher Education.* Sterling, VA: Trentham Books.

Roksa, Josipa, Eric Grodsky, Richard Arum, and Adam Gamoran. 2007. "United States: Changes in Higher Education and Social Stratification." In *Stratification in Higher Education: A Comparative Study,* ed. Yossi Shavit, Richard Arum, and Adam Gamoran, pp. 165–191. Stanford, CA: Stanford University Press.

Roscigno, Vincent, and James Ainsworth-Darnell. 1999. "Race, Cultural Capital, and Educational Resources: Persistent Inequalities and Achievement Returns." *Sociology of Education* 72(3): 158–178.

Rose, Mike. 2008. "Intelligence, Knowledge, and the Hand/Brain Divide." *Phi Delta Kappa International* 89(9): 632–639.

Rosenbaum, James E. 1997. "College-for-All: Do Students Understand What College Demands?" *Social Psychology of Education* 2: 55–80.

———. 2001. *Beyond College for All: Career Paths for the Forgotten Half.* Rose Series in Sociology. New York: Russell Sage Foundation.

Sanderson, Michael. 1993. "Vocational and Liberal Education: A Historian's View." *European Journal of Education* 28(2): 189–196.

Sax, Linda J., Alexander W. Astin, William S. Korn, and Kathryn M. Mahoney. 1996. *The American Freshman National Norms for Fall 1996.* Los Angeles: University of California, Los Angeles, Graduate School of Education, Higher Education Research Institute.

Seifert, Tricia A., Kathleen M. Goodman, Nathan Lindsay, James D. Jorgensen, Gregory C. Wolniak, Ernest T. Pascarella, and Charles Blaich. 2008. "The Effects of Liberal Arts Experiences on Liberal Arts Outcomes." *Research in Higher Education* 49(2): 107–125.

Shavit, Yossi, Richard Arum, and Adam Gamoran, eds. 2007. *Stratification in Higher Education: A Comparative Study.* Stanford, CA: Stanford University Press.

Shavit, Yossi, and Hans-Peter Blossfeld, eds. 1993. *Persistent Inequality: Changing Educational Attainment in Thirteen Countries.* Boulder, CO: Westview Press.

Shulman, James L., and William G. Bowen. 2001. *The Game of Life: College Sports and Educational Values.* Princeton, NJ: Princeton University Press.

Sigel, Laura. 1997. "All in the Power of a Name." *Yale Herald,* Vol. 23, No. 8, March 6.

Smart, John C. 1986. "College Effects on Occupational Status Attainment." *Research in Higher Education* 24: 73–93.

———. 1988. "College Influences on Graduates' Income Levels." *Research in Higher Education* 29: 41–59.

Smeeding, Timothy M. 2005. "Public Policy, Economic Inequality, and Poverty: The United States in Comparative Perspective." *Social Science Quarterly* 86(5): 955–983.

Snyder, Thomas D. 1993. *120 Years of American Education: A Statistical Portrait.* NCES 93-442. Washington, DC: U.S. Department of Education, National Center for Education Statistics, Institute of Education Sciences.

———. 2007. *Digest of Education Statistics, 2006.* NCES 2007-017. Washington, DC: U.S. Department of Education, National Center for Education Statistics, Institute of Education Sciences.

Snyder, Thomas D., Sally A. Dillow, and Charlene M. Hoffman. 2009. *Digest of Education Statistics, 2008.* NCES 2009-020. Washington, DC: U.S. Department of Education, National Center for Education Statistics, Institute of Education Sciences.

Snyder, Thomas D., and Charlene M. Hoffman. 2002. *Digest of Education Statistics, 2001.* NCES 2002-130. Washington, DC: U.S. Department of Education, National Center for Education Statistics, Institute of Education Sciences.

Snyder, Thomas D., Alexandra G. Tan, and Charlene M. Hoffman. 2006. *Digest of Education Statistics, 2005.* NCES 2006-030. Washington, DC: U.S. Department of Education, National Center for Education Statistics, Institute of Education Sciences.

Soares, Joseph A. 1999. *The Decline of Privilege: The Modernization of Oxford University.* Stanford, CA: Stanford University Press.

———. 2007. *The Power of Privilege: Yale and America's Elite Colleges.* Stanford, CA: Stanford University Press.

Southern Connecticut State University. 1983. *The All-University Curriculum: Southern Connecticut State University.* www.southernct.edu/UCF/importantdocuments/, as "The 1983 document on All University Requirements."

———. 2002. *General Education Review: Final Report to the UCF [Undergraduate Curriculum Forum].* Prepared by the General Education Subcommittee of UWIC [University Wide Impact Committee]. www.southernct.edu/UCF/importantdocuments/, as "General Education Committee Final Report (05/08/2002)."

———. 2009a. "Admissions: Freshmen & Transfers—Applied, Accepted, Enrolled—Fall." www.southernct.edu/departments/research/ [accessed June 15, 2009].

———. 2009b. "The Fine Arts." www.southernct.edu/artssciences/finearts/ [accessed June 15, 2009].

———. 2009c. "The Humanities." www.southernct.edu/artssciences/humanities/ [accessed June 15, 2009].

Spies, Richard R. 1973. *The Effects of Rising Costs on College Choice.* Research Report Series No. 117. Princeton, NJ: Princeton University, Industrial Relations Section, Department of Economics.

Stevens, Mitchell L. 2007. *Creating a Class: College Admissions and the Education of Elites.* Cambridge, MA: Harvard University Press.

Students Helping Students. 2005. *Navigating Your Freshman Year: How to Make the Leap to College Life and Land on Your Feet.* New York: Prentice Hall Press.

Swartz, David. 1997. *Culture and Power: The Sociology of Pierre Bourdieu.* Chicago: University of Chicago Press.

Swidler, Ann. 1986. "Culture in Action: Symbols and Strategies." *American Sociological Review* 51 (April): 273–286.

———. 2001 *Talk of Love: How Culture Matters.* Chicago: University of Chicago Press.

Thomas, Kim. 1990. *Gender and Subject in Higher Education.* Bristol, PA: Open University Press.

Time Magazine. 1972. "Woman & Man at Yale." *Time Magazine,* March 20.

Tinto, Vincent, and Anne Goodsell. 1994. "Freshman Interest Groups and the First-Year Experience: Constructing Student Communities in a Large University." *Journal of the Freshman Year Experience* 6(1): 7–28.

Tinto, Vincent, and Diane Lebo Wallace. 1985. "Studies of College Choice: A Review." *American Journal of Education* 94(1): 120.

Turley, Ruth N. López. 2006. "When Parents Want Children to Stay Home for College." *Research in Higher Education* 47(7): 823–846.

Turner, Sarah W., and William G. Bowen. 1999. "Choice of Major: the Changing (Unchanging) Gender Gap." *Industrial and Labor Relations Review* 52: 289–313.

U.S. Bureau of Labor Statistics. 2007. *Women in the Labor Force: A Databook (2007 Edition)*. Report 1002. U.S. Department of Labor, U.S. Bureau of Labor Statistics. www.bls.gov/cps/wlf-databook2007.htm.

———. 2009. *Highlights of Women's Earnings in 2008*. Report 1017. U.S. Department of Labor, U.S. Bureau of Labor Statistics. www.bls.gov/cps/cpswom2008.pdf.

U.S. Census Bureau. 2000. "PCT 112: Family Income in 1999," *Census 2000 Summary File 4 (SF 4)—Sample Data*. Census 2000 United States, U.S. Census Bureau. http://factfinder.census.gov/servlet/MetadataBrowserServlet?type=DTtable&id=DEC_2000_SF4_U&table=DEC_2000_SF4_U_PCT112&_lang=en.

Useem, Michael. 1989. *Liberal Education and the Corporation: The Hiring and Advancement of College Graduates*. New York: Aldine de Gruyter.

Useem, Michael, and Jerome Karabel. 1990. "Pathways to Top Corporate Management." In *The High-Status Track: Studies of Elite Schools and Stratification*, ed. Paul W. Kingston and Lionel S. Lewis, pp. 175–207. Albany: New York University Press.

Van de Werfhorst, Herman G. 2002. "A Detailed Examination of the Role of Education in Intergenerational Social-Class Mobility." *Social Science Information* 41(3): 407–438.

Williams, Christine L. 1995. *Still a Man's World: Men Who Do "Women's Work."* Men and Masculinity, No. 1. Berkeley: University of California Press.

Willis, Paul. 1977. *Learning to Labour: How Working Class Kids Get Working Class Jobs*. Farnborough, UK: Saxon House.

Wilson, Kenneth L. 1978. "Toward an Improved Explanation of Income Attainment: Recalibrating Education and Occupation." *American Journal of Sociology* 84(3): 684–697.

Wolfe, Tom. 2004. *I Am Charlotte Simmons: A Novel*. New York: Farrar, Straus and Giroux.

Wolff, Tobias. 2003. *Old School*. New York: Knopf.

Wootton, Barbara H. 1997. "Gender Differences in Occupational Employment." *Monthly Labor Review* (April): 15–24.

Yale University. 2005a. *Standard One: Mission and Purposes*. Yale NEASC Self-Study. www.yale.edu/accreditation/1999/accred/standards/standards.html [accessed August 3, 2005].

Yale University. 2005b. *Yale College Programs of Study: Chapter I—Yale College; The Undergraduate Curriculum*. www.yale.edu/yalecollege/publications/ycps/ [accessed August 3, 2005].

Yale University. 2007a. "Enrollment (Headcount) Minority and International." *Yale University Ongoing Book of Numbers*. www.yale.edu/oir/open/index.html [accessed June 1, 2007].

Yale University. 2007b. *Factsheet: Post-Graduation Activities of Yale College Classes*. www.yale.edu/oir/ [accessed July 27, 2009].

Yale University. 2007c. *Factsheet: University-Wide Enrollment by Ethnicity*. www.yale.edu/oir/ [accessed June 17, 2007].

Zhou, Min. 1997. "Social Capital in Chinatown: The Role of Community-Based Organization in the Adaptation of the Younger Generation." In *Beyond Black and White: New Voices, New Faces in the United States Schools*, ed. Lois Weis and Maxine S. Seller, pp. 181–206. Albany: State University of New York Press.

Index

Southern Connecticut State University
students (*cont.*)
161, 164, 201, 210; and hands-on training, 174–75; high school as motivating, 40,
41, 46, 48, 49–50, 51, 67, 69–70; and high
school as work, 70; high school athletic
involvement of, 47–48; and high school
curriculum, 55–57; high school enjoyed by,
48–49; high school expectations of, 46–50,
51, 55–56; high school experience of, 39,
40–41, 79; high school extracurricular activities of, 51, 57; high school grades of, 40,
49–50, 51, 69, 106, 113; high school identity of, 47, 51; and high school peers, 65,
67; high schools attended, 106; and high
school social aspects, 47; and high school
teachers, 58, 61–62, 63–64; high school
test scores of, 51, 106, 113; and high school
type, 107; identification with schooling by,
69–70; and knowledge of college options,
111–12, 113, 114; as labor power, 30; and
learning for its own sake, 151–52; and
liberal arts and practical/preprofessional
considerations, 19, 20–21, 23–24, 29, 30,
72, 160, 162, 163, 167, 173–74, 176, 183,
199, 200, 201, 207, 208, 209; majors of,
160, 161, 162–72, 179, 199, 201, 207, 208,
209; occupational goals of, 2, 73, 77, 79–81,
82–83, 110, 116, 142, 151, 161, 162–64,
165, 172–73, 175, 178, 199, 200, 206, 207,
209; and occupational knowledge, 165–66;
and parental education, 15, 25, 26, 79, 107,
113, 214; and parental expectations, 46–47,
81; and parental/family income, 25–26,
107, 206; and parental occupations, 2, 25,
79–80, 165; and personal change, 150–52;
postgraduate careers of, 12–13; post-high
schools expectations for, 52, 54; and professors, 144–46; and program offerings,
110, 111, 115; and public vs. private high
schools, 51; and residence on campus vs.
at home, 107, 110, 113, 119–20, 143, 153;
SAT scores of, 25, 49; and self-betterment,
82–83; and sense of belonging at college,
115; and social background, 15; and social
class dynamics, 109–10; and social mobility,
214; and social networks, 111; and status of

college, 108, 109, 116; and status of degree,
82; and teacher expectations, 81–82; and
time for completion, 25, 164; and transfer
credits, 148; transfers by, 105–6, 112, 113,
114–15; and two-year colleges, 105, 115;
and up-to-date curriculum, 173, 197; and
value of knowledge, 172–76, 192, 197, 198,
200; and vocationalist narratives, 72; and
white-collar jobs, 12, 210; and work before
college, 105; and work during college, 2,
120, 143, 146, 153; and working-class, 165
Southern Connecticut State University students (men), 13, 14; and choice of major,
167–68, 169–70, 171–72, 203; family backgrounds of, 107; and graduate degrees, 160,
161; and high school athletics, 47–48; and
income, 210; and success, 192; transfers
by, 106
Southern Connecticut State University
students (women), 13, 14; and choice of
major, 167–72, 203; family backgrounds
of, 107; and future family, 192; and graduate degrees, 160, 161; and income, 210; as
percentage of student body, 25; transfers
by, 106
student-athletes, and Ivy League, 27–28. *See
also* Yale University students (athletes)
students: individual choices of, 14; interviews
with, 14–15; lived experiences of, 10; structural constraints facing, 14
students, first-generation: academic and social
involvement of, 153; and college transfer,
105–6, 115; and desire to fit in, 140; and
family income, 25–26; and identity, 98–99;
and occupational considerations, 179, 180–
81, 185, 200, 209; and residence at home,
113; and sense of self, 213–14; and social
networks, 178; and Southern students,
25–26, 105, 106, 113, 115, 167, 200; and
Yale students, 25, 27, 98–99, 140, 178, 179,
180–81, 185, 200, 209, 213–14

whites, 7, 27, 30, 35, 141, 142, 227
women. *See* gender, women

Yale University: admissions committees at, 44;
curriculum at, 19, 197–98; educational phi-

21833401R00142

Made in the USA
Charleston, SC
01 September 2013